Go Public!

Go Public!

Encouraging Student Writers to Publish

Susanne Rubenstein
Wachusett Regional High School
Holden, Massachusetts

National Council of Teachers of English
1111 W. Kenyon Road, Urbana, Illinois 61801-1096

Staff Editor: Kurt Austin

Interior Design: Doug Burnett

Cover Design: Joellen Bryant

Cover Photographs: Thompson - McClellan Photography

NCTE Stock Number: 18623-3050

Library of Congress Cataloging-in-Publication Data

Rubenstein, Susan, 1954–
    Go public!: encouraging student writers to publish / Susanne Rubenstein.
        p.   cm.
    ISBN 0-8141-1862-3
    1. English language—Composition and exercises—Study and teaching (Secondary) 2. High school students' writings—Publishing.
3. School prose—Publishing. 4. School verse—Publishing.
5. Authorship—Marketing.   I. Title.
LB1631.R83 1998
808'.02—dc21   97-43721
                                                                                    CIP

For my students,
who give me the wonder of their words

Contents

Acknowledgments

We are not born knowing the power of words. We learn from good teachers, those individuals who lead us to appreciate the voices around us and who help us to strengthen our own. My teachers include my parents, who taught me to love books and who always listened to my voice; Elinor Erickson, whose passion for words and ideas inspired me in adolescence and in all the years since; Tom Moore, who made me understand that you teach best when you love the words you are teaching; and Bette Fauteux, whose wit and wisdom and love of language guided me through every page of this book. And my best teachers will always be my students—the Wylies, the Keiths, the Marcys, and the Meghans—who daily remind me of the courage it takes to write from the heart. I thank all of my teachers.

I also thank Tom Seavey, who first encouraged me to pursue the idea for this book; Bob Trikakis, who provided invaluable technical support; Kurt Austin, who shared with me his enthusiasm and expertise; and all those at the Massachusetts Field Center for Teaching and Learning whose trust in teachers' voices gives teachers the confidence to speak.

And of course, Skip.

I An Introduction

In the curious and convoluted way that teachers and students—leaders and learners—are connected, it is my students who have taught me to be a teacher of writing. Although I began my teaching career believing I could show them the way, I have learned that it is far better for me to follow, perhaps pushing and prodding a bit from behind, but letting my students decide what path toward self-expression to take. I may guide them toward subjects and styles and standards, but if their writing is to come from their hearts, as truly powerful writing does, then they must make their own choices. Though the path and pace each student chooses is different, the destination, I have discovered, is the same. When students write from their hearts, they want to be heard. They want to be read.

This book begins with Wylie's story, a story about the power of published words and about where the words our students write can take all of us. It is in some ways an unfinished story, for Wylie continues to shape her words and seek her audience. Yet already, Wylie's writing has changed her world and that of her readers. This is the power of publication. This is the power we can give our students.

1 Wylie's Story

The doughnut boxes are empty; the cider jugs have been drained. I look out at the circle of sophomores, sugary faces and all. "O.K., people," I say, "let's get the crumbs cleaned up. I think we're all anxious to begin!"

They are. There is a flurry of activity, cups crumple and napkins fly into the wastebasket, and suddenly on each desk papers appear. I move about the room, smiling a bit at the jelly stains on the desks and the worn edges on the papers. I can tell these papers have been read and reread and read again. They bear the mark of their writers not only in words but also in thumbprints.

"Ms. Rubenstein." The voice is soft. I turn to Wylie, one of my favorite students. Her desk is immaculate, no doughnuts there. The papers she holds in her hand are pristine. "Can you read this before we start? I . . .," she pauses, and I hear the catch in her throat. "It's what I want to read, but I'm not sure it's . . ." she looks away, "appropriate."

I am puzzled. I take the pages from her, wondering why at this last minute she is having second thoughts. For weeks we have been preparing for this morning in June, when all of us, teacher and students alike, share our work with one another in celebration of the community of writers we have worked all year to become. Since September we have struggled together, working as writers and readers and editors, learning to trust our words and each other. We are not unfamiliar with sharing. We read in response groups; we collaborate as peer editors; we hang our words on the classroom walls. But this is different. This is the culmination, the true publication. This is the moment when each of us says, "I am a writer. This is my work. Remember me by it." For weeks the students have been fluttering with indecision. *Which piece shall I pick?* They rustle through their writing folders, choosing first one piece and then another, asking my opinion, their best friend's opinion, their response group's opinion, and ultimately, I am glad to say, realizing that the choice is theirs alone. If I have given them nothing else this year, I hope I have given them the freedom to feel responsible for their work, to believe that each word they put on paper is their own. For some it is a new sensation, this sense of ownership. I have seen the quizzical look in their eyes when they hold a paper out to me and say, "Do you like it?" and I answer, "Do you?"

I am about to respond in kind to Wylie. I am ready to say, "Do *you* think it's appropriate?" but something in her eyes stops me. Wylie is a talented writer—and a somewhat dramatic one. Many times throughout the year, I have seen her throw up her hands at the word processor and announce, "I can't do this!" She's right; at that moment she can't. Wylie is the kind of writer who must sit and sweat and stew before she can put herself on paper. For her, writing is not a facile activity; it is a commitment. She puts her heart and her soul and her self on paper, and so the words do not come easily. But both Wylie and I have learned that they do come—and when they come, they are powerful.

In the blur of voices about me, I begin to read Wylie's story. "Mirror, Mirror" she calls it. The beginning makes me smile: *My ears awake to one of the many nauseating songs of Michael Bolton.* I read on, skimming a bit, aware of the rising restlessness in the room, the students eager and anxious to begin the reading. But then a line jumps out at me—*I pop a Dexatrim in my mouth like it's candy and I'm out the door to school*—and I blink and begin to read more slowly. Wylie sits staring straight ahead, her face composed, and she is for all the world the girl she describes in her piece. *As I sit there I know what everyone in the room thinks of me. I'm obviously a confident, happy girl with a boyfriend and a snobby circle of friends. But they don't know the truth, and this makes me smile even more.* The noise in the room is growing, but I cannot stop reading. *I walk upstairs and flop down on my bed with my newest magazine. Like always I look at all of the gorgeous, perfect people that fill the pages before me. Sometimes I'll disfigure their faces and bodies with a pen, or sometimes I'll cut them out and hang them on my wall for motivation. . . .* I turn the final page, not wanting to believe what's coming—but Wylie is too honest a writer to hide the truth. I read the final paragraph, swallow hard and put the paper on her desk.

"This will take courage," I say. She nods. "Do you have it?"

She nods again almost imperceptibly. "I think so," she says.

The reading takes three days. No one has been given a time limit, and there are twenty-five writers, all, even those who at first balked at this public activity, now beaming with pride, luxuriating in this moment of recognition. Some of their pieces make us laugh, stories of childhood pranks and embarrassing moments, and some, like the tales of parents who *never* understand, make us nod our heads in empathic agreement. Some pieces leave us silent, a girl's voice breaking when she describes the boy who hurt her. But each piece is received with wild applause, and though perhaps sometimes it is not the quality of the writing which is so lauded, the applause is sincere, for every piece bears the stamp of its writer and every piece comes from the writer's heart. Each of us knows the effort that went into each piece of writing, and each of us understands the courage it takes to make the piece public. I am pleased by the comments I hear as the kids leave class each day. "That was great! You should send it to *'Teen*!" "I liked what you read. Can I have a copy?" "Hey, Pete, I didn't know you could write like that!" They are generous with their praise, and I am delighted to see that though I too congratulate each writer, my words are almost superfluous. They don't need to please the teacher. They have pleased the writing community—and themselves.

But still Wylie has not read. Each morning she takes the clean white pages from her book bag and places them on her desk. Each morning her classmates charge themselves on cider and snacks—though the adrenaline runs so high they need neither—but Wylie sits quietly smiling that smile. I sense her struggle, and I half suspect that buried in that book bag is another story, an escape-hatch story, the one she will read if her courage fails her, and part of me wants to give her permission to relax and read that piece. But, I remind myself, that is something a teacher would do, and here in this room at this time we have dropped those labels. We are all simply writers, and we are responsible for our own words.

Midway through day three Wylie's hand goes up. I smile at her encouragingly. "Your turn, Wylie."

She clears her throat softly and begins reading. Her voice is breathy and her words slide into one another, a blur of phrases, *snarly hair, feeling sorry for myself, shades of pink.* . . . I feel her classmates leaning forward, straining to hear, and she senses it too. She takes a huge breath. "Wait," she says. She closes her eyes for a second, and I watch her features settle. "O.K.," she says, "I'm ready." Then once again she begins to read, her voice now her own, clear and true, but there is no one in the room who does not understand what this is costing her.

High praise for my students is when I say, "Your piece took my breath away." In the time it takes Wylie to read the five pages of "Mirror, Mirror," it seems as if we all stop breathing. The students are transfixed. They are watching a transformation, and some stare at the product of it as if hypnotized. Others, perhaps disquieted by the change, look away from Wylie, but it is clear that they are listening to her every word. She has been for them all year long the proverbial popular girl, the epitome of teenage triumph: bright and beautiful, a success in school and on the ski slopes, someone on the inside of what Wylie herself calls *that circle.* Some of these students are her friends; some wish they could call themselves that. Even those who perhaps have called her a snob would, I think, change places with her in an instant. I know I would have when I was fifteen. But as Wylie reads her story—and it is indeed *her* story—a different Wylie appears, and she looks to her listeners much more like themselves—and perhaps even sadder. *I need to stop. I need to stop thinking and feeling bad for myself. I need to stop staring, worrying, hiding, eating, breathing and hurting.* I see Lee's eyes fill with tears. I see Dan bite his lip. And I see the flush in Wylie's cheeks and wait for her final words. *I get up and put on my bathing suit. I frown, suck in my stomach, and look hard at the person in the mirror. I wonder who she is and why she's hurting me. I can feel it beginning to happen again. I can't stand being in front of that mirror any longer. I run to the bathroom and shove my toothbrush down my throat. I feel everything leave my body—the guilt, the shame and the hurt. And for that one moment, lying there on the cold, white floor in my black bathing suit, I'm happy.*

She does not cry until she has spoken the last words. Then tears slide down her beautiful face. I suspect we all want to comfort her, to tell her that no matter what her mirror tells her, she is the fairest of them all, but we realize that it is not the moment for comfort. That will come later and in ways I cannot even begin to imagine. Instead we sit in silence in tribute to her work, and then suddenly the applause begins, and it takes a long, long time for it to end. Wylie wipes her eyes and almost smiles, but her hands do not stop shaking. When the bell rings, she gets up, a huddle of girls around her. I look at her over their heads. "Thank you," I say. She nods.

That is not the end of Wylie's story. It could have been. For me, it would have been enough to know that Wylie, at fifteen, made a leap of faith all committed writers must make. She put her true self on the page and sent it out in the world—and once she began she didn't look back. She sacrificed all else for the power of the published word. She trusted her readers, her listeners, to respect that word—and they didn't let her down. That could have been a satisfactory ending. And yet, as the final few days of the school year wound down, Wylie—and I—learned even more about the power of publishing.

I sit reading final exams. Prior to the exam, I have asked my sophomores to work on a piece of writing that answers the questions "Where are you now? Where have you been?"—a loose paraphrase of the title of a Joyce Carol Oates story, "Where Are You Going, Where Have You Been?", we read earlier that term. As part of the exam the students must revise their earlier drafts and hand in a polished piece of writing. As I turn the page of Meghan's exam, I am surprised to see her piece begin "Dear Wylie." Meghan, like Wylie, is pretty and popular, and from my vantage point as teacher it would seem to me that they would travel in similar spheres. Meghan's letter assures me I am wrong:

. . . I have always thought that you were a snob and only interested in how your hair looks and where you buy your clothes. I never realized you were just an average person inside with average problems. At the beginning of the year I felt awkward reading my stories because I thought that you would laugh in my face and tell your friends how stupid my writings are. But as the year went on I felt less awkward and more secure reading what I had written. Just a few days ago I remember feeling very ashamed to think of you as a snob. That was when you read your personal essay. I realized more than ever that you were sick of people thinking you were a snob . . . I was one of those people. I am sorry I thought of you in that way. In the past year you have taught me not to judge people by their friends but to get to know them. Thank you for opening my eyes to a whole new way of looking at things.

Meg

The letter does indeed answer the questions posed on the exam assignment, but clearly its audience should be Wylie, not me. I approach Meghan. "It's a beautiful letter," I tell her. "Can Wylie read it? I think it would mean a lot to her."

Meghan smiles and nods in agreement, and as I carefully ease the paper from the stapled pages of her exam, I realize that Meghan too has learned what it means to write "for real." Like Wylie, she has put her self on the page—and signed her name. Her work is going out into the world where it will make a difference. In September she could not have taken this risk. What if her words were misunderstood? What if her readers did in fact "laugh in her face"? But it is June, and in these nine months Meghan has learned to put her heart into her writing and to believe that when her writing says what her heart feels, its power is extraordinary. She has learned that such writing deserves to be read, and she has no fear of audience.

The next day I ask Wylie about Meghan's letter. It's clear that Wylie is overwhelmed, that even though she read her work and shared her self, she never expected such a return. Meghan's letter is not the only response she has received. Lee too has written Wylie a letter and handed it to her. Other classmates have spoken to her, wanting to talk about her writing and her feelings. She shakes her head in wonderment. "I didn't know something I wrote could matter that much."

"But it has," I say, "and maybe it can make an even larger difference. What would you think about sending your story to a magazine?" It is not an idle suggestion. All year I have encouraged my students to send their writing to publications and contests, and many have responded with enthusiasm. But not Wylie. Not yet. The furthest she has gone outside the classroom is the school literary magazine.

"I don't know," she says, her eyes darting nervously about the classroom. "Some of the kids say I should send it to *Seventeen,* but. . . ."

"It's a good suggestion," I say. "Certainly it's a story that teenagers can relate to. You saw it happen here." She nods, a small smile of pleasure playing at her lips, so I add, "Why don't I bring you the guidelines and address, and you can think about it?"

On the final day of school, Wylie rushes into the room. I am taking down the writing board, already missing this year's classes. She is breathless, hurrying into summer. "Do you have that stuff?" she says.

I give Wylie the packet of information. "Thanks," she says, stuffing it into her already overflowing book bag. She pauses for a minute and looks me straight in the eye. "I'm going to try," she says. "But it's scary. *Seventeen* . . . I'm not that good, and—do I really want *everyone* to know about me?"

"I don't know," I say. "Maybe not right now. But someday I think. And your words will last until you do."

She smiles, grateful, I think, for the reprieve. Then waving good-bye, she is out the door, leaving me with thumbtacks and thoughts.

Now, months later, Wylie still works on her story. She has rewritten and revised, carrying her manuscript back and forth to me, to her mother, to her trusted friends. All of us have offered suggestions and comments. All of us have penciled in editorial marks. At times our ideas have conflicted, and Wylie has looked at the story in dismay, unsure what the *right* revision may be. "There's no way to know for sure," I tell her, "but remember, this is *your* story. You are the writer. In the end, the words belong to you." She sighs, bites her lip, and carries her story home to make her own decisions. While words brew in her head, she takes on the practical tasks, learning about manuscript format and cover letters. I give her more guidelines and samples, and she studies them like blueprints, making notes to herself on the margins. Then one day she appears with a perfectly printed manuscript—heading, word count, and all—and I compliment her on it. "You look professional," I tell her.

Meanwhile she continues to peruse *Writer's Market,* for though her classmates suggested she send her story to *Seventeen,* she's just not sure. She grows absorbed in the thick book, fascinated by the possibilities. "I never knew there were so many magazines in the world," she says. "Hmmm . . . *Highlights.* Maybe I could send one of my kids' stories to that." True, she still has not put the story—*her* story—in an envelope, but she will—when she is ready. In the meantime she has mastered the nuts and bolts of manuscript preparation, discovered a myriad of publishing opportunities, and polished "Mirror, Mirror" to a brilliant shine. The overwhelming response her story received months ago has also fired her love for writing. Since last June she has worked on many other pieces, participated in a Young Writer's conference, signed up for Creative Writing in school. When she breezes into my classroom to say hello, she is full of new stories and only bemoans the fact that she never has enough time to get them all on paper. We end almost every conversation with her words, "I'm going to send my story out *soon*. I'm almost ready." I know she is telling the truth. Publishing, be it in the classroom or in the literary world, is risky business, and the writer has to be ready to take the risk. When you offer a piece of writing to an audience, you are offering a piece of yourself—and that is never easy.

Almost ready. I think of that as I face a new year of students, as I am about to challenge them with this risk. In my classroom, a classroom-turned-writing-community, students are encouraged to publish. We believe in writing for real. We do not believe writing should languish in a teacher's gradebook or lie in a student's notebook. We believe in an audience.

I tell my students, "Go public!" Indeed, the bulletin board in the corner, filled with publishing opportunities, shouts that advice in bright yellow letters. But it is not a challenge that all students undertake with enthusiasm, nor is it one that even the most eager students always know how to approach. *Almost ready.* As a writing teacher, I believe it is my responsibility to guide my students to this edge, to make them "almost ready" to publish. I can't make them take that final step, but within the classroom-turned-writing-community I can provide an environment that makes it possible to take that last leap.

Publishing can take many forms. When you open your mouth to read your work to a group, when you press a heartfelt letter into someone's hand, when you seal an envelope and send your story to *Seventeen* . . . all those acts and others along the way are what it means to publish. To be a writer is one thing; to be a published writer is another. I believe that writing teachers owe their students the opportunity to become published writers, to experience firsthand the power their words can have in the world. Furthermore, I believe that when the ultimate goal of writing is publication, the quality of the writing improves dramatically. For teachers who struggle daily to help their students grow as writers, that is very convincing reason to shout, "Go public!"

This book reflects my steadfast belief that students should—and *can*—publish their writing. Like many writing teachers firmly committed to the process-writing model, I see the writing classroom as a writing community with students and teacher turned writers and readers and editors, joined in a collaborative effort to recognize the worth of all. I believe that this recognition should be nurtured within the walls of the classroom to ultimately bloom in the world outside. Like writing itself, publishing is a process, and we must guide our students through that process, offering them encouragement, information, and opportunities every step of the way. Publication begins the moment a student shares his writing with the members of his response group. The support he receives there may encourage him to hang a piece of his writing on the classroom wall or to allow it to be printed in a class anthology. Maybe later he will decide to submit his work to an in-school literary magazine. And sometime he may just find himself ready to send a piece off to one of the publications posted on the bulletin board or to a contest the teacher has announced to the class. Each time a student shares his words with readers, be it one or many, be it strangers or peers, he experiences what it means to be a published writer, and he discovers the power his words possess. That is the wonder and joy of publication. As teachers of writing, we can offer our students a variety of opportunities to experience the thrill of publication, and so we can show them that their words do have value in the world. At the same time I realize that as middle and high school teachers we also have a responsibility to a curriculum, to a body of literature and writing that students are supposed to study. But these two responsibilities are not exclusive; they can co-exist peacefully, indeed complement each other, in the classroom-turned-writing-community. In such an environment, students are always aware that the world is full of readers, "real" readers who don't own red pens but who certainly appreciate good writing.

This book offers the writing teacher both a continuing rationale for fostering the publication of student work and very specific classroom suggestions and assignments that will promote such publication. Many of these ideas are neither new nor startling, and many teachers will have experimented with some before. I offer them here as a collection, a compilation of techniques I use with my students in my endeavor to make them published writers. I offer these techniques quite humbly, realizing that my students, not I, make them work. Perhaps that is the central characteristic of all these ideas: they demand that students take responsibility for their own success—and for their own failure—as writers. I think of Wylie as she began to read her story in class. "I'm ready," she said. I see her now, standing in my classroom, a magazine address in her hand. "I'm almost ready," she says. To get our students ready to publish—that is the teacher's task. We can trust them to do the rest.

II Beyond the Gradebook

It is one thing to want to guide students and their writing out of the classroom and into the world; it is another to find the means to encourage those first steps. A lack of class time, an excess of curriculum demands, and a basic unfamiliarity with the publishing opportunities available to young writers combine to make the task of moving writing beyond the gradebook seem a difficult one. It is not. In the next three chapters I offer practical suggestions and specific classroom ideas to promote "real writing"—writing that the students are committed to and that they direct to an audience that goes beyond the teacher and beyond the classroom walls.

Chapter 2, "Sincerely Yours," presents the letter form as a means of inspiring "real writing." Letters are perfectly suited to students who are just beginning to write for an audience outside the classroom because letters are by nature directed to someone in the world. This chapter emphasizes the idea of audience, an important concept when guiding young writers toward publication. Divided into two parts, the chapter focuses first on informal letter writing, generally directed to a familiar audience, and then moves into formal/business letter writing.

If letter writing can be a stepping stone to a wider arena of publication, so too can be the writing students do in connection to the literature they study. Chapter 3, "Making the Connection," offers an approach to literature that combines the study of literature with the challenge of publishing. Part One of this chapter suggests ways of studying the style, genre, and intended audience of a piece of literature in order to gain a deeper understanding of the work *and* of the qualities that make that piece marketable. Part Two focuses on writing *about* literature and the importance of individual response to and reflection on a piece of literature. Such response and reflection lead to the writing of reviews—and a discussion of markets for these reviews—as well as to other opportunities for publishable pieces about the literature students read.

With skills, confidence, and enthusiasm strengthened by the activities suggested in Chapters 2 and 3, students can move on to "The World of Published Writing," described in Chapter 4. This chapter presents first a detailed discussion of both the risks and the rewards involved in any attempt to publish. Following that is a section offering the "nuts and bolts" of manuscript preparation and marketing concerns in a question-and-answer format. The chapter also includes discussion of various potential markets and contests for young writers which are then described in detail in the Market List and Contest List in the Appendix.

2 Sincerely Yours

From the first day of school in September, the "Go Public!" board flashes its message in bright yellow letters. When my students troop in to the classroom on that first day, it is perhaps the one thing their eyes linger on, for the rest of the walls are bare, awaiting their writing. I watch as some students pause by the board, wondering what they are thinking as they read the notices posted there.

> "Send us a letter describing the adventure of your dreams. Think big and original. Send your entry to The Adventure Grants, *Outside Magazine*."

> "Your writing, ideas, and artwork are important to us . . . Welcome to *New Moon: The Magazine for Girls and Their Dreams,* the exciting new magazine where girls like you are in charge."

> "Just write and enter the *Seventeen* fiction contest. Attention, all writers: we're looking for a few good short stories. Send us your fabulous fiction and take a shot at winning, money, fame . . . ."

Experience has taught me that within a day or two, a few of these curious students will come to me, full of questions about these opportunities, eager to send the stories that fill their heads and their notebooks off into the world. But most of the students will not. For them the board barely exists, and if they consider it at all, they suppose that it is there for some other class, the older students perhaps, or maybe the Honors class, or most likely those Creative Writing kids. For many of my students, their last experience with "publishing" was a paper hung years ago on the refrigerator door. Now they're not kids anymore; they're young adults who write for *school,* who write for the *teacher*—and they believe that's the way it's supposed to be.

A writing teacher who takes on the job of fostering student publication can't simply design a bulletin board full of exciting opportunities and sit back and await the results. She will wait forever. Given inspiration, encouragement, and instruction, students can and will publish, but before a teacher undertakes the challenge of getting students to publish, it is important that she understand the obstacles that stand in her way.

First a simple reality: it is writers who publish, not students, but by the time children reach middle school, many of them have forgotten what it means to be a writer. They knew when they were very young; young children love to write stories. Their writing is colorful and original and close to their hearts. They write about purple cats, princesses in Nikes, and bratty baby brothers. They trust in a world of interested readers, imagining their work pinned to the bulletin board, hung on the refrigerator, and sent to Grandma. Unaware of the "rules" the grammarians espouse, they play with language, turning nouns into verbs, stringing long lists of adjectives together, and beginning sentences with *and*. And for a long time no one tells them no. Then one day, maybe in a fifth-grade classroom, something changes. Suddenly you can't write about your little brother; you have to write about products produced in Idaho. And you must write five paragraphs, and every one has to have a topic sentence, and commas need to go around words in apposition, and you need to use more conjunctions, and your teacher circled six words with a red pen, and if you don't fix all your errors you'll get a C, and . . . . If you're smart, you very quickly forget about being a writer because you realize that success comes to students. For many adolescents that means that they sacrifice what they have to say for what they think the teacher wants to hear. The sad result is inevitable: stilted, spurious, schoolroom writing, writing without heart, writing that won't ever be published.

In truth, for most middle and high school students, the idea of publishing their writing, particularly outside of the classroom, is a foreign one. They are not naive; they realize that publishing is a business and that the writing world is a competitive one. In their minds it is adults who get published—people like Stephen King, or Judy Blume, or the local sportswriter—not schoolkids. Certainly, then, their eyes can be opened by a myriad of publishing possibilities placed before them, but even if the teacher stands beside that bulletin board pointing to opportunity after opportunity open to anyone, most kids will shrug and say, "It's only the good writers who'll maybe get published—not me."

That's another obstacle. It takes an enormous amount of confidence in oneself and one's writing to compete in the publishing world. The risk is a paradoxical one. First, of course, there is the fear of rejection. Sadly, many students by the age of twelve have already had their confidence in themselves as writers shaken. The teacher does not give them A's. Their stories are not chosen to hang on the classroom walls. No one has ever taught them to take pride in their words. When you haven't even had success in the limited arena of the classroom, why would you take on the challenge of a much larger world? And what if you *have* succeeded in the classroom? What if your papers *are* the ones the teacher reads aloud or the ones that get published in the school literary magazine? Why not settle for that much success? Why risk rejection in a much more competitive world? And what if—just maybe—you do get published out there in the world? That's frightening too. Wylie asked, "Do I really want *everyone* to know about me?" For some students the classroom is a safe place where teacher and students together have created a community of trusted, sympathetic readers, but outside those walls the audience may not be so kind. For any writer, even the most adult and the most experienced, offering one's work in a competitive market is a perilous undertaking. For adolescents, by nature insecure and self-conscious, the risk grows.

The writing teacher must work to overcome these obstacles. She must create a classroom environment that allows her students to see themselves and each other as writers, not students. In this classroom-turned-writing-community, the writers support and encourage each other, and through their efforts, not only as fellow writers but also as readers and as editors, they work to strengthen both the quality of each other's work and the confidence of the writer. In Chapter 6 I elaborate on this idea of the writing community and discuss the principles upon which such a community is based. At this point, however, it is important to understand that within this classroom-turned-writing-community, writers are engaged in work that has meaning outside of the classroom. Only when adolescents are involved in writing that matters—and matters beyond the quest for the almighty A—can they produce work that speaks from their hearts and that speaks to an audience beyond that of the teacher. Unfortunately, most students are all too comfortable with "school writing." Tell them to write a five-hundred-word essay on "My Most Important Decision" and they'll spew it out with ease, the bright ones even remembering to use that sacred five-paragraph format! And when the teacher reads these essays, some will be "good" and some will be "poor," but rarely will one take her breath away. Even if there is one essay that does, where will it go from there? Maybe it will hang on the wall, maybe it will be read aloud in class, maybe it will even circulate in the Teachers' Room—but it deserves more attention, and perhaps it would receive more were it not in that "textbook form." Certainly there is nothing wrong with teaching students to write personal essays, and indeed the personal essay is a perfectly viable genre in the publishing world too. But as a form it is perhaps overused in middle and high school classrooms, and when students begin to see it as "the way one writes in school," they adopt a writing voice that is academic and artificial and calculated to please the teacher alone.

The teacher's task, then, is to design assignments that will have a natural audience—and one that extends beyond the classroom. When the audience is real—and red-penless—so too does the writing become real, free of the classroom clichés and studentspeak that spoils good writing. When students write for a wide audience—perhaps that which reads *Merlyn's Pen* or *Outside* or the local paper—they cannot rely on the "tricks" that have earned them A's in the classroom. Now the judging is more difficult and the audience far less easy to figure out.

But certainly not all students are ready or able to tackle the commercial publishing world, and to send them unprepared into that competitive arena is counterproductive. Young writers need stepping stones before they can begin to consider commercial markets and/or writing contests. One of the most effective stepping stones is the simple letter form. Letters, by nature, are directed to someone in the world, so the form is perfectly suited to students who are just beginning to write for a wider audience than that of the classroom. Letters can be divided into two general categories, the personal letter and the business letter, with a variety of opportunities for good writing inspired by each.

The Personal Letter

Take, for example, the "My Most Important Decision" assignment. The topic itself is interesting in that it prompts students to consider the power they have over their own lives and the importance of the choices they make. So why do the essays students write in response often sound stilted, "schoolish," and untrue? I suspect it is because these essays are so obviously written for the teacher—and most young people figure out quite quickly what each year's teacher wants to hear. What would happen, then, if the assignment were this: *Think about—and discuss with your classmates— the important decisions you've made in your life. Then write a letter to someone who has helped you work through a decision and tell this person how he/she influenced you. Make a copy of this letter and mail it to this person.* Suddenly the assignment has changed. Suddenly there is a real audience out there, maybe a well-loved grandparent, a favorite coach, or a fifth-grade best friend, who is going to receive this letter in the mail and for whom each word will have real impact. Suddenly the words matter, suddenly they have meaning, and suddenly they come from the writer's heart.

Keith writes a letter to his father recreating a hot Sunday night when together they stood *at the top of, what seemed to me, the largest hill in Holden with a small bright blue bike.* The letter goes on to describe the agony of learning to ride this two-wheeler:

> I wondered how you could do this to me, when in reality I was doing this to myself. Through the tears and pain, time after time, I got back on that bike. It's not that you forced me onto the bike. It's that you didn't stop me from getting on it. You egged me on! You knew that I wouldn't let myself down, and so you, my father,

on that twentieth time down, taught me to ride. . . . What I was too
naive to figure out at that time was that what you had taught me
went much further than just riding a bike. Like a good father, you
taught me a lifelong lesson. You taught me to pick myself up when
I was down. You taught me not to be a quitter. So many times in my
life, I've decided to "get back on the bike" instead of giving up,
because of you.

Keith

I have used this personal letter format in a variety of ways, and each
time I use it I am heartened by its success, by the pleasure students take
in the writing and by the sincerity of their words. For example, instead
of writing essays about childhood memories, my students write letters to
someone who shared a memory with them, and they send these letters
off to trigger that moment of memory with someone else. Almost without exception their letters are alive with detail, and it is clear that these
memories are truly significant ones.

Do you remember in the sixth grade when we were going out? Do
you remember when we used to dance at the school dances? Do
you remember how we used to dance? Close together and holding
on tight. I remember. Do you remember when you used to sing in
my ear while we were dancing? I always made you stop but inside I
was loving everything about it. . . .

Cassandra

If I had asked Cassie to write an essay about first love, I doubt she would
have done it with such poignancy. But when she writes to the young man
who inspires it, the feeling is there.

Jen sends a letter to her grandmother. It is inspired by a snapshot
she has carried with her while she works on the letter, but her writing is
so vivid her readers do not need to see the photograph. She describes a
memorable winter night years ago:

. . .Then Greg made the statement, "I wonder what it's like run-
ning in the snow with no shoes on."
"Probably cold," Grandpa said.
I giggled. Then Greg and I looked at Mom at the same time
with pleading eyes.
"Do you really want to?" she asked. We both nodded with excitement. "You guys are nuts," Mom added.
We started to take off our shoes and socks. Then you stood up.
"I'm nuts too!" you exclaimed.
Mom dashed for the camera as the three of us flew out the
door. As soon as we hit the freezing snow, we screeched with laughter. We scurried around on our tiptoes, just long enough for Mom
to snap two shots with the camera and for Grandpa to cringe, as if

he actually felt the cold. Then we hopped into the house, one by
one, dragging chunks of white snow on the carpet. . . And even to
this day, when I look at those pictures, a smile spreads across my
face.

Jen

I imagine that when Jen's grandmother read that letter, she smiled too.

In a variation on this idea of personal essay turned letter, I also
ask my students to write introspective letters, letters they write to themselves in order to confront and clarify many of the complex issues they
face both as students and simply as adolescents. Although these letters
are not published per se, they do have a very important audience—the
writer—and students understand that they can learn a great deal from
themselves if only they are honest with their words.

Frequently, for example, at the beginning of a course, I will ask
students to write letters to themselves describing their strengths and their
struggles as writers. They are welcome to share these letters with me or
with each other—or they can simply tuck the letter away in the back of
their writing folder until the end of the semester, when I again ask them
to write a letter assessing their growth as writers. They are unflinchingly
honest, perhaps because it is not so easy to lie to oneself.

> I've learned a lot, mostly from just listening to other people's writ-
> ing. . . . My writing is purely improvisational. I begin with an idea
> and spit out the story. Unfortunately idea continuity suffers this
> way. After taking this course I've learned to build a frame of the
> basic points and write within that frame. It's like building a house.
> My writing voice is like my speaking voice, mumbled and some-
> times incoherent. . . . Unlike most people in the class who know
> what they want to say but don't know how, I know how to say it and
> I would—if I was sure of what I wanted to say in the first place!
>
> Matt

Though Matt may find his situation frustrating, I am pleased that
he has begun to build that frame on which to hang his words—and that
he is making connections between himself and other writers in the class.
He can look back at the letter he wrote at the beginning of the semester
and see that he has grown and is still growing. Matt is truly invested in
the writing community, and in writing this letter I think he sees himself
as an integral part of it.

In one of my favorite letter-to-yourself assignments, the audience
reads the letter long after the semester ends. I call this my "Poem of Possibilities" assignment because it was originally modeled after John
Updike's poem "Ex-Basketball Player," the story of Flick Webb, once a

high school hero, now a grease monkey, a boy-man who spends his days pumping gas and remembering his glories on the basketball court. Each May I ask my seniors to write a letter to themselves, in either poem or prose form, in which they describe the kind of lives they imagine they will be leading five years after their graduation from high school. In order to help them achieve a certain distance, I encourage them to write about themselves in the third person, just as Flick himself is described. Even though these students are in the last throes of "senioritis," they always tackle this writing with enthusiasm—because they know how real the audience will be. They know that they will put these letter-poems in envelopes, sealed and stamped and addressed, and I will store them away. Then one day in May five years in the future, the letters will find their way back to their writers, once high school seniors, now young adults. It is always gratifying to me to discover how many of these students then "go public" with their writing, sending me copies of their poems with updates of their lives. I think of that when I read Jen's letter-poem, and I hope the future finds her less torn than she imagines it will.

> Jen Cutting drives aimlessly down the road,
> Enjoying her first brand new car,
> But not forgetting her first car accident.
> She stops at a Mobil station to get a fill-up,
> Only with super premium plus, of course,
> And she couldn't forget her pack of Marlboros. . .
>
> . . . Without thinking she screeches her car
> To a stop and turns it around.
> Her career can wait; not her family.
> Med school doesn't need her; her father does.
> She must put her priorities in order.
> She's never been able to do so; it's time to learn.

Recently I used a variation of this assignment, partly to alleviate my own frustrations and partly to offer my students a vivid example of how our views change, depending upon where we are standing. In my Contemporary American Culture class, we discuss feminism, reading a variety of nonfiction and fiction pieces that address the issue. This particular year we focused on Mary Grimm's short story "We" as well as the introductory chapter, "The Problem That Has No Name," from Betty Friedan's *The Feminine Mystique*. Early on, it was clear that I was meeting resistance, not toward the works themselves but toward the issue of feminism. My students, juniors and seniors, males and females, could not see its relevance in their lives. The young women believed that the important victories ensuring them equality in school, in sports, and in the workplace had been won. The young men simply didn't see how the issues of childcare or domestic abuse or abortion concerned them. I was frustrated dealing with their indifference, and I had to continually remind myself that they stood at a very different vantage point than I. They had not been part of the movement that fought so hard for the rights my female students take for granted, nor have they yet come up against any of the barriers which still exist that no legal system can completely break down. I knew the futility of trying to enlighten them. I could tell them that they were too young and inexperienced to understand the issue, and I could give them examples from my own experience in an attempt to change their views, but if it were that easy there would be no such thing as a generation gap. I realized they simply had to grow up and experience the world on their own—and that was not going to happen in one semester.

But I could not let it go. I wanted my students to at least consider the issue seriously, and I wanted them to recognize how much one's views are determined by one's vantage point. So I handed them paper and an envelope, and I asked them a series of questions that focused on the issues involved in the feminist movement. *Do you consider yourself a feminist? How do you define the term feminist? Which of these issues are of importance to you, and why: Equal pay? Equal opportunity in education? Equal opportunity in employment? Sexual freedom? Violence against women? Maternity leave? Child care? What problems do you imagine encountering in the future in working out your role as a woman or man?* They seemed to respond to the questions quite seriously, thinking a lot and writing furiously. When they were finished, I told them to date the papers, fold them, and seal them in the envelope. Puzzled, they did as they were told, and then I asked them to address these letters to themselves, guessing at an address that might reach them in five years.

Those letters are piled in the back of my closet, next to five years' worth of Flick Webb-inspired poems. The writing served a purpose that day. It made each of my students consider the issue of feminism seriously and made them put their opinions in black and white, which often have more validity than the half-formed thoughts students toss about in class discussion. It also did generate discussion. Students who had previously dismissed the topic, sure they had nothing in common with those "radical women," now at least had something solid to say, even if they still saw themselves on the other side. And I suspect, in five years, when these students open the envelopes, many—especially those who are struggling to balance marriage, career, and family—will have a moment of bittersweet laughter as they remember how the world seemed much simpler at seventeen.

For middle and high school writing teachers, the possibilities for such letter-writing assignments are endless—and I have included a list of ideas at the end of this section. Most of these ideas can be molded and shaped to fit any English/language arts curriculum. The positive features of such an assignment are evident.

First, letter writers seem to find their subjects easily, perhaps because suddenly the idea is concrete. When I say, "Write a letter to someone to whom you owe an apology," I quickly see traces of shame on their faces—light blushes, embarrassed smiles, downcast eyes—and I know ideas are coming to them. But if I were to say, "Write an essay about a time you were wrong," I am sure the boy in the back would respond, "I've never been wrong" and the rest of the class would see him as their spokesperson! All writers need to make connections with the world. Their ideas need to be grounded in experience, and, for young writers, experience is generally associated with another human being.

A second positive outcome of letter writing is that it creates writing that is alive. It is direct and honest and clear, and it rings with the voice of its author. Only Keith would say, *What it all boils down to is you're the person I try to model my life after,* and sign his letter *Your son and buddy always.* It's one thing to try to fool the teacher; it's another to try to fool your dad, or your first boyfriend. Moreover, letter writers rarely have to be encouraged to *Show, don't tell,* for they are eager to bring to life a shared experience, to communicate vividly what is on their minds. Ironically, I have on occasion read a student's letter and commented that perhaps a certain section could use more detail, that I'm not exactly sure I understand. I'm usually pleased when the writer challenges me. "Dad [Grandpa, or whoever the recipient of the letter is] will understand. He's the audience!" I consider that a valuable lesson for my students to have learned, for writing must always be geared to a specific audience, and often it is the nature of the audience that determines the content of the writing.

Certainly this concept of audience is crucial too, for it is the students' introduction to the idea of publishing. After students mail their letters, they wait eagerly for a response. Sometimes it comes in the form of a conversation, a friend who stops the writer in the hall to communicate her surprise and pleasure at the letter. Or maybe it comes as a phone call, perhaps from a grandparent who was touched by the letter from a grandchild. Sometimes it comes as another letter, perhaps from a first-grade teacher or a Girl Scout leader, and my students are most pleased by that. When they hold a written response to their words, they learn more about the power of words on a page. There is energy in the writer-to-writer relationship, and sometimes the communication continues long after the class has ended. Of course, sometimes there is no response at all, and students have to learn to understand that. They must realize that perhaps the recipient of their letter is unsure of how to respond, but that does not mean that she was not moved by the letter, for it is unlikely that a letter written from the heart could have no impact at all. All of this waiting for response prefigures in many respects the waiting that hoping-to-be-published writers endure when they send their manuscripts out. One hopes, of course, that the writer of a letter will receive something warmer than a printed rejection slip!—but the concept is the same. When you write for a real audience, you expect a response—and that response will come in something other than the letters A, B, C, D, or F.

There is another significant benefit of letter writing and one that involves an issue with which many writing teachers struggle. We all want our students to write well, and though perhaps most of us agree that content is most important, still we know that young writers must learn to write *correctly* if they are to write well. Grammar, spelling, and punctuation all contribute to good writing, yet many students fail to produce papers that are mechanically/grammatically correct, and in fact these students are relatively unperturbed about the teacher's correction marks that litter their graded papers. Yet, I have found that when students send letters to friends, family, real people in their lives, they suddenly are concerned that their writing is "right." Some students understand that their meanings may be lost if their grammar is muddled or their spelling incorrect. Others simply develop a sense of pride in their writing once they realize that their words are making connections in the real world, and they do not want to send out sloppy work. And generally all agree that they respect their audience—this coach, this ex-baby-sitter, this big sister—and they want to offer their own best work.

Isn't this what we as writing teachers want to create—young writers who have something to say and who want to say it well? Isn't that where publishing begins? I believe that the personal letter is that beginning. True, it is publishing on a very small scale, but it is a start, an important first step, a way to reawaken in young writers a belief in the power of their very own words.

More Suggested Topics for Personal Letters

1. Write a letter to the most memorable person you have known. Tell this person why he or she is so memorable to you. [The goal here is to create a character sketch—and it generally happens without my ever having to say those two words!]

2. Write a letter to the best teacher you have ever had, telling him or her what he or she taught you—and remember, not all teachers are in a classroom.

3. Write a letter to someone you have *almost* forgotten. Tell this person why you have suddenly remembered him or her or why he or she lingers in your memory.

4. Write a letter to someone with whom you are engaged in a long-standing argument. Defend your viewpoint, and, at the same time, consider your opponent's arguments and try to refute them. [This letter frequently gets sent to a parent, and issues like curfews, dating privileges, etc., abound! What is important is that students learn to support their opinions in a clear and coherent manner.]

5. Write a letter to someone to whom you might turn for advice. Explain clearly the situation for which you are seeking advice.

6. Write a letter to someone who has asked your advice.

7. Write a letter you would *never* send! This might be directed to someone with whom you are very angry, or to someone whom you are shy about approaching, or to someone who might not want to hear what you have to say. (Despite the fact that these letters are not sent, they are often the most powerful!)

The Business Letter

Students gravitate quite naturally to the personal letter. It allows them to be themselves on paper and to develop a writing voice that is comfortable and real. But the business letter—and I'm assuming a broad definition of that term—is also very accessible to adolescents, and it encourages a clarity of expression that is integral to good writing. My students see the difference between personal and business letters as a degree of formality. Both forms demand good writing—clear, concise, vivid writing. Both demand correct writing—writing that conforms to the standards of good English. And of primary importance, both demand honest and sincere writing; the words and the voice these words are written in must ring true. But, I tell my students, there is one very significant difference. In the case of the business letter—be it a letter to the editor, a complaint to a company, or a query to a publisher—the writer is generally a stranger to her audience, and so she must put her best foot forward and present herself in a polite and polished manner. The words on the paper are the handshake and the smile, the first and perhaps only picture of the writer her audience sees.

Most students learn to write business letters when they are in fourth or fifth grade. They learn about headings, correct salutations, and proper punctuation. For older students, then, the format is less challenging than the content. I use the business-letter form as a vehicle for helping my students practice concise writing and for helping them develop a voice that is both decorous and their own. "All business letters sound the same," they initially tell me, offering a plethora of phrases they believe belong in the business letter: *Enclosed is . . . Thank you for your attention . . . I would like to express my opinion. . . .* "No," I tell them. A business letter, like any communication, should bear the mark of its creator, and it should be fresh and engaging. Moreover, I tell my students, a formal letter *is* a piece of publication. It will be read by someone in the "real" world, and it will hopefully evoke a response. The business letter then, in all its variations, is another stepping stone to the publishing world, and it is one that most students are comfortable taking.

Certainly there are the obvious uses for a business letter. Perhaps a student wishes to receive a pamphlet on car care from the Consumer Information Center, or perhaps she is requesting an application for a summer writing program at Bread Loaf. Those letters are quite straight-forward and demand little inspiration on the part of their writers, but, I remind my students, they are still pieces of writing that will be read in the world and will present an image of the person who wrote them; thus anything less than one's best writing is unacceptable.

There are many other ways that the business-letter form can be employed that do permit more creativity and that may in fact lead to actual publication. For example, I point out to my students that they hold many opinions—be it on the quality of a new soft drink, a television sitcom, or a bill a local legislator is supporting. I ask them to write letters stating and defending their opinions, positive or negative, and I encourage them to mail their letters off to the company, the network, or the individual. (In fact, years ago when *Cagney and Lacey* was about to be taken off the air for the first time, I suspect it was a class of my senior girls who helped to save the show, so ardent were they in their letters!) This sort of letter writing isn't easy. Students realize that they must present their opinions clearly, that they must offer solid support for their ideas, and that the tone must be both courteous and sincere. They also realize that some-one—often someone of importance—is going to take time from a busy day to read this letter, and maybe to compose a response, in words or in action. I think of one student who had written very little all year until he was inspired to write to a town official about public space for paintball games, and I remember how eagerly he awaited some reaction. I remind my students that the impact of their letters may not stop at the name on the envelope. Perhaps a letter criticizing the treatment teenagers receive in a local restaurant will hang on the wall in the employees' lounge, or perhaps the letter of praise written to the principal for her handling of a tense school issue will be circulated within the School Committee. Writers can, of course, set out to make their opinions very public, and I am always pleased by students who decide to express their views in a "letter to the editor." Some send their letters to the school newspaper, while others seek a wider forum through city newspapers or national magazines. I have found that, unhampered by many of the conventions adults seem to hold, young people often write the most heartfelt and meaningful letters. For example, when school funding was tight, it seemed that letters to the editor which were written by students and appeared in the city newspaper were the ones that people talked most about. Certainly for many writers, adults as well as teenagers, the "letter to the editor" forum, either in newspapers or magazines, is a doorway to wider publication. It is a way of making yourself known, of having your voice heard, and of building the confidence to go a step further.

There are opportunities out there that make that step an exciting one. Publications and organizations that sponsor writing contests for students recognize that the letter format is popular with students, and they often design their contests accordingly, as a look at the Contest List (see Appendix) indicates. One of the most interesting contest opportunities employing the letter format is that offered by RespecTeen for students in grades 7 and 8. The contest requires students to write and send a letter to their U.S. representative discussing an issue that affects young people on a national level and suggesting a solution. RespecTeen offers teachers a detailed curriculum guide focusing both on letter-writing skills and on the legislative process. Given this chance to be heard by someone in power—as well as to win U.S. Savings Bonds, trips to Washington, D.C., and the chance to participate in the RespecTeen National Youth Forum—students are often motivated to think seriously about issues they may generally ignore, and to put their thoughts into words that matter.

Sometimes such opportunities arrive in unexpected ways, and a teacher of writing should watch for unique chances for student publication that may cross her desk. Recently my students participated in a letter-writing/publication project that may or may not come to fruition but, in the meantime, taught them a great deal about writing and publishing. I was fortunate to receive an appeal from a writer in California who is at work on a book composed of "problem" letters written by teenagers across the country. These letters cover a wide range of adolescent problems, including health concerns, family conflicts, and school difficulties. My students, and many others, were asked to write thoughtful and honest responses to these individual letters with the hope that these questions and their responses might be the material for a published book that would address adolescent issues in a way that teenagers could understand. My students, in all grades and all levels, took to the writing with extraordinary enthusiasm, and I knew why.

First, my students had something to say. They fight with their parents, debate about drugs, and know how it feels to be unpopular. They did not have to struggle for words because these issues are ones they live with each day. Second, this was writing for real at its best. Someone, age fifteen in New Jersey, was agonizing about an unwanted pregnancy and she wanted advice. My students, realizing that although their responses would likely never help this particular girl, knew that someone, a year or two from now, would be in the same dilemma and might find help and support from this book. And that—The Book—was the third thing that made this writing so powerful. Though there was no firm guarantee, they nevertheless imagined their words on the printed page, part of a real book in a bookstore display or on a library shelf. For them, the possibility of publication is the best proof there is that their words matter! Even now, months after their letters have been sent to California, they ask, "Have you heard about The Book?" It is definitely a teachable moment, a chance for me to show them with a concrete example how exciting—and uncertain—the business of publishing is and how writing to publish—be it a story, an article, or a book—takes much time and effort and more than a little luck.

It is not often that such unique opportunities as this present themselves to the teacher, and sometimes she must create her own. One project I have had good success with involves writing to writers. Like all of us, teenagers are fascinated by famous people and they see such people as far removed from themselves. Yet that's not really the case, as many writers have proven to my students. I ask students to compose a letter to a writer to whom they truly have something to say, or better yet, something to ask. I advise them to avoid simple fan mail, for generally that elicits little response, and I am hoping through this activity to reinforce for my students the idea that their words do have power in the world. Their choices show real variety. There are always two or three who want to write to Stephen King, some who write to favorite childhood authors, others who pick a magazine columnist whom they read avidly each month. Generally, each year through their letters, I meet a writer or two whom I have never read, and I consider this an added bonus. Once they have made their choices, we work on letters, and as always, the commandments of good writing hold. All the letters are clear and concise, and questions are phrased in a courteous manner. All the letters are read and revised and reworked and edited, and the final copy, complete with a self-addressed stamped envelope, is letter perfect. But—and this, I tell my students, is the challenge—each letter must, despite its adherence to form and figure, attract the attention of its audience. Surely Stephen King and Robert Cormier and Susan Minot receive many letters from their readers. What would motivate the writer to respond to *your* letter? It all comes back to writing for real, presenting yourself on paper in a way that makes your words—your self—come alive.

Though I caution students not to expect a response, reminding them that published authors would have little time for their own work if they were to reply to every letter from a reader, many students do receive responses. Jay McInerney scrawled a message about the writing life on the back of a postcard picturing Truman Capote. On a piece of stationery from the University of Wisconsin, where she was teaching, Lorrie Moore discussed the narrator of her story "The Kid's Guide to Divorce." On an actual Dandelion Wine label, Ray Bradbury wrote a note about the power of word association in the struggle to get writing ideas. Together these writers and many others have taught us much about writing and the profession itself, and they have made my students realize that real writers are in fact real people. With this in mind, I suggest that students write brief thank-you notes to writers who do take the time to respond to their letters. In this very human connection made possible by the U.S. mail, the act of publishing one's writing begins to seem less mysterious, more possible. Excited as we all are by the replies (and there are students who become obsessed with the arrival of the morning mail!), I am most pleased by the unspoken message that these replies are the result of good writing—of letters that came from young writers who truly cared about words, their own and those of the published writer.

As students get closer to the challenge of actual publication, the opportunities for letter writing become more focused. When students begin to study *Writer's Market, Poets & Writers,* or other publications that list potential markets, they start to come across words like "query" and "cover letter." Certainly the teacher must think in terms of teachable moments and give students information and guidance when it is needed. Not all students need to know how to write a query letter perhaps, but to compose a cover letter that accompanies a manuscript is, I think, a very useful skill. It is not, I remind my students, so different from the letter one might include with an application to a select soccer camp or to the college one hopes to attend next year. Quite simply a cover letter is a way of introducing oneself; it is indeed that handshake and smile, and it just might change the attitude with which the editor reads all else in the envelope.

Cover letters should never be long, and in fact for most young writers the letter will be very brief. Professional writers frequently use a cover letter to list their credentials in terms of experience and/or publishing credits, and most beginning writers have few credentials. In some cases I encourage my students to mention their age in their letter, but only when the market has specifically stated an interest in publishing the work of young writers. Otherwise I suggest to my students that they want to appear as professional as any other writer submitting a story or article. The letter should simply state that the enclosed manuscript is being offered for consideration and that the writer looks forward to hearing from the editor (see sample cover letter in the Appendix). I always tell my students to send the letter to a specific editor and to address him or her by name. This information can generally be found in the current market listing. Although usually not a necessity, a cover letter is also a nice addition to a contest entry, and when students are preparing manuscripts for contests such as those sponsored by colleges or community groups, I suggest that they take time to write a courteous cover letter. The task of writing a cover letter provides students with another opportunity to hone their writing skills, and it also challenges them to present themselves as professional writers do.

Within the classroom there are fewer occasions for writing query letters, but some students do need to learn how to do so—the girl, for example, who has written a profile about her saxophone instructor and wants to send it to *Jazziz Magazine*. The listing in *Writer's Market* informs her that the magazine does publish such pieces and in fact encourages articles by beginning writers but states that a query is essential.

A query letter is a concise but detailed letter intended to kindle the interest of an editor in hopes that he or she will want to see the entire manuscript. Query letters are rarely requested for fiction; most editors prefer to see the entire manuscript. But for magazine articles—a market that certainly has potential for young writers—queries are often required. As any writer knows, query letters are not easy to compose; in fact sometimes they seem more difficult to write than the article that inspires them! Because a query letter is brief (generally only one page in length), the writer must catch the editor's interest immediately with a powerful and compelling opening. The query should go on to offer the basic design of the article, a projected length, and enough information to convince the editor that the writer is both knowledgeable about the subject and capable of writing a first-rate piece on it. Certainly, then, the style of the query is as important as its content.

Such a task is difficult for most young writers, and they need guidance if they are to write queries that can compete with those of much more established writers. I generally guide my students to *Writer's Market* with its specific section on query letters, and for those who become more engrossed in the task, I suggest, as does *Writer's Market*, that they refer to *How to Write Irresistible Query Letters* by Lisa Collier Cool. Often these sorts of reference books are available in the public library, but I try to maintain a personal library of such books which I make readily available to my students. I also encourage students to talk to other teachers who are involved in professional writing. They are often surprised—and impressed—to find that Mr. Biology Teacher has had his work published in *Popular Science* or that Ms. English Teacher is sending queries on her mystery novel to publishers in New York, and they are equally surprised, and in a curious way heartened, to learn that many adults have struggled for years to publish their work without growing discouraged. Although we learn much from the books and magazines that guide us in the craft of writing, we also learn much from one another, and I want my students to understand that although we as a class comprise a writing community, our boundaries are fluid and we can go outside the classroom walls for assistance as we struggle to make our words read in the world.

Through these sorts of letter-writing activities, students begin to send their words out into the world. They begin to see themselves as writers, and they begin to anticipate an audience of readers. True, letters are only a beginning, and it is quite different to send a letter recreating a shared memory to a favorite aunt than it is to send a story to a glossy magazine. But first steps are crucial steps in that they create the confidence and the enthusiasm to go further. Start here and one day your students will say, "We're ready to go on." There is a wide, wide world waiting for their words.

3 Making the Connection

My sophomores are reading *Siddhartha*. Though less than eager at first, finding both Hermann Hesse's style and the Eastern culture described within the novel a bit baffling, they have come to appreciate the book, seeing in this bildungsroman a rough parallel to their own journey toward maturity. We talk about the people who help Siddhartha along the way, including his best friend Govinda, the beautiful Kamala, and the wise ferryman Vasudeva. We discuss how each influences Siddhartha, teaching him things about himself and about the world that he might not have discovered on his own. We agree that the people in our lives have an extraordinary effect on our own development.

My sophomores are not surprised when I suggest they write a chapter from the book of their own lives, giving the chapter the name of a person who has had a strong influence on them. In it, they will write about themselves in the third person, and they will describe an encounter with someone who has truly had an impact on their lives. Each piece will have the flavor of fiction—and, I tell them, they are free to use a bit of poetic license if they desire—but the heart of the piece will be truthful.

There is at first the requisite number of groans. Sophomores by nature are not the most cooperative bunch; at fifteen, anything that smacks of enthusiasm for schoolwork is less than cool. But I can see by the glint in some of their eyes that they are thinking and, more important, that they are reliving some powerful moments in their lives. Before long, the room comes to life with the start of stories.

"I knew this kid where I used to live who. . . ."

"I used to think my brother Danny was like a god."

"Hey, does anybody remember Coach Hayes?"

Suddenly out of the chatter comes a question.

"Does the person have to have had a *good* impact on you?" Mark asks.

I suspect he has in mind a rather wicked story about someone whom his parents have likely deemed a "bad influence."

I shrug. "It's up to you. Good and bad are relative terms. Was Kamala a good influence on Siddhartha?"

There is a great blur of voices, yeses and nos coming from all corners of the room. We are back on a discussion of *Siddhartha*, which is where I hoped we would be, and we are headed toward an interesting piece of writing, one that combines the students' interest in their own lives with a comparison to a piece of literature and an exploration into the techniques of writing fiction as well. It is all coming together.

A coming together. A connection. That is what teachers hope to achieve when they make the study of literature a part of the challenge of publishing. They want their curriculum to be one that intertwines the study of literature with writing that has the potential for publication. In truth, the two are not always easily joined. Much of the writing we ask our students to do in conjunction with the books they read is pure "school writing"—writing that would be of little interest to anyone outside the classroom—and, if teachers are honest, is frequently of little interest there!

We ask students to write short answers to quiz questions to prove that they have read the material. *The merchant's name was Kamaswami. Kamala was killed by a poisonous snake.* We ask them to write longer, more sophisticated essays, often in the five-paragraph format, exploring themes or explaining symbols. *Siddhartha dreams of a dead songbird in a golden cage. The bird represents* . . . . We ask them to write critiques, formal papers with thesis statements and documentation. *In the novel* Siddhartha, *Hermann Hesse proves that* . . . . All of these exercises have value and teach certain skills, but it is rare for any of them to result in publishable writing, and, even if the teacher makes the effort to publish such work within the classroom, perhaps on the back wall, it is unlikely to attract a large audience.

Writing does not have to be published to be of value, but the desire for publication often inspires young writers to do their best work. Some students are inspired by a grade, but certainly many, particularly those of high school age, are all too easily satisfied with a mediocre grade. Moreover, writing that has a place in the world outside the classroom, writing that matters beyond the gradebook, is more authentic writing and is generally more powerful, more persuasive, and more meaningful than its classroom counterpart. The challenge for the teacher, then, is to create opportunities for students to connect "real writing" with the study of literature.

This chapter is divided into two parts, each offering a different approach to that challenge. Part One focuses on using literature to teach writing skills and to learn what makes a piece publishable. Part Two suggests various writing ideas that encourage students to write about literature and offers possible publication opportunities for their work.

Part One

When I design writing assignments to supplement the literature my students are reading, I am always thinking about publication. That does not mean that every piece my students write in conjunction with *A Raisin in the Sun, Franny and Zooey, The Things They Carried,* or any of the other literature we read is sent out into the world. What it does mean is that most of the writing my students do has the potential for publication, sometimes in a wide sphere, sometimes in a narrow one. The stories they write in connection with *Siddhartha* may become pieces they can send to publications like *Blue Jean Magazine* or *360° Magazine* that are looking for true-life stories that appeal to their teenage audience, or they may be pieces that the writers decide to send to the very people who inspired the story. More than one student has done so and received a touching letter in return, revealing the pleasure a grandparent, ex-coach, or former teacher felt in learning what a powerful influence he or she has been in a young person's life.

I'm sure there are teachers who would ask, "But what does a writing assignment like this teach about the literature? While the students are busy with their stories about themselves, are they learning anything about *Siddhartha*?"

I am convinced they are. Over the course of the days that they are working on their pieces—thinking, writing, sharing, revising—we are continuing to talk about the novel. As we explore its content, structure, and style, the discoveries we make begin to inform the students' writing. We discuss the chapter in which Siddhartha's son comes to live with him, and my students tell me that young Siddhartha finds life with his father unbearable.

"How do you know that?" I ask them.

They rattle off reasons, proving to me that they have read the novel closely. Young Siddhartha hates his father's thrifty ways; he is unused to the work his father expects of him; he suffers from the guilt his father's enduring patience provokes.

"Those details," I say, "are Hesse's way of showing us, rather than telling us, how unhappy the son is with his father. Now, go back to your own writing and find places where you have told your readers things that you need to show them."

The next day, when I ask for volunteers, writers will read revisions they have made. Hopefully, their stories will have grown richer with detail and description, giving the reader vivid pictures of the people they describe. The Aunt Nancy in Kevin's piece will no longer simply be a "fun aunt." Now she will be someone who knew how to build great kites, loved knock-knock jokes, and took her nephew to a baseball game every time she visited. And Mark will take us behind the bleachers in the schoolyard and let us share the first puff of the cigarette he took with that "bad influence."

I am not trying to turn my students into young Hermann Hesses, nor am I trying to get them to mimic the work of any other writer. Every writer, no matter how young, has his or her own personal style that needs to be appreciated and nurtured. But there are basic techniques involved in all good writing that young writers should be acquainted with and should integrate into their own writing. "Show, don't tell" is one of the great commandments of good writing. Taking that commandment to heart, I show my students, through Hesse's words, how much more powerful it is to show readers something than to tell them about it. With luck, through such attention to the author's words, my students come away with a deeper understanding both of the novel and of the skills involved in writing well.

This exercise demonstrates one approach to combining the study of literature with the challenge of publishing. It suggests that as students read various pieces of literature, they will examine the particular characteristics of the genre and, in doing so, identify the qualities that make a piece marketable. To do so demands very close reading of each individual work and ongoing comparisons of different works. Students quickly come to recognize the striking differences in the writing styles of someone like Charles Dickens as compared to someone like Raymond Carver, and they eventually begin to see the subtle differences between Carver's minimalist style and that of Ann Beattie. They read two plays, Arthur Miller's *All My Sons* and August Wilson's *Fences*, and find similar themes in the father-son conflicts explored in each, but they begin to see how each playwright has a unique voice and uses different stylistic devices. They read poetry— free verse and sonnets, ballads and haiku—and come to appreciate the advantages—as well as the limitations—of each form. And all the while they are experimenting with their own writing through a variety of exercises, using the literature as inspiration.

These exercises can certainly vary, depending on the particular literature in any given curriculum. I offer below a number of examples to demonstrate how teachers can create meaningful connections between the study of literature and writing for publication, and I suggest that teachers adapt these exercises according to the literature their students read. The examples are grouped into three categories focusing on the topics of style, genre, and audience.

Studying Style

The first example aims to teach students about that elusive quality of style. Younger students especially have difficulty recognizing what it is that writers do with words to give their writing a particular style. They know, for example, that Dickens does not sound like Hemingway, but they often are not sure why.

Having read some works of both authors, perhaps *A Tale of Two Cities* and *The Sun Also Rises*, students are ready for this exercise. I give them each a piece of paper and ask them to describe something quite concrete and well within their experience—a sunset, the school cafeteria, the convenience store across the street. I give them no other directions; they simply must write a description of whatever we have chosen.

When they have completed this, they are ready to try it again—in a different way.

"Imagine you have suddenly become Charles Dickens," I tell them, "and you are standing in the middle of the school cafeteria. Write a description of the caf the way Charles Dickens would."

It's not an easy task for many, nor is it intended to be. Suddenly they are struggling to use rich language and vocabulary they are not entirely comfortable with. Their sentences grow more dense and more complex. They feel they need to write *more*, and they think hard, trying to imagine things about the cafeteria they may not have considered in their first descriptions.

I let them write until they feel they have done their best, and then I say, "Transformation time again! You're no longer Dickens. Now you're Ernest Hemingway! How would he describe the caf?"

They breathe a small sigh of relief. This seems easier. They understand Hemingway's stripped-down style, his straightforward declarative sentences, his unadorned vocabulary. But as they get involved in the writing, they find it isn't all that easy, that what looks simplistic on paper is rooted in something much deeper. And once again they struggle.

When all of them have completed these three pieces of description, we read many of the pieces aloud, and we compare and contrast the work we have done. We make lists of phrases on the board to describe the different styles of Dickens and of Hemingway, and as students read their own pieces to the group, we try to find words to characterize each student's style. I am always amused to see how pleased they are to discover that they have a style, but I remind them that, for most of them, their style is still evolving. Who knows? Maybe they will find themselves becoming more descriptive like Dickens or perhaps more minimalist like Hemingway. Now is a time to experiment.

The point of this exercise is threefold. First, it makes students recognize—and remember—the unique styles of important writers, for it obviously demands that they read the works of these writers closely if they are to imitate their styles. Second, it gives students an opportunity to experiment with the technique of style in a context they understand. Were I to tell them to describe the school cafeteria in three different writing styles, they would look at me blankly. This exercise makes them see that they *do* know how to write in different styles, and it allows them to take the risk and do so. Third, it enlightens students as to who they themselves are as writers. Do they write more like Dickens or more like Hemingway? What are the particular qualities of their own style? How does their work differ from that of other members of the class? Most young writers simply think they do schoolwork just like every other student in the class. An exercise like this shows them that they write in a style that is all their own.

Again, I would remind teachers that this one exercise can be adapted in many ways. Certainly the writers can be changed. Students discover extraordinary things when they try to write like Salinger or Vonnegut or Morrison. Or instead of asking students to describe a particular thing not connected to the literature, a passage could be taken from one author's work and rewritten in another author's voice as well as in the young writer's voice. Though *The Catcher in the Rye* and *Huckleberry Finn* are frequently compared both in themes and in the use of the vernacular, the vernacular from each time and place is very different, and a student trying to describe Holden Caulfield's adventures in New York City using Twain's style would certainly have some fun with language. Rewriting that scene again, this time in the voice of a '90s teenager, would be another interesting challenge. These sorts of activities can also be turned into games, in which students write short pieces in the style of a writer they select and then read their pieces aloud, letting other students guess which writer they are imitating.

Similar work can be done as students read poetry. Clearly the poetic style of William Carlos Williams is very different from that of Walt Whitman, but that truth—as well as an appreciation for each poet's unique style—never becomes clearer than when students try to imitate the poets on paper.

However the activity is adapted, the effect is the same: students develop a deeper appreciation for the literature they read and they themselves grow as writers.

Of course, these exercises are only that—exercises, designed to offer students writing practice that will help them grow into writers whose work has publishing potential. I have, however, had students so taken with the challenge of writing like Hemingway that they have gone on to enter the annual International Imitation Hemingway Competition, which challenges entrants to write a five-hundred-word parody of Hemingway. Others, having fun with writing styles they rarely associate with school writing, have sent entries to the Bulwer-Lytton Fiction Contest, an annual competition that asks writers to submit the worst possible opening line to a novel in a variety of genres. Though these activities are enjoyable, they also give students real practice with style and voice and help them to strengthen their own writing styles.

Experimenting with Genre

If I were to ask my students what kind of writing they were most comfortable with, most of them would say letter writing or personal essay writing. They are intimidated by analytical essay writing, feeling sure that it demands some complicated formula that only the teacher truly knows; they are put off by poetry and the rules of rhyme and meter they have come to believe it must obey; and they have grown too old and jaded to tell made-up stories with the wonderful abandon of young children. Letters and personal essays, however, allow them to write in a voice that comes naturally to them about topics that interest them.

I am glad that students enjoy writing letters and personal essays, and I encourage them to do so, knowing that any writing students do is valuable in that it builds confidence and sharpens writing skills. I recognize, though, that neither of these genres is highly marketable in the publishing world. Certainly, as described in the previous chapter, letters do go out into the world and have an effect on the reader to whom they are sent, but they less frequently generate payment or publishing credits! Personal essays do a bit better. Some magazines and newspapers, and especially those that are student-written, do publish first-person essays, but frequently the pieces students write in class need major revision and often expansion in order to make them interesting and appropriate for a wide audience.

One need only scan a page of market listings to see that editors seek particular genres—fiction and poetry, especially in the literary journals, and a range of articles from feature stories to opinion pieces to how-to's in many of the commercial and trade publications.

If young writers want to compete in these markets, they must submit work that fits the editorial needs. That means they have to move beyond the letters and personal essays with which they are comfortable and tackle new territory. For the teacher that means introducing students to the various genres and explaining the characteristics of each. This is certainly what we do as teachers of literature. When we introduce a play, novel, short story, or poem, we talk about its structure, and often we ask students to memorize terms—*exposition, climax, scene, stanza*—in order to demonstrate their understanding of its structure. As we get further into a piece of literature, we ask students to examine other literary devices—the symbols interwoven throughout a poem, the dialect in a short story, the foreshadowing employed in a novel. What students need to realize is that these literary techniques are not the exclusive property of established writers—nor are they simply terms to trip up students on final exams. Literary techniques are essential to good writing, and young writers can learn to use these techniques to improve their own writing and to make it marketable.

My sophomores generally agree that *Monkeys* is the best book we read in class. A contemporary work by Susan Minot, the novel describes the Vincent family, parents and seven children, over the course of thirteen years. The problems that plague the family are ones that my students deal with daily, and more than one student has said, "My father's just like Mr. Vincent," or "Sometimes I feel like I'm Sophie." It is that ring of truth that gives the novel its strength, and though Minot has said it is not strictly autobiographical, the work my students have done in searching out reviews of the work as well as biographical information on Minot reveal that there are definite connections between her life and the fictional work. Though the chapters are woven together beautifully to produce a novel, each of the nine chapters could stand on its own as a short story, and in fact some were published as such in the *New Yorker* and *Grand Street*.

Teaching this work gives me a perfect opportunity to lead my students toward fiction writing. Many of them may have lost the wild imaginations they possessed as young children and find themselves unable to invent stories out of thin air, but all of them have stories to tell. I know that from the conversations they share every day and from the letters and personal essays they write. Teenagers today live rich and complex lives, but lives often marked by chaos and pain. When my students write about their experiences, I realize that they know grief and joy, loss and acceptance, fear and courage as well as any fictional character ever has, and that the stories they live are the stuff of contemporary fiction. They need only learn how to turn their autobiographical essays into short stories by learning the techniques of fiction, such things as when and how to turn summary into drama, how to write dialogue, and how to create a moment of crisis.

When we read *Monkeys*, we consider all this. We read the chapter in which the family is vacationing in Bermuda and the oldest boy Gus is seeking his father's approval in increasingly desperate ways. Students recognize that this story could easily come from a personal experience (they have many of their own family vacation stories to tell!), so we discuss how the story would be told differently were it written as an essay. As they point out which scenes are told in summary and which are played out with dialogue and brilliant detail, they begin to get a feel for the shape of a short story. As they search through the chapter looking for lines that reveal character, lines that show us how Gus is different from his brothers and that help us understand the kind of man the father is and the things that he is hiding, they start to see how character is at the heart of a short story and that the reader must know and care about the characters if he or she is to care about the story. As they look for details that they think might have been invented or imagine those from the real-life story that might have been left out, they get a sense that fiction, though it replicates life, is not life and must be made that little bit more interesting for it to hold its readers.

Clearly this sort of exercise forces students to know the text inside out, and isn't that what teachers of literature want? Armed with this new knowledge and understanding of a genre that is marketable, students can then go forward and experiment with this sort of writing. That is generally what I ask my students to do. As we read and discuss *Monkeys*, I ask them to work on their own short stories, adapted from personal experience. Before we begin the writing, they tell each other their stories, trying, through the telling, to find a dramatic structure that works and that keeps the audience involved in the story. For many students, fiction writing is a new and difficult challenge, something they have been given little opportunity to do in school. For me to simply tell them "Write a short story" would be unfair and unproductive. I need to show them how to do so, and what better way to demonstrate fiction writing techniques than through the close examination of the literature they read.

This method can be used just as effectively with other genres. A student might, for example, want to turn her personal essay into a one-act play, perhaps to submit to a contest such as the Young Playwrights Festival National Playwriting Competition or Very Special Arts Playwright Discovery Program. Playwriting is a skill not often taught in school, and though it looks easy to young writers—many of my students are lulled by the fact that there is none of that detailed description to do—it is not as easy as it appears. When my students read plays, then, perhaps *The Glass Menagerie* or *A Raisin in the Sun*, we discuss the techniques involved in writing a play—the principles of economy and credibility, the need for authentic dialogue, the use of stage directions. I might then ask a group of students to collaborate on the writing of a one-act play, or I might ask each student individually to turn one of his or her own life experiences into a drama. One of my recent students wanted to write everything as a play, and I gave him free rein to do so, letting him discover on his own the limitations of that particular genre. At one point he turned to writing poetry.

"If I want to write about what I feel, it doesn't always work in a play," he said. "Unless," and he grinned, "I'm the only character."

I have also had students practice playwriting skills by turning sections of novels and short stories into play scenes. This works particularly well when students can compare their finished products with the work of experienced scriptwriters. So, for example, I have had students who were reading *Ethan Frome* work in small groups to choose a section of the book and turn it into a dramatic sequence, putting words into Ethan's mouth that Edith Wharton never did. Later, after the groups have read or performed their scenes for one another, we see the movie version of the novel, and students can compare their efforts to the screenwriter's approach. Another piece of literature this exercise works especially well with is Joyce Carol Oates's short story, "Where Are You Going, Where Have You Been?" and its film version, *Smooth Talk.* Not only are students particularly drawn in by the teenage protagonist who is very much like themselves, but they are also intrigued by the story's unresolved ending and the liberties taken with it in the film. The scenes they write—and many of them choose to focus on the tension between fifteen-year-old Connie and her mother—are usually exceptional, indicating not only obvious experience with parent-child conflict but an ability to capture the voice of both generations.

Not having a background or training in drama, I have done only minimal work with the actual performance of such pieces outside the classroom, but I have colleagues whose students stage extraordinary productions of their written work, inviting students, teachers, parents, and the community to see their performances. These students, trained in the elements of drama as well as in stage techniques through the plays they read, work collaboratively to adapt their writing, often pieces that began as personal essays, into a montage of short pieces, usually in a thematic design, that they can perform on stage. These performances require only minimal costuming and simple sets. Their power lies in the students' words, and that power is tremendous. Certainly it is important to remember that performance is a very meaningful method of publication. Words do not have to be printed on a page to have an impact on an audience, and that audience may be as small as the classroom or as wide as the world can offer. The point is that students learn through the works of the masters—the Millers, the Wilsons, the Chekhovs, and certainly the Shakespeares—how to put their ideas in words that could hold their own on a stage.

The personal essays students write also have a place in the world, but often require extensive revisions to make them fit the needs of editors. The first concern revolves around the issue of topic. In the personal essays students write for class assignments, they typically describe a personal experience based on a theme the teacher offers: *Describe your most frightening experience. Write about a time when you learned the meaning of courage. Tell about a moment when you discovered you were no longer a child.* Sometimes the teacher's directions lead students to write quasi-opinion pieces. *Who is your hero? What is the most interesting place you've ever been—and why? Write about the biggest problem facing teenagers today.* There is nothing wrong with any of these assignments—as long as they generate truly heartfelt responses—but I am willing to bet that in a class of twenty-five, it is very likely that at least a couple of students have yet to learn the meaning of courage or have no heroes or do not care about contemporary problems in any real way and will end up inventing "appropriate" experiences. I caution teachers, then, against being too dogmatic in their need to assign topics. I see nothing wrong with suggesting topics, particularly for younger students who benefit from some sort of direction, finding themselves either overwhelmed or underwhelmed by possibilities when they must make entirely their own choices. Even when I do make a specific assignment, perhaps seeing a need to make a close connection with a piece of literature, I always leave the door wide open for individual choice and modification. When I created the assignment described above in conjunction with *Siddhartha,* I admit I was imagining that students would write about someone who was a positive influence in their lives. Mark quickly showed me there were other options, and his final piece proved these options were very viable ones.

The point is, unless students care about what they are writing about, there is little chance the writing will be any good, let alone publishable. Consider, for example, a class of students who are reading Greek mythology and discussing the concept of the hero. Perhaps the teacher makes the seemingly logical decision to have her students write about the heroes in their lives. But maybe few students have a hero—and the sad truth is that in the '90s heroes are hard to come by. If a teacher were to demand that every student nevertheless write a personal essay about his or her hero, most students would do it, simply because the teacher, the person holding the gradebook, said to do it. And maybe there would be one or two brilliant essays about Mother Teresa, or Magic Johnson, or a loving grandparent, but I suspect most of the essays would be stilted and pedantic and hardly memorable, simply because the topic has no authentic meaning to the writers and so their response to it is false. They would hardly give their best effort to a piece that really did not matter to them, nor would they have any real motivation to attempt to publish such work. The essays would become simply a stack of papers to be read and graded by the teacher. The essays would become simply schoolwork.

So what is a teacher to do? Abandon all assignments? Have her students read the required mythology and then go on and write about absolutely anything they desire? I don't think the alternative to the "Write about Your Hero" assignment has to be that drastic. What the teacher can do is offer the word *hero* as the focus of a writing assignment and allow students to take off from there. Some may in fact decide to write about their heroes—family members or the people whose faces appear on the posters that paper their bedroom walls. Others may want to write about their own heroic moments, actions they themselves have taken that proved to be heroic. Some may move beyond the personal experience and write more of an opinion piece—perhaps an essay on why there are so few heroes in our time, or one that examines our need for heroes. Whatever approach each writer takes, he or she will gain a greater understanding of the concept of the hero and see that it has validity in a world very different from that of the ancient Greeks. That is the sort of knowledge we want our students to take from the literature they read. We want them to see that great works of literature have a meaning that reaches beyond their pages, that it is the universal truths that they reveal that make these works great and lasting.

When students are given a certain amount of freedom to write about topics that interest them, they are likely to produce pieces that have publishing potential. A stack of twenty-five similar essays on "My Hero" has no obvious market; two or three of the best, written by the students who truly have a hero, might be marketable in certain teenage journals or be appropriate for a particular contest. And certainly a well-written piece about a hero in the writer's immediate life could be sent to him or her and would surely generate a very positive response. But what about the other twenty-two essays, the ones that lack heart and substance simply because the topic had no real meaning to the writers? Those essays, with grades that indicate their mediocre quality, are apt to disappear into the students' writing folders, having had no real impact in the world.

But change the assignment a little bit—simply ask students to use the word *hero* as a focus—and that scenario will change in many ways. First and foremost, the work will be of better quality as more of the students will be writing about something that matters to them. A student, for example, may not have a hero because he does not believe in them. The essay he writes describing his distrust of heroes could be a powerful piece, one that could find its way into an op-ed section of a local newspaper or into an opinion column of a magazine. Second, the twenty-five pieces will no longer be carbon copies of one another, with one or two standing out as the best, the ones that most closely fulfill the teacher's expectations of topic, style, and form, and the others ranked in descending order along the way. When students are given freedom of expression in subject and style, there are apt to be many outstanding pieces, each stamped with the writer's unique voice. Third, when pieces are so individual, each appeals to a different market. Twenty-five students will not be clamoring to send their work to one contest where only one piece can be a winner. Instead, each student can search for the particular market that best suits his or her work, work that he or she has invested real thought and effort in and that is worthy to submit to a publication.

Of course I am not so idealistic as to think that *every* student in a class would ever have a heartfelt response to the word *hero* or any other broad topic. But I do know the chances are better with the topic broadened in that way than if the students are given the much more narrow assignment of "Write about Your Hero." I also know that some students will fail to respond even then and will need other options, ones that are still in keeping with the literature. Perhaps such a student would want to create a contemporary myth in the spirit of one of the Greek myths, complete with contemporary hero. Perhaps she would want to determine what it means to be the opposite of a hero and explore that character in our society. Certainly each teacher has to decide individually how much freedom he or she wants to give students in terms of the work they do. We all know that some students can manipulate situations and might take advantage of the teacher's willingness to make the work interesting in order to avoid challenges that are essential to their growth as writers. As in many classroom situations, teachers need to make wise judgment calls, ones that they are comfortable with and ones that best serve their students' needs.

Just as I generally give students much choice in their selection of topic, so, too, do I try to give them the freedom to work in the genre they prefer. So, to go back to the "hero" assignment, unless I were specifically trying to teach the entire class a specific essay writing skill—the design of the thesis statement, perhaps, or the need for examples to support a topic sentence—I would give my students the opportunity to do their pieces in another genre, such as poetry or drama. Some students are, by nature and by plain hard work, gifted poets, and they thrive when allowed to express themselves in poetry. Others, like the boy in my sophomore class who was into writing plays, get "hooked" on a genre, and their work grows steadily better as they work on piece after piece in that genre. I encourage the work of such students, recognizing that most adult writers would certainly be able to identify one particular genre with which they are most comfortable and skilled. But, and this is a large *but*, I also realize that young writers are still in the formative stages and that they need experience in all genres in order to legitimately determine which is their forte. So yes, I let Steve write everything in play form for a while, because I loved the enthusiasm he suddenly had for writing, and because I knew he would soon discover the limitations of the form on his own and bring his new passion for words to another genre. But I certainly do not think a student can be allowed to write free verse forever, refusing, for example, to master the elements of essay writing. Like the parent who tells the child he must at least try everything on his plate, so, too, do I tell my students that they must give each genre we study a try and be sure they do not reject it without a clear understanding of its strengths.

In keeping with that, I offer my students a variety of writing challenges so that they do not become too comfortable with the sort of essay writing they tend to do most often in school. Not only does this sort of writing become tedious and almost automatic after a while, but it surely cannot be the specialty of every writer, young or old. Different writers have different skills, and I want to give my students every chance of success as writers by letting them experiment with different genres to find their strong suit. Sometimes there are pleasant surprises.

Kelly's work produced one such surprise, and led to an equally surprising connection for me. Early in September, I ask my students to write feature stories about one another. My purpose is two-fold: 1) I want them to get to know each other and begin to build a community within the classroom; and 2) I want to get a sense of their writing ability.

First I introduce the concept of a feature story, bringing in samples fortuitously provided by the local paper which highlights some of the community's teenagers in its back-to-school issue. I suggest too that students bring in models they find, and usually we end up with an interesting assortment of pieces from *Sports Illustrated*, *Rolling Stone*, and *Glamour* about athletes, rock stars, and supermodels. As a class we then discuss interviewing techniques and work on generating interesting interview questions, ones that will tell us more about the subject than his or her favorite color. Always we are thinking of a focus or a hook, something that will draw the reader in and convince him or her that the subject is indeed worthy of a feature story. When this preliminary work is done, students randomly pick numbers that put them into pairs, and they spend the next few periods interviewing each other. Though they are guided by their interview questions, I remind them to be open to new ideas and to follow through on any interesting leads. They take notes on their interviews, being particularly careful to record some quotations. When they have gathered sufficient information, they begin writing the feature story, working both at home and in class. Like all other pieces of writing we do, these are read in response groups and revised and reworked accordingly. Ultimately the finished stories are mounted on a class bulletin board complete with accompanying photo which each writer takes of his or her subject with a disposable camera that I provide. Through the writing and reading of each story, students come to learn a lot about each other in a very short time, and we are well on our way to becoming a community of writers.

Sometimes, such as the year that Kelly was my student, there are added benefits. Though Kelly started out quite eager about the interview process, she became dejected once she had amassed all the information her subject was willing to offer.

"I can't do this," she wailed. "There's nothing to write about!"

In truth, her subject was not a high school hero, not a soccer star or president of the class or straight-A student. Her subject provided her with very little in terms of a hook. He was someone who generally disliked school and did not have a band or a job or a cool car to talk about. In fact, the only one more dejected than Kelly was her subject. I tried to help her and to prod him by suggesting more questions, but none of my efforts helped. It was not that either of them was being uncooperative; it was simply that the interviewee was an all-too-average teenager who had not found a focus in his own life, and I could hardly expect the interviewer to do that for him!

Then Kelly did something rather remarkable. Without a word to me, she abandoned the idea of writing a feature story and turned her subject's life into fiction. She did not glamorize it; he did not suddenly become a teenage superhero or even, for that matter, a happy and successful young man. Instead, he remained who he was, a rather confused fifteen-year-old, bored with school, itching for independence, and wondering what his place in the world was. It was a poignant story, real enough to touch the hearts of her classmates who suffered similar feelings, fictitious enough to protect her subject's privacy. The protagonist of her story became something of a teenage Everyboy or Everygirl, loved by the readers.

So Kelly did not write a feature story that year, and though maybe she did not acquire the skills to do so, I do not worry about it. Kelly proved herself to be a fiction writer, not only by talent but by instinct. She quickly realized that the material she had collected was not the stuff of great journalism, but it was the stuff of fiction, and she used it accordingly. In the process, she opened the door for herself and her classmates to enjoy another writer's story, one which they appreciated because Kelly's work had created one of those rare and wondrous "teachable moments."

Kelly's writing led us to Peter Cameron's "Homework." Originally appearing in the *New Yorker* and later published in Cameron's short-story collection *One Way or Another,* "Homework" was also printed in *Literary Cavalcade,* and it remains one of my favorite stories to teach. "Homework" is the story of a teenage boy who simply and temporarily stops going to school. The adults in his life attribute his actions to the grief he feels over the death of his dog, but there is more troubling Michael. In a very few pages, Cameron captures the angst of adolescence. It is a powerful story both in the quality of the writing and in the issues it addresses. Though my sophomores always read this story, never did it work so well as when Kelly set the stage for it with her feature-turned-fiction story. It was another time when the literature and the writing came together in a way I did not expect but try always to remain ready for.

Anticipating Audience

Every writer needs to anticipate the audience he or she is writing for. A clear image of the reader helps to clarify the writing. Sadly, our students have a rather limited view of audience. Having been trained for so long to write for the teacher, they are barely cognizant of an audience beyond the person wielding the red pen. Though that red pen may be a motivator of young writers, it is hardly the best kind. It is far better for them to be inspired to write because they imagine a world of interested readers waiting for their words.

The literature students read in class can help them develop an understanding of the importance of audience and make them better able to direct their own writing to a particular audience. With that sort of focus, students produce writing that is interesting and marketable—and that demands far less attention from the teacher's red pen!

Just as students struggle with the concept of audience for their own work, so too are they sometimes confounded by the notion that the work they read in class was originally destined for a particular audience—and not one confined to desks and chairs. Younger students especially tend to think that the books and stories they read in school were created to fill the hours of English class, and they look astounded when I tell them that generations of people spent pleasant evening hours enjoying *The Red Badge of Courage* or *Walden*. Contemporary literature fares somewhat better in that they can see its authors' names in the copies of the *New Yorker* or *Harper's* that I bring into class, but still, to most of them, school reading is one thing, pleasure reading something else. One student even looked somewhat betrayed when she discovered an issue of *Seventeen* with a Joyce Carol Oates story in it. It was a bit hard for her to reconcile the fact that the same writer we were studying in class was appearing in her favorite magazine. In Lisa's mind, it appeared some unspoken boundary had been crossed!

When students read literature in class, I think it is important for them to realize that few, if any, writers imagine their audience to be a classroom full of adolescents who have been told this work is good for them. Rather, writers imagine an audience of perfect readers, perceptive and empathetic human beings who appreciate the writer's skill and sensitivity and ability to communicate ideas clearly. They imagine readers who love their work. I try to give my students a sense of the authors they read as people who do dream of such perfect readers. I give them biographical information on the authors, emphasizing especially the struggle most face in getting their work published, and I stress that the ability to write well is not a gift but a goal, and one that takes much hard work and determination as well as the courage to risk failure. Not only is specific information about each writer's individual struggle important in order to bring his or her work to life, but it also paves the way for my students' own publishing challenges. It is far easier to accept rejection from a major magazine if you know the writer you are reading in school once suffered her own rejection from that same publication.

I also ask my students to think about the audience for whom a particular work was intended. Who was Fitzgerald writing for when he penned *The Great Gatsby* or Willa Cather when she wrote *My Ántonia?* What about poets like Lawrence Ferlinghetti or playwrights like August Wilson? Are they thinking of a reading audience at all, or are they imagining an audience sitting in the dark hearing the words loud and clear? What about contemporary writers like Jay McInerney and Lorrie Moore, whose work peppers the pages of national magazines? How about writers who have come to represent the "new voices"—minority voices or those long silenced—writers like Amy Tan, Jamaica Kincaid, and David Leavitt? Whom are they all speaking to?

Certainly there is no one correct answer in any of these cases. A writer like Fitzgerald who could spew out short "formula" stories for slick magazines while working on a masterpiece clearly has more than one audience in mind, but the point is, each work does have an audience, and its author has a vision of that audience. In a world where commercial considerations are an important factor, the purity of that vision may be compromised, but the fact remains that if a writer expects to be published, he must never lose sight of whom he is writing for.

It is not easy to wean my students away from the practice of writing for the teacher alone. Though I try, through the rapid establishment of response groups, to forestall their even starting to write just for me, they have had too many years of experience to easily abandon the idea of Teacher as Reader. Projects like the feature story described above may help, because the subject of each story naturally becomes its most fascinated reader, but sometimes an even more dramatic approach is needed.

Picture book writing is one such approach. Middle and high school students may be years beyond the reading of picture books, but they are not beyond loving them. It is a rare student, even among those who in their adolescent years have become reluctant readers, who cannot remember a picture book that, as a child, she loved desperately. Many students can still quote lines from books that were read to them over and over again, and some, the packrats or those with younger siblings, can even produce these beloved books. I love the shrieks of delight that greet *Curious George* or *The Saggy Baggy Elephant* when the book appears in class and is immediately pounced upon by those students who also remember it well.

Much can be learned from children's books. Though one would hardly build a middle or secondary school English curriculum around them, neither would one deny that the best children's books contain all the elements of good literature—well-drawn characters, a vivid setting, a carefully constructed plot, a strong sense of voice, and the clever use of language. When students examine them carefully, they begin to see the parallels in the design of such seemingly simple books and the adult works they read in class. When I ask my students to write their own children's stories, which will ultimately be made into picture books, I am asking them to explore those parallels as well as to come face to face with the concept of audience. At the same time, they are engaged in a real-life publishing venture. Things are coming together.

This picture book project can be designed in a variety of ways. Each student can write his or her own story, or a group of students can collaborate on a story. Usually I leave that decision to the students themselves. Some prefer to work alone, liking the freedom to go off in their own direction; others like the creative support offered by a small group. However the students choose to work, the task is the same: they must write a children's story that is appropriate for, and interesting to, a particular age group. Their audience is not an imaginary one either, although here again the approach in terms of who the audience is can be altered.

One easy and highly effective means of getting a real audience is through a connection with a primary-grade teacher. In some school systems, this means walking down the hall; in others, it means making a phone call to a school some distance away. Either way, it is a relatively easy task to find a classroom of first or second graders who would delight in reading stories written expressly for them by "the big kids." But if this approach is impractical, there are other possibilities. A teacher can appeal to a neighborhood nursery school or day care center, some of which are housed in public schools. Students can even find their own audiences in younger brothers and sisters, neighborhood kids, or the children they baby-sit. The audience does not even have to be a local one. I have known teachers who have hooked up with an elementary school colleague in another state and have conducted the project by mail.

Once an audience is selected, students need to develop a clear understanding of what is appropriate and interesting to the particular audience. Certainly what works for a four-year-old would likely strike a "grown-up" seven-year-old as babyish. Students themselves can be resources in determining what is right. Those with young siblings might bring in their favorite books or even hold "interviews" with their brothers and sisters, asking them what they like stories to be about. If the audience is right down the hall in school, then a class visit might be effective in order for the authors to talk to their audience and see the books they are reading. And certainly, too, students' own memories of the books they loved provide valuable insights.

It is possible, and also very exciting, to use the audience as more than a reading audience. Children's books contain more than words: the pictures on the pages are equally important to their young readers. Though older students love to do the artwork for their picture books, sometimes they can be persuaded to turn that task over to the children, and the cooperation and collaboration that results is a wonderful thing. Imagine a six-year-old's delight at being asked to draw the pictures to show just what did happen to Louisa with the Lollipop Legs or the Sulking Sun and the Merry Moon. Again, writer and illustrator can work closely together through scheduled class visits, or they can work independently, sending pages of the book back and forth between them. Although I generally ask that the writing be done before the illustrating begins so that my students can engage in the necessary reading, responding, and revising, it is not uncommon for other revisions to take place as writer and reader/illustrator collaborate on the finished product. The young readers are unabashedly candid in their appraisal of what is good about the book and what is not, and the older students generally take their comments to heart and make changes accordingly. In that way student writers are far more fortunate than published writers who only know what displeases their audience after the book is in print!

But these children's books *can* go into print; how elaborately depends on the teacher and the classes involved. The text can be handwritten or computer-printed; the illustrations done by a six-year-old's crayons or a fifteen-year-old's oil paints. The pages can be tied together with brightly colored yarn, clipped together with brass fasteners, or bound in a sophisticated bookmaking process. The choices depend on the time and energy a teacher wants her class to devote to the project. No matter how the books are finally published, I predict they will be presented with great pride by their authors and received with great enthusiasm by their readers. And that is the point of the activity: to give students a project that lets them connect the skills of good writing, and specifically good storytelling, with a focus on an audience and a desire to create work that has a real place in the world.

Indeed, one of the biggest dilemmas following the publication of these books is what to do with them next. Usually the student writers are quite generous in letting their young readers keep the books and share them with each other. The writers wait anxiously to hear which are the favorite books within the group—a bit like waiting for word from the reviewers—and these responses seem to carry more weight than any teacher's grade. Sometimes, if the work has been done with a primary class, that teacher will decide to keep the books as part of the class library, and sometimes the books are sent to the real school library and even given their own check-out cards. What's important is that the writers see that their work has continuing meaning; it is not simply a school project to be finished, graded, and tossed away. Writing a book means putting your words into the world, where they may last for a long, long time.

There is even in this project the potential for much greater fame and fortune. Some companies, among them Landmark Books, Raspberry

Publications, and Tyketoon Publishing Company, offer publishing contracts to young writers who produce quality books for young readers. These opportunities are listed in the Market List and Contest List in the Appendix. I advise teachers to send for information and submission guidelines because there are very specific instructions to follow in order for a work to be eligible. Companies interested in such student-written ventures often also publish books that aid teachers in such a class project, and these resources can be very valuable, particularly in the technical aspect of book production. Certainly these outlets offer extraordinary chances for student writers, and those students willing to take on the work involved should be encouraged to do so. Whether they earn a publishing contract or not, they will benefit greatly from the work involved in the project and from the sudden awareness that someone outside the classroom is waiting for their words.

Studying style, experimenting with genre, anticipating audience: all of the work students do around these activities strengthens the connection between the literature they read and the words they write. No longer are the two disciplines distinct and different. Great literature may be writing that is "done," but learning what went into the "doing" makes young writers better able to do their own work, writing that may not have yet earned the adjective "great," but may well be worthy of the word "good."

Part Two

The exercises above ask students to consider the genre of a piece and the stylistic devices its author employs. This, to me, is of primary importance in any study of literature. I want my students to leave my class with an appreciation for each writer that we read, and I am far more concerned that they leave carrying with them an understanding of his or her unique style and voice than that they remember factual details from the text. I recognize, though, that many teachers feel a need to determine if their students have "learned" certain material, particularly factual material, from the literature, and they feel that they cannot go forward into a deeper, more rewarding exploration of the work until they are sure that all students have, quite simply, done their reading. This is generally ascertained by a quiz or a test, which is clearly the most efficient method. What teachers need to realize, however, is that even when such quiz or test questions demand written responses beyond a *true* or *false* or multiple-choice letter, the writing is not the focus; the facts are. True, some teachers refuse to give credit if an answer is not written in a complete sentence or if it includes certain grammatical mistakes, but that is more an editing concern. I think, however, it is quite possible to combine the goals teachers attempt to achieve through reading quizzes and tests with more meaningful writing—writing that even has the potential to be published.

What I am referring to is writing *about* literature. Writing about literature goes far beyond outlining the facts in a short story, novel, or play—summarizing the plot, listing the characters, stating the setting. Though the ability to do so may confirm that a student has read a piece of literature, it does little else. It certainly does not allow for individual response and reflection. Writing *about* literature does both. When a student writes about a piece of literature, she can express an opinion about the work, explore her questions about the work, or reflect on the work's connection to her own world. All of those activities demand that she read the work closely and prove that she has done so through specific references to the text. All of those activities generate writing that comes not only from her mind but from her heart. And all of those activities produce writing that has publishing potential.

One of the most powerful, but, I believe, underused kinds of writing that students can do to demonstrate their factual knowledge, as well as their individual opinions, is the review. Students are surprisingly familiar with reviews. They read them all the time to determine what movies to see or what videos and CDs to buy. Of course, a page taken from the *New York Times Book Review* or the "Books" section of the *Atlantic* is a bit more daunting for most adolescents, but the point is, they understand what reviews are supposed to do, and they see them as a valuable resource.

Teachers can start by asking students to bring in reviews of films they have seen or music they enjoy, and, through a close study of this material, they can guide students to an awareness of the qualities of a good review. Students come to understand that the reviewer must take a stand on the work and though any opinion, positive or negative, is valid, it must be substantiated by specific examples. Examples must be clear and memorable, and they must be precise. No one will believe a reviewer who offers erroneous information. The review must be tightly constructed, and it must say enough, but not too much. Who wants to see a movie or read a book if all the suspense has been taken away?

The review must also be interesting, not only in content but in style and voice, and it must sustain the reader's attention throughout. In short, the review must have all the characteristics of good writing, and the reviewer must do all the things we want our students to do—read closely, think carefully, write coherently.

Reviews, then, are an excellent writing activity for students to engage in. When students are asked to write a review of a piece of literature they have read—be it a novel, a short story, a play, or a poem—they have to be critical readers of the work and astute observers of its strengths and weaknesses. They then have to make a judgment about the work and support that judgment with material from the text. This activity gives students a sense of power, the power any reader has the right to. I do not mind at all if a student writes a negative review of *Billy Budd, The Scarlet Letter,* or any other book that does not appeal to his taste and sensibility—but he cannot simply say it was boring. He has to prove it was boring by discussing the style or what he sees as the lack of action. Sometimes in attempting to do so, he realizes that the book was not so bad after all and that his aversion to it was more a function of his expectations as a '90s reader. Sometimes he makes a good case against the novel and writes a review that would trigger much intelligent discussion were it published for a wider audience.

Like all other writing we do in class, the reviews my students write are read in response groups and receive feedback from the group to use in revision. The sharing that goes on in response groups has another function here as well. In the process of talking about a student's work, the group also engages in a discussion of the literary work. For example, imagine a student review of J. D. Salinger's *Nine Stories.* A student might write a negative review based on her opinion that the endings of the stories are left unresolved. She might offer as evidence two stories, "Teddy" and "The Laughing Man," both of which do leave the reader puzzling about the outcome. But another student, responding to the review, might rise to Salinger's defense, perhaps maintaining that it is quite clear what happens at the end of "A Perfect Day for Bananafish," or he might feel that the ambiguity in certain stories is purposeful and effective and he might offer specific reasons why. Whatever the discussion, the fact is, it *is* discussion, which is what we as teachers of literature want our students to engage in. A student who has not read and remembered the material cannot participate in such a discussion, and that usually becomes very clear both to the group and to the teacher. Generally, as a result, students either feel pressured by their peers to read and participate, or, even better, they are inspired to read by the enthusiasm the work has generated in their classmates. And certainly too they have their own reviews to write and defend!

It is interesting to watch students create their own rating scales and methods of measuring one work against another. My New Literature students generally begin the year reading Raymond Carver, the "father" of minimalist writing. They adore him—for precisely the same reasons so many critics do: for his ability to speak the plain truth about real people and real life. Their love of Carver then becomes a standard against which all other writers are measured. We read other early minimalists—Mary Robison, Ann Beattie, and Grace Paley—and they shake their heads. "Not as good as Ray," they say. (To my students, Carver seems so approachable, they can only call him Ray!) When they write reviews of these other writers' works, I let them make specific comparisons between each writer and Carver. Though that might not always be appropriate for a review published in the *New York Times,* it works for my students and helps them see how literature is a movement and how writers are part of a community, each struggling to find a place in it. These four writers were all writing at the same time in a similar style for a similar audience, and yet each was distinct from the rest because of the type of characters that peopled the pages, the concerns reflected in the plot, or the voice used to tell the story. To recognize and appreciate the similarities and the differences that exist among writers and to understand how their work reflects the society in which they write is what it means to study literature. When students write reviews that compare and contrast writers' works, they are doing that sort of study.

And students do not even have to like the writers. Todd was one such student. Todd hated everything we read sophomore year, from the generally loved *Monkeys* to the less popular *Siddhartha.* He did all the reading—probably because he knew I would not listen to his complaints otherwise—but he claimed to hate it all. "It's *sooo* boring," he would groan, occasionally supplementing his oral critique with an "It's dumb." But on paper Todd had to be more specific; he had to *prove* that Alice Hoffman's *Illumination Night* was dumb or that Jack London's stories were boring. And he could not quite do it. When he had to put his whines into written words, he found that he did like some things better than others, that he did not hate them all equally, and that maybe that Ethan Canin story was not as bad as he thought; it *was* better than the Faulkner one, and, in Todd's mind, for very definite reasons. Had Todd not had to write reviews, had he only had to take quizzes and write essays about the reading, I suspect he never would have discovered that all things are relative, and that if you despise one book enough, the others are bound to seem better! As a student Todd was not an enthusiastic reader, and the mere fact that a book was assigned in school assured him that it would be "boring and dumb." As a reviewer, however, he gained a more open mind and began to see something of value in some of the works.

These reviews my students write are not just an in-class activity, designed simply to encourage reading and reflection. Reviews of literature have publishing potential, both within the classroom and far outside of it. Thus they also become vehicles to improve student writing.

In one of my favorite activities, students contribute to a collection of reviews that grows over the years. After students have shared with one another their reviews of a work we are reading in class, I ask them to select among themselves three or four of the best reviews to be added to an ongoing anthology of reviews to be read by future classes. I ask students to determine which reviews should be included, partly to remind them that I am not the ultimate judge of quality writing, but also because I think they will choose reviews that are meaningful to their peers. I am always pleased when they select reviews that offer contradictory opinions because I know differing views will also be voiced by future students. I do caution students against selecting simple book-report-like pieces to go in the collection. After all, I tell them, we are not creating our own version of Cliffs Notes for the lazy readers, nor do we want to ruin the suspense of any piece for the readers. The reviews that go in the class collection should be like any review—not a plot summary but an intelligent evaluation of the work, marked by the style and voice of the reviewer.

Book reviews also have publishing potential in a wider sphere. Certain publications, especially those geared to young readers, are in the market for book reviews written by students. *Writing!*, for example, publishes book reviews by students in its "Reader's Choice" department, stressing that the choice of the book is always made by the student submitting the review. Eager to encourage more reading by a generation known for its lack of interest in that activity, many editors obviously realize that the best encouragement comes from adolescents themselves. When students write compelling reviews of works that we read in class, I suggest they send them off to these publications. I also encourage students who are avid readers to share their pleasure in the books they have read on their own with readers of the magazines. At the end of this section is a list of markets interested in book reviews written by students. More specific information on each publication can be found in the Market List in the Appendix.

There are other ways students can demonstrate through meaningful writing their knowledge of a text as well as their opinions and feelings about it. One such approach is to let students write letters back and forth to each other in an attempt to clarify the ideas in a work. This works particularly well when the letters go between classes, with students from one group exchanging their ideas with students in another. Often two classes, engaged in reading the same work, express radically different opinions on it. When two of my New Literature classes read "Little Things" by Raymond Carver, they came up with strongly opposing views as to how the issue *was* decided at the end. They also differed in their opinion of who was the "villain" in the story and why. Certainly as the teacher I could have gone back and forth between the two classes, telling each group what the other thought. But it was far more effective to let each group of students put their thoughts into words. Within each class, small subgroups of students formed, each responsible for addressing one concern. The class that maintained that the baby was killed at the end had a group responsible for convincing the other class of that, by means of persuasive arguments drawn from the text. The class that believed that the mother let go before harm was done to her child did the same. One class believed that the man's infidelity was the reason for the fight in the first place; the other saw the woman as the culprit. Again, within each class, a group set out to prove that their interpretation was the correct one.

None of this was simple. It is far easier to carry on a spirited discussion when all participants are present and able to speak, building on to each others' words and reacting to comments as they come. It is more difficult when you have to anticipate arguments in advance and express yourself clearly and succinctly in an organized statement. Yet that is a skill which young people need; it is a skill which life demands. When, for example, you write a letter to an editor about a community problem or one to a company expressing your displeasure with a product, you have to make yourself heard without the aid of qualifying questions and answers. So, too, when a writer publishes a piece must she assume that this is her one shot, that she isn't going to have the chance to respond to her readers' confusion, to make her point clearer, to say it all again and better.

When students are confused about a published writer's work, I sometimes employ a similar technique. The reading of poetry, something most students are not naturally attuned to, presents many such opportunities. Say, for example, my students read Emily Dickinson's "Much Madness is Divinest Sense" as an introduction to reading the play *Man of La Mancha.* Typically, that poem, its title alone a paradox, evokes a certain amount of confusion among my students, a confusion that I see as positive in that it leads to curiosity and a need to make sense of it all. I might start that search for understanding by asking three or four students in the class to pose a question on a piece of paper, the answer to which would definitely aid them in their comprehension of the poem. The question, however, cannot be something as general as "What does this poem mean?", because presumably no one in class knows what it means. Rather, the question should be more pointed and perceptive—for example, "What *is* divinest sense? Does it have to do with something spiritual?"—giving the responder, the next student in line, at least a chance of offering an intelligent answer. As the three or four questions circulate around the room, students compose responses, write them down, and sign them. If Kate writes that she thinks divinest sense has to do with intuition, then Alex might write that sometimes people who are perceived as mad appear to have a powerful intuition. That might then lead Candace to say that having such a sixth sense might make you better able to cope with life—or she might backtrack and ask what intuition is, leaving the next student to find a clear definition for her. Certainly all of this could be conducted in a verbal discussion and probably in a more timely fashion. But a verbal discussion would not permit two important things to happen. First, it would generally not allow all students to be equally involved. As all teachers know, in any discussion there are those students who dominate while the more reticent students sit silent unless the teacher specifically calls on them. Second, having to put their ideas into written words forces students to use language more efficiently and effectively than they might in speech. I imagine most students who know what intuition is would somehow find a way of conveying that knowledge aloud, perhaps with a little help from their friends who could fill in the gaps. But to define intuition succinctly on a piece of paper, without the help of a dictionary, is much more difficult. The writer cannot try to gauge how much a reader understands, as can the speaker with a listener. The writer has to say it once and say it well.

Though obviously an exercise of this sort is not publishable outside the classroom, it does generate much student involvement and is a sort of mini-publication within the group. A writer's words are on paper, his or her name accompanying them, and they are read by the group. That is often enough to encourage students to give the work their best effort, which is the primary goal of publication. Beyond this, however, the exercise may lead to a more formal effort that is worthy of publication outside the classroom. There are contests with literature at their center which ask students to express ideas about specific literary works. (See the Contest List in the Appendix.)

One of the most well known is the essay contest sponsored by the Ayn Rand Institute. This annual contest, offering over $20,000 in prize money, features two divisions, one for ninth and tenth graders focusing on the novel *Anthem*, and the other for eleventh and twelfth graders focusing on *The Fountainhead*. Each year specific essay topics are offered, and students must select one to respond to. Essays are judged on both style and content with a particular emphasis on understanding of the philosophies inherent in each novel. Certainly students need not have discussed either of these works in an English class to do well on such an essay, but they do need to have learned to express and support their opinions on paper in a convincing and articulate manner. Exercises like the ones described above can give students practice in exactly that and can lead to bigger projects.

Another contest opportunity that connects writing with the study of literature is the "Letters About Literature" Contest sponsored by *Read*. This competition, open to students in grades 6-12, asks students to choose a book they have read and feel strongly about and then to write a letter to its author, explaining what the book taught them about themselves. This is an interesting assignment to give to students at the end of a semester, allowing them to choose from the books read in class or those many have read on their own. Not all students will want to submit their letters to the competition, but simply writing the letter will strengthen students' writing skills while reminding them that good writing touches the reader's heart.

These connections between writers and readers are what we seek when we make literature and writing one in our classrooms. We want our students to be writers. We want our students to be readers. I truly do not believe they can be one without being the other.

Suggested Markets for Student Reviews

The following is a list of magazines/publications that publish student reviews. They may be interested in book reviews, movie reviews, music reviews, or even food reviews. See the Market List for specific information on each publication, and send a SASE for specific guidelines for writing reviews for the publication.

Hobson's Choice

How On Earth!

Iowa Woman

Merlyn's Pen

The New Girl Times

New Moon: The Magazine for Girls and Their Dreams

Seventeen

Stone Soup, The Magazine By Young Writers and Artists

360° Magazine

The 21st Century

The Writers' Slate

Writes of Passage

Writing!

Young Voices

4 The World of Published Writing

Student writer as published writer. This idea seems natural to me, but it is not a universally accepted one. Some of my colleagues consider my confidence in the student writer as published writer to be foolish; those who are kinder substitute the word idealistic. Whatever their words, their message is clear: a lot of student writing isn't very good, and as a teacher I'm wasting my time encouraging students to pursue publication. Any teacher who does encourage her students to publish their work, and who creates a classroom that fosters that activity, is likely to incur similar resistance. Perhaps the best arguments for this practice are anecdotal. I offer two of my stories, certain that the teacher who does become an advocate of student publishing will very quickly collect her own.

I ran into Dina not too long ago. She was pushing a grocery cart, three little boys clutching its sides. I smiled at her, the sympathetic smile I send to harried mothers with children, and headed toward the cereal aisle. But a voice, tentative and a bit quizzical, followed me.

"Ms. Rubenstein?"

I turned around, focusing on her face. She *did* look familiar, but. . . .

"I'm Dina," she said. "Dina Andrews. Well, Dina Cassidy now," she smiled at the boys," but I was Dina Andrews back in 1982. Creative Writing? Remember?"

I *do* remember. More than a dozen years have passed, yet I do remember that young blonde girl in Room 231, always polite and smiling, not the best writer in the class maybe, but sure, I remember Dina.

We exchanged warm smiles and pleasantries, and then I began to push my cart forward. She stopped me with her words. "I'm working on a book," she said, "a children's book. Would you . . . would you read it?"

Sometimes when students leave my class, I banter with them, telling them I expect a dedication in their first novel or collection of poetry. Those are the students whose papers are splashed with the yellow highlights I use to mark lines I particularly like, who come to me after class bearing notebooks full of stories, who scan the bulletin board every day looking for new contests to enter.

Dina was not such a student. Dina was a quiet, reserved seventeen-year-old, who, if I recall correctly, was interested mainly in horses and the dress she was wearing to the Senior Prom. I don't recall her writing, and, as she reminded me slyly as we leaned against our grocery carts, I gave her a B- for the course. But somehow in that class the seed was planted. Somewhere in the jumble of handouts—market lists, cover letters, and manuscript preparation guidelines ("I still have those," she tells me. "Are they outdated?")—Dina found something that would never become passé. She found a reason to believe in the power of her own words. Years ago I told Dina that when you have something to say that comes from your heart, there is a whole world waiting for your words. Now, as a mother, Dina's heart is full of children and she has something to say to them. It may have taken more than a dozen years for her ability and her confidence to come to fruition, but, in the course of a lifetime, that isn't very long.

Sometimes it doesn't take that long. I think of Brian, a hulking sophomore who hung out in my classroom before school with his pals, tossing wisecracks and elbows at one another as only sophomores can. It was always Brian's elbow that got caught on the bulletin board, tearing a flyer or sending an envelope of entry forms to the floor. It was always Brian who picked absent-mindedly at the staples while he listened to the bluster of his buddies. None of the damage was intentional. I knew Brian's mind was far removed from my bulletin board. It was just something that got in his way while he was being what he was, a fifteen-year-old kid charged with the energy of adolescence. But it made me crazy. And he wasn't even my student.

One day I had had enough. My polite requests to *please be careful of the bulletin board* had gone unheeded one morning too many. I stomped to the back of the room, looked Brian in the eye, and pointed to a page taken from *The 21st Century* posted on the board.

"Read this," I said.

His friends snickered, but Brian did as he was told.

"'Enter Virgin Records' Contest: Fight For Your Mind. $800.00 in cash to be awarded. . . .'"

I stopped him. "That's enough. Thank you. The point is, there are announcements here that students are interested in. I'd appreciate it if you'd leave them intact long enough for them to read them!"

The boys laughed again, but they moved a few steps away from the bulletin board. Brian ducked his head, seemingly abashed, and I went back to my desk, hoping the matter was settled, at least for a few days.

I was wrong. Brian was back at the bulletin board the next morning, even before his friends arrived. But this time he was studying it intently, and, had I not known better, I would have thought he had never seen that board before in his life.

Then suddenly he was in front of me. "Eight hundred bucks?" he said. "They give you eight hundred bucks?!"

"It's not quite that easy," I cautioned. "It's a national contest. There'll be a lot of entries. There are rules to follow. And you have to have something you really want to say."

I am adamant that students not be led to believe that entering a writing contest is like buying a lottery ticket. But a dreamy look had already come into Brian's eyes, and, though I am realistic enough to know it was at that point the look of someone counting crisp one hundred dollar bills, I encouraged him to write down all the necessary information and give it a try. *Write a letter, essay, or poem about your feeling and opinions on "Freedom of Expression."* More than once that morning while his friends jostled and joked before the first bell rang, I caught him staring at the paper in his hand. When he headed out of the room, he gave me a small wave.

To be honest, I didn't expect to hear any more about Brian's literary pursuits. Experience has taught me that though students are often tempted by the publishing opportunities available to them, they often fail to follow through on them unless steadily encouraged by a teacher, another adult, or a fellow writer. They dream of the winning but are often discouraged by the work. Brian struck me as such a student.

I was wrong. Within a few days, Brian was back in front of my desk, an essay in hand. It wasn't a great essay and it certainly wasn't an award-winning essay, but Brian knew that. He held it out to me and said, "What can I do to make it better?"

"You want to win?" I asked him.

"Yeah," he said, "but I want to say what's in my head too, and I don't know how."

I wondered if the words that were in his head had ever mattered to him before.

Sometimes I wonder if I am too idealistic (I won't admit to being foolish!) in my attempt to turn my students into published writers. On those days I think of Dina and Brian. They reassure me. Neither Dina nor Brian showed great youthful promise as writers. Neither exhibited a gift that any teacher would feel particularly privileged to nurture. Yet both of them saw themselves as writers. Dina grew into that identity. Brian stumbled upon it. Presented with an opportunity and with the knowledge and skills—and encouragement—needed to make their words public, both found they were writers, real writers, pursuing the path to publication.

Students who have something to say, who take pride in their work, and who commit themselves to the painstaking writing and revision that professionals undertake (and that English teachers demand) ought to give that writing a chance to "make it" in the world outside the classroom. That is not idealistic; that is practical. For good writing to languish in a gradebook or in a folder marked "Student Writing" or even to hang on the bulletin board (subject to the mischief of the Brians of the world!) is sad and senseless. Good writing deserves the widest possible audience, one that goes beyond the classroom walls and even beyond the school building walls.

The preceding chapters have suggested ways to begin to build a wide audience, an audience of readers for whom the writing has real meaning. As students grow comfortable with the idea of an expanded audience through their letters and reviews and shared papers, they develop the confidence and the writing skills to move naturally into a much wider sphere—the world of published writing. It is an exciting world, where one's words can reach thousands of readers. It is a world filled with possibilities for the proverbial fame and fortune. It can also be a cold world, where rejection comes in the form of a printed slip clipped to the manuscript with no kind words penned by a teacher to soften the rebuff. For that reason, I caution teachers about *requiring* students to attempt to publish their work in a competitive market. Not all students are emotionally ready to face flat-out rejection, and to put them in such a situation is to jeopardize their growth as writers.

Teachers who encourage their students to publish work in a competitive market need to be very aware of both the rewards and the risks of such a pursuit. In fact, I would suggest that teachers who undertake this activity be *personally* cognizant of the rewards and risks; that is, that they be writers themselves. They should know what it feels like to struggle with words, and they should understand the thrill a writer feels when finally she's got it right. They should be familiar with markets, own the yearly *Writer's Market*, and subscribe to magazines like *Poets & Writers* and *Writer's Digest*. And, most important, they should know what it feels like to have their work rejected. It's one thing to tell a student not to be discouraged when her story is turned down by *Story* or *Skylark*. It's another to truly know that sinking feeling when you see a big brown envelope in your mailbox. In the world of athletics, it is generally agreed that to be a good coach you have to know what it's like to play the game. It's no different for a writing teacher. To be an effective and empathic "coach" in the game of publishing, it's best if you've taken a few knocks on the field yourself.

Armed with that personal knowledge of the experience of trying to publish, there are things a teacher should consider to help make her students' experience in the publishing world a positive one. First, as Part One of this chapter indicates, teachers, as well as students, need to be aware of both The Risks and The Rewards involved in attempting to publish. Then, when the decision has been made to go forward, to send words into the world, students need to know how to do it right, to produce a professional manuscript. Part Two addresses those concerns.

Part One

The Risks

Rejection

Rejection is demoralizing; there's no refuting that. When as writers we send our work out into the world, we send pieces of ourselves, and when those pieces come back marked *Thanks but no thanks*, we can't help but lose a little confidence in our work and feel hurt. For young writers, unused to such unqualified rejection, the blow can be quite damaging and make them wary of ever submitting their work anywhere again. For that reason, it's important to make students understand that rejection is just part of the game. To return to the sports analogy, in every game there are winners and losers, but just because you didn't win—your name isn't on the front page, you didn't take home the trophy—doesn't mean you're not a player. As long as you're out there on that field kicking a soccer ball, you're a soccer player, and as long as you're putting words on a page and sending those words out into the world, you're a writer. Winning or losing—being published or being rejected—doesn't change that.

My students know I'm a writer. They know it because I talk about my works-in-progress, because I tell them about writing workshops I attend, because I grow excited when one of us discovers a new market. But often they naively assume that because I am a writer, my work is always published. The day I bring in an envelope—a very large envelope, I'm afraid—filled with my own rejection slips is an eye-opening day for them. Students find it hard at first to fathom that a teacher—*their* teacher— could be such a failure!

That's the teacher's task: to make her students realize that in the publishing world rejection is not synonymous with failure. I spread out my rejection slips and let my students shuffle through them, reading the messages. From *The Sun, A Magazine of Ideas*: "Thanks for sending us your work, but it's not what we're looking for. This isn't meant as a reflection on your writing . . ." From *Agni,* a journal out of Boston University: "Thank you for letting us consider your work—The Editors." From *Seventeen,* a handwritten rejection letter: "Sorry to have taken so long to respond. Sorry too that your story 'Mother Love' isn't right for *Seventeen.*" From the *Iowa Review:* "We've filled our next several issues and won't be reading again until September. Thanks for thinking of us and we hope you'll consider sending us more work next year."

What I want to impress upon my students is not only the number of rejections I have received (and yet I still consider myself a writer), but also the impersonal nature of the notes. Students need to understand that when their work is taken from the slush pile—that enormous heap of unsolicited manuscripts the staff of every magazine and journal faces— and read, the editor has absolutely no personal connection with the writer. The work is judged purely as a piece of writing, and if and when it is rejected, it means simply that at that time the piece is not suitable for that publication. The work has been rejected; the writer has not.

At the same time, student writers need to realize that there are a number of reasons why a manuscript may be rejected, and not all have to do with the quality of the piece. For example, a particular piece of writing may be rejected because it is not appropriate for a certain magazine. That's one reason why it's essential that young writers choose their markets carefully. In other instances a very good piece may be rejected because it is similar to something the magazine has recently published. In that case, the piece will likely find a home elsewhere. And sometimes good pieces are simply overlooked. We all know the stories of now-famous pieces of literature whose authors collected numerous rejection slips before some perceptive editor spotted the piece's worth. I discuss honestly all these situations with my students in hopes that they can then face the all-too-common rejection slip with equanimity.

And I discuss another truth with them: that certainly in many cases a manuscript isn't accepted for publication simply because it isn't good enough. That's a hard truth but an important one. Until students accept this reality, attempting to publish really is little more than buying a lottery ticket, hoping for a "win" on luck alone. I encourage my students to publish because I believe it will make them more enthusiastic writers and *better* writers. Each time their work is rejected, I tell them to take a long, hard look at that work, to examine it for flaws and failings, and to ask themselves, "What can I do to make this piece so good that an editor will want to publish it?"

Sometimes they are aided in this undertaking. I encourage my students, particularly those who are just beginning to market their work, to send to publications that may comment on the work they reject. Many of the literary journals and small-circulation magazines note this practice in their listings in *The Writer's Market*. Other magazines take an even more concrete approach. *ByLine*, a monthly magazine with a special interest in new writers, sends a rejection slip that lists a number of reasons why a piece might be rejected and the editors check off the appropriate reasons. Not surprisingly, my students seem far more impressed when *ByLine* says of a piece "Too much editing needed (grammar/spelling errors, manuscript preparation errors or problems in the writing)" than when I make similar suggestions! *Merlyn's Pen, The National Magazine of Student Writing*, receives over 15,000 manuscripts by students per year, accepts approximately 200 as written, asks another 100 authors to make revisions before publication, and returns the remaining 14,700-plus with a critique from a *Merlyn's Pen* editor. The important point is that though rejection is disappointing, it should not be defeating. All writers—professional writers, teacher writers, and student writers—grow *as* writers if they understand that rejection of a piece is not rejection of a person and that rejection of a piece is simply a call for revision.

Revelation

Writing is revelation. When we write we often discover things about ourselves and others that we've never quite realized before. So too when we write do we reveal things about ourselves and the people in our lives who make up our stories. Even when we turn the truth into fiction, fragments of the truth, often very recognizable, remain. For these reasons, writing is risk-taking. It's putting yourself—and sometimes others—on the line through your lines. That's not an easy thing to do, and sometimes the ramifications are serious.

For students, the greatest risk is usually self-revelation. We all have students who, a bit embarrassed, squirm when we read their papers aloud in class or encourage them to hang their work on the classroom wall. Usually that squirm comes partly from pleasure at being singled out and complimented on their work. But often, too, there's an element of discomfort, for when a writer's words are made public, so too is his or her heart. I think of Wylie considering the publication of her intensely personal essay and the look in her eyes when she says, "*Seventeen* . . . I don't know, do I really want *everyone* to know about me?" In the classroom she felt safe to reveal her feelings and the insecurities that plague her. Enough trust had been built within that small community of writers to make such honesty possible. At that point, however, she was not ready to offer her self to a national publication.

When students seek to publish their work, they need to seriously consider what it would mean to them—and to others—for their words to be very public. Publication in even the smallest, most obscure literary journal is still publication, and I challenge any writer not to want to tell the world, "I've been published!" when his work appears. Though I explain to students about the use of pen names and tell them it's certainly an option in their work, I also tell them that it's unlikely that they can keep secret the work they publish, nor in fact would they really want to. Writers write because they want to be heard, because they want to give voice to the feelings inside of them. I think of the young woman who, using a pseudonym, publishes a wonderful poem in our school literary magazine about an unnamed boy she is attracted to. Before the poem is printed, I ask her if she's sure she wants to do this. She thinks about it a bit and then nods. When the poem is published I hear students buzzing about it and its author. Many of them have guessed the author and her subject correctly. I wonder if she regrets her decision, but when I ask her about it, she smiles. Apparently for her that poem was a love letter to be shared with the world.

Sometimes though, the situation is not so pleasantly adolescent. Student writers are generally very candid writers, particularly if they are part of a classroom-turned-writing-community that fosters trust and honesty. In such a classroom students feel safe to write about the difficulties in their lives: dysfunctional families, friends with drug and alcohol problems, their own insecurities. The papers they produce are often extremely powerful because of their candor. Recently Carrie wrote of the dissolution of her family in a piece that I found heart-wrenching and that her classmates, many struggling with similar situations, listened to in rapt silence: "A few months after Amy went to school, my dad explained that he really felt as if he didn't belong and he left. There was no more cooking meat and sautéing vegetables. There was no more WGBH echoing through the house. There was no more dinner and there was no more family."

I wish Carrie could publish the piece, partly because it's just so good it deserves to be published, but also because I suspect it would have a significant impact on teenage readers who would find in Carrie's words not only an echo of their own lives but empathy as well. But in good conscience I can't encourage Carrie to send this piece off to *Writes of Passage* or *360° Magazine*, not unless her family, the people so poignantly portrayed in the piece, are completely comfortable with that. Nor do I want to suggest that Carrie turn this autobiographical piece into fiction, which is one way of protecting those involved. Carrie put her heart into her essay, and in doing so, I think she confronted some feelings and issues that had been buried inside of her. She's not ready to turn that hard-earned truth into fiction.

On Parents' Night her mother speaks to me about the piece. Her voice trembles a bit, perhaps with pride in her daughter's work, perhaps with pain. "It was all *right there*, wasn't it? It was good . . . and, you know, I never knew before why Carrie stopped eating at the kitchen table."

Teachers who encourage students to publish their work need to discuss issues of privacy with their students. Students need to understand that there are legal issues as well as moral issues involved in revealing truths about the lives of others. Though I've told my students about famous writers, Flannery O'Connor and Tennessee Williams among them, who did in fact use the lives of their families and friends as fodder for their work, I suggest that at fourteen or fifteen one might not want to alienate those closest to them! I want my students to be risk-takers. I know great writing doesn't happen by playing it safe. But students who are used to writing for the teacher alone frequently don't realize just how powerful their words may be. So when a student wants to try to publish an essay or poem that speaks candidly about a difficult family situation, for example, I always ask the student to bring the piece home, to let the family read it before it goes out in the mail. Sometimes students balk at first, uncomfortable about sharing their words with those closest to the experience, but they soon realize that if the piece does get published, there will be no hiding it anyway. Other times I suggest that students change the most telling details to protect the privacy of those involved. That might mean simply altering names, dates, certain events, or it may mean turning a nonfiction piece into a work of fiction. And sometimes, when the piece is self-revelatory, I just encourage the writer to wait a bit before sending it out, good advice in general in that most pieces of writing improve by "aging." Young writers can be very impulsive, loving a piece they wrote one day, hating it the next. Worse than not having your work published is having work you're no longer proud of in print! Sometimes a "cooling off" period is necessary for a student writer to clearly evaluate a work and its potential impact on others.

None of this is meant to discourage either teachers or their students in the publication of student work. It is simply a caution, a reminder that good writing, writing from the heart, has extraordinary power, and, like any sort of power, it must be used responsibly.

Rivalry

Writing may not be a competitive activity; publication is. That is the cold, hard truth. You need only read a market listing for any publication—commercial, literary, or small circulation—to realize just how fierce the competition for space on the printed page is. *Seventeen* receives 350 unsolicited fiction manuscripts per month and generally buys only one per issue. *Boys' Life* receives 150 unsolicited short stories and publishes 12–18 per year. Even the so-called "little and literary" magazines are inundated with submissions—fiction, nonfiction, and poetry—and can publish only a fraction of them. Within these adult markets, young writers must also compete with older, experienced writers, many of whom already have publishing credits.

Even if students confine themselves to student-written magazines, there is no guarantee that they will be published. There are a limited number of such publications and, as the fifteen thousand yearly submissions to *Merlyn's Pen* indicate, there are many, many young writers eager to see their work in print. That number is growing, as editors of these publications realize. The *21st Century*, a monthly newspaper of student work, now also offers a separate publication, the *21st Century Poetry Journal*, to keep up with the flood of poetry submissions, over four thousand per year. Students who send their work out to *any* magazine need to understand that they are vying with many other writers for a place on a page.

But if the world of publishing is necessarily competitive, the writing classroom need not be. In the classroom students should feel safe to experiment with their writing, to try out new styles, play with new voices, and take all the risks that apprentice writers need to take in order to develop their craft. I tell my students that in the world of published writing there are basically two grades: an A, you get published; an F, you don't. In the writing classroom, however, there should be an endless number of grades, or, in an ideal world, perhaps no grades at all. In the next chapter I will talk in detail about the issue of evaluating writing, but for now let me say that it is of utmost importance that student writers feel that, in the classroom, they are competing only against themselves and their own previous efforts.

As a teacher, I believe my job is to encourage all students to grow as writers from whatever point they begin. Early on in my writing classes I find that students preface every piece they read aloud in class with a line like, "This is terrible but . . . ." I joke with them, tell them that we will begin every class with that line, all of us repeating it together like a mantra. In fact that disclaimer is an excellent means of relieving the pressure of publication, even when the publication is only in front of peers, and it seems to serve as an "equalizer" among the students, making them all feel they're on the same ground as writers. Every one of them can get better. No one's work is perfect, and they are all there to help each other improve. Certainly when students read their work in response groups, they recognize that some pieces are "better" than others, but response to writing is highly subjective, and what one reader enjoys, another may not. And sometimes there are wonderful surprises. The student who never quite measures up in terms of analytical writing, or whose voice is non-existent during class discussions often produces the most powerful po-etry or prose. I love the look of amazement in the other students' eyes when the quietest kid in the corner shares a story they never expected could come from him. It is the teacher's job to create a classroom where every student's potential is recognized, where every student is a "writer-in-progress." When the writing community is nurturing, the praise lav-ish, the criticism specific and constructive, students feel comfortable as writers and begin to take those risks that allow their work to develop. That's when they start heading toward publishing success.

But sometimes one student finds that success more quickly than her peers. This was the case with Anne, a young woman who sat in my sophomore class a few years ago. Anne was a talented writer, but beyond that she was a hard-working, disciplined writer, someone who took on a writing project with enthusiasm and followed it through to the end, motivated by her own high expectations for herself. That spring Anne independently decided to enter a contest sponsored by Scholastic, Inc. Certainly she was lured by the face on the advertising materials—a soul-ful image of Tom Cruise—but it was also the headline that attracted her. "Send your story to the *Far and Away* Creative Writing Contest. Win a chance to meet Tom Cruise, Nicole Kidman, and Ron Howard." The story was to be about a voyage to America and could be based on family his-tory or be a purely fictional account. Anne had a story to tell—the remi-niscences of an elderly woman who fled Poland and the Nazis during World War II—and she set to telling it. A few other students in my class also began working on stories. Not all followed through, but by the dead-line date, four stories were in the mail.

The happy outcome was that Anne won. As the state winner from Massachusetts, she earned an interview, via satellite, with Cruise, Kidman, and Howard, as well as the admiration and celebrity that comes with such an honor. I was thrilled for Anne, thrilled to watch her grow in her glory. Almost overnight she turned into a person who radiated confidence in herself as a writer. So delighted was I that I bought an enormous sheet cake emblazoned with the words "Congratulations, Anne!" for her to share with the class. It was on the day that I picked up the cake and gazed at the bright yellow frosting that shouted her name that I realized how suddenly and completely competition had come into our classroom. To their credit, none of the other students who had entered the contest begrudged Anne her moment of fame; in fact, they seemed to be quite happy just knowing someone who had spoken to Tom Cruise! But the fact was that suddenly the stakes had grown higher than who had received an A and who a B or C. Suddenly there were larger prizes to claim, and I realized that if I were to keep my classroom a community, I had to find a way to recognize Anne's accomplishments without slighting her peers.

Over the years I've worked to find ways to let the spotlight shine on those young writers privileged to earn its light without letting their peers feel lost in the shadows. When one student's work is published, I always congratulate the class, particularly those students who worked closely with the writer on revision and editing. When a student discovers a "friendly" market, a publication that appreciates his or her work, I encourage other students whose work might also be recognized there to submit their pieces. Kate sends a short story to Majestic Books and promptly receives an acceptance letter and a contract. They want her piece to appear in an upcoming anthology of student works. I am delighted for Kate and also delighted to find this new, receptive market, and I begin to think of other students whose work might be appropriate for it. I am always on the lookout for markets for my students' work, and I gear my search to the level of competition I feel each individual writer is at.

For some students, particularly those who have never imagined themselves as writers, publication in the school's literary magazine is just as wonderful and rewarding as publication in a national magazine. I think of Bryan, a pseudo-tough senior, who couldn't quite keep the grin off his face when a story about his father was printed in *rhubarb pie*, my school's magazine.

"Wait 'til my folks see this," he said, a gleam in his eye. "They'll be off my back about my grades!"

Obviously some student writers have their own idea of rewards! And in all my classes, I end the year with a class reading, a time for us to celebrate the work of all the writers, published or unpublished. When I carry to class the cake for that event, I'm always pleased to see it say, "Congratulations, Class!"

The Rewards

Glory

Were I to ask my students what they feel are the rewards of being published, I imagine most of them would tell me that the greatest reward is glory, the "fame" that comes with being published.

When a student's work is published, be it in a school literary magazine or in a major publication, immediately that student gains a measure of celebrity. For Anne that fame came in the form of a write-up in the city paper as well as an interview on local cable news and that, she told me, led to many conversations with people she had never spoken to before who wanted to know what *he* (Tom Cruise) and *she* (Nicole Kidman) were *really* like! When Jen's essay on a near-tragic experience with alcohol was published in the "First Person" column of *Worcester Magazine*, she found her teachers and her peers looked at her with new respect. And Dan's letter to the editor brought a flurry of responses in the days that followed that made him the talk of the local paper as well as of the community.

For many teenagers this Warhol fifteen-minutes-of-fame can be a heady experience, but also one that contributes to a more permanent sense of self-esteem. As all teachers know, it is not unusual for their best student writers to be the more quiet, introverted students, those who generally don't find glory on the athletic field or on the school stage. They are the students whose talents can go unnoticed in a typical high school or middle school environment. For that reason, I particularly enjoy watching students bask in the acclaim—however short-lived—that publication brings them. Although I offer a gentle reminder that you're only a writer as long as you keep on writing, for most students that warning is unnecessary. Once students have tasted success in the form of publication, they rarely stop writing.

Gain

Next to glory, my students would probably name "gain" as the best reward of publication. Gain can come in many forms: monetary awards, scholarships, all-expenses-paid trips, books, computers, even interviews with people like Tom Cruise. Certainly many of my students are initially motivated by the "prize," and when they scan the bulletin board in the back of my room for potential publishing opportunities, I know their attention will be drawn first to those that offer the most extravagant concrete rewards.

I don't condone this interest, but I understand it is human and can even be quite practical. Adult writers consider the compensation they will receive from various publications when they set out to market their work. Writing is work and does deserve compensation. For that reason I don't discourage my students from considering the payment they will receive as one factor when they are deciding where to send their writing. But I remind them, there are other important points to take into consideration.

One is that they are very much beginners, particularly if they are competing in an adult market. For that reason, sending their stories to a highly competitive and very well paying publication is perhaps imprudent. Their time and effort (and postage!) might be better spent on sending their work to a smaller, less prestigious publication, one that may only pay in copies of the magazine. Some students, however, simply want to try the big magazines, and, as long as I feel confident that they will not be permanently discouraged by likely rejection, I don't dissuade them. In fact, I share a bit of their optimism and figure that rejection is rejection and you might as well be rejected a time or two by the best! In my own experience, too, I have found that sometimes the bigger magazines, which are perhaps better staffed than their smaller counterparts, do take the time to offer a comment or two that aids in later revision. Such a personal response is invaluable, not only in terms of reworking a piece, but also in letting the writer feel that she is truly a writer and part of the whole writing enterprise.

My other caution to student writers who are lured by big prizes is this: sometimes prestige itself is a prize, maybe more valuable than any material award. In the writing world, *where* you have been published is a very important issue, and even student writers are not too young to begin to amass writing "credits." As all writers know, that first sale is the hardest. Once you have "cracked" the market and found your way into print, then you are a writer by commercial standards and can use that first publishing credit, revealed in your cover letter, as a way to open other doors. Clearly, certain publications, even those written exclusively by young people, carry more weight than others, and while I would never disparage publication in any legitimate market, I want my students to understand that some magazines/journals/contests are more respected and better recognized than others. Publication in such arenas then is very valuable, regardless of what other rewards are, or are not, offered.

In terms of financial rewards, any market guide will provide up-to-date information on payment for accepted pieces. Some smaller journals pay only in copies called contributor's copies or offer only minimum compensation, as an honorarium. Some periodicals pay by the word, generally three cents on up. Others offer a broad payment range, from twenty-five to more than one thousand dollars. Payment rates depend on the commercial success of the publication itself and on the type and length of the piece accepted for publication. As a general rule, nonfiction pays more than fiction and everything pays more than poetry!

For publications written exclusively by students, financial remuneration is usually minimal, under $25, and writers are basically rewarded by seeing their words in print. They may receive complimentary copies of the issue in which their work appears as well. Detailed information as to what certain publications pay appears in the Market List in the Appendix.

Students motivated by grander awards might want to consider one of the many writing contests that seek student work. Details about these many contests are included in the Contest List section in the Appendix. A sampling of such contests reveals a wide variety of prizes for an equally wide variety of types of writing.

EF Educational Tours sponsors an EF Ambassador Scholarship Program for students in grades 9–12. Scholarships for an educational tour in Europe are awarded to students who, in poetry, prose or artwork, best describe a plan for global or local change.

Young Playwrights Inc. offers the Young Playwrights Festival National Playwriting Competition for students ages eighteen or under. Playwrights are asked to submit one or more plays of any length, style, or subject and compete for the opportunity to participate in the professional production of their plays in New York City. As an added incentive, each entrant receives a written evaluation of his or her play.

America's Best High School Scholastic Writing Competition is presented annually by the Writers Foundation, Inc. This competition judges work in six categories—Scriptwriting, Short Fiction, Poetry, Original Sitcom, Novel, and Songwriting—and awards computers, savings bonds, and autographed copies of work by celebrity writers in each category.

Landmark Editions, Inc. sponsors the National Written and Illustrated By . . . Awards Contest for Students, offering the publication of winning books in three age categories. Student writers receive publication contracts and are paid royalties annually. They also win a trip to Kansas City to participate in the production of their books.

Opportunities for students abound, and the rewards are often impressive. Of course the competition is also fierce since most of these contests are offered on a national level, but, as I always remind my students, someone has to win and it might just as well be someone sitting in my class. But, as I tell students who are often quite dizzy with excitement when they hear of a new contest, one that offers a trip to Europe perhaps, thinking about winning a contest is one thing; doing the writing is another. I remember all of my sophomore girls ooohing and aaahing over the possibility of meeting Tom Cruise, but by deadline day only four stories made it to the mailbox. If it's human nature to procrastinate, then that tendency is born in adolescence, and student writers can use that to their advantage when they enter competitions. Getting your entry in on time, in a polished, professional form that adheres to the contest's rules, is half the battle. Once you have done that, I tell my students, you have earned the right to daydream about winning.

Growth

The rewards of fame and fortune are certainly attractive, and I understand why students find them such powerful motivators. But in my mind the greatest reward of publication for students is growth. When students seek to publish their writing, they suddenly begin to grow as writers, producing work of a much higher quality than even they thought themselves capable of creating.

The growth in these would-be published writers seems sometimes miraculous, but there are very solid reasons for such improvement. First, when a writer sends a piece of writing out into the world, he has to imagine on some level that it may actually be published. Even in a national competition where the chance of publication is slim, that chance still exists, and it is that possibility, that knowledge that one's words may appear in print for all the world to see, that spurs young writers to do their best work. Students may share mediocre work with their response groups or turn in "C" quality work to their teachers, but when their audience grows, so too does their desire to produce work they are proud of.

Competition itself can be a great motivator. Students know that to get their work in a major magazine or to win a prize in a writing contest, they have to produce exceptional work. Even when I distribute copies of solely student-written publications like the school literary magazine or national publications like *Writes of Passage*, students recognize that the work within these pages is of top quality. Only occasionally do I hear a student say, "Oh, I can write better stuff than that!" When I do, I seize the moment to offer that student a challenge. "Prove it," I tell him or her. "Let's see you get your work in print." Sometimes they meet my challenge head on and successfully submit their work. It's a confrontation I'm happy to lose.

Cognizant of the competition they face, students are far more willing to revise when they are working toward publication. "Oh, it's good enough," they often tell me when they hand in a paper they believe is destined for my eyes alone. When I ask if they made the changes suggested by their response groups or peer editors, they shrug, and that shrug is an eloquent statement of their belief that they've given enough attention to that particular paper. After all, a grade by any other name is still a grade, isn't it? B or B+, what's the difference?

Getting students to revise is an extraordinarily difficult task. Even though revision has been made easier by the word processor, it nevertheless is a tedious and exacting chore, one that young writers shy away from. The best revision my students do comes when they are working on a piece that they want to send out for publication. The most compelling reason for this is that the piece matters to them; if it didn't, they wouldn't be putting the time and effort into preparing it for publication. Because they truly care about what they are saying, they want to say it right. Second, knowing how hard it is to get work into print, they are willing to put extra effort into the final piece and welcome, even seek out, suggestions from their peers and from me. They seem to understand that every improvement, however minor it may seem, increases their chance of publication. And last, but hardly least, is the fact that when they are working on a piece, for *The Claremont Review* perhaps or maybe *New Moon* or *How on Earth!*, suddenly they feel like real writers, not students writing for the teacher but writers writing for the world. They understand that writers revise and that revising is part of the job of being a writer. Now it has a purpose: it makes your writing good, it makes it publishable, and it makes you a writer.

And there is another kind of growth that comes from putting yourself on a page. That's personal growth, the kind of growing we all do when we confront head-on the problems in our lives. As teachers we know that our students' lives are far more complicated and difficult than children's lives ought to be. They struggle daily with adult issues—poverty, violence, divorce, death—and their ability to function effectively in school is impeded by the weight of these problems. Writing that allows students to address these problems is powerful, not only for the reader but for the writer as well. When a student can put the pain in his life into words, he gains some control over it.

The student who taught me that lesson best was a young man of nineteen, a quadriplegic since the age of seven. He came to me in a wheelchair with a ventilator and a nurse and a mouthstick with which to type his words. During the months he was in my class, he began to tap out the story of his accident, the family problems it provoked, the years spent in hospitals and rehabilitation centers, the losses he lives with daily. Writing those pieces was slow going for Chris, both physically and emotionally, but he had a story he wanted, no, *needed,* to tell. He wanted to enlighten those who don't understand what it means to be a seriously disabled person, and he wanted to encourage those who know all too well. And I think he knew too that he needed to finally put the years of pain and grief and ultimately courage into words on a screen, on a printed page, perhaps maybe even one day in a book. That was part of his recovery, to see for himself where he had been and just how far he had come.

Certainly not all the writing our students do about the problems in their lives is worthy of publication. Some of it is simply therapeutic for the writer, and he or she has neither the interest nor perhaps the emotional energy to take it farther, to turn it into publishable material. But the personal problems young people describe in their writing are ones often experienced by many of their peers, and when they are able to share their words in a published piece, the impact can be extraordinary. When my students pick up a magazine or journal filled with student work, they generally go directly to the personal essays. That is where they find their connection. That is where they feel the pulse of the publication. That is the place where the writer's heart beats best. Just as my students grow emotionally from putting their own problems into words, so too do they find comfort and wisdom from the words of their peers as they recognize that their problems are universal ones. They learn that solutions come slowly with patience and effort, just like words on a page.

Goals

We live in a "quick-fix" society. Today's Americans are not known for their patience. We want our rewards and reinforcements to come quickly; we want to see results. Such drive is not an entirely negative quality. But in our young people this eagerness, this itchiness, this out-and-out impatience is often counterproductive, and many adolescents find it hard to set, and follow through on, long-term goals.

As any published writer will attest, writing for publication is most definitely a long-term goal. From the moment a writer has the first glimmer of an idea to the day he sees a finished piece in print, an enormous amount of time may elapse. The writing itself can take weeks, months, or years, during which time the writer rethinks, revises, and rewrites and sometimes just lets the piece sit in a drawer for a while so that he can see it again through fresh eyes. Once the piece has been sent out for publication, it's not unusual for a magazine to take months to respond to it, and even if the work is then accepted, many more months may pass before it actually appears on the printed page.

My students are often taken aback when I explain this long process to them, and indeed many of them challenge it. I post a notice for the Nicholas A. Virgilio Memorial Haiku Competition for High School Students on the bulletin board on Tuesday. On Wednesday, some of my students come in with three typed haiku ready to send off. "They're short," one student tells me nonchalantly. "I wrote 'em in ten minutes."

The truth is, he probably did, and it becomes my job to explain why a haiku written in 3.3 minutes is most likely not a prize-winning haiku nor the poet's best work. It is hard to explain to an eager young writer that writing takes time and that sometimes the best writing happens not when you're holding a pen or when your hands are poised on a keyboard, but when you give your mind and heart time to wrestle with your subject, when you let your creative imagination work its magic on its own. I delight in those students who tell me sincerely, "I'm working!" when I see them gazing into space during a classroom writing session. I know they're telling the truth. They are the kind of writers who need to let their ideas brew in their heads before they ever begin to put words on a page. I wish more of their peers would follow their patient example.

I tell the boy with the haiku that writers need feedback, that before he sends his poetry out to face a real editor, he needs to get feedback from "pseudo-editors," his classmates, a trusted reader, me. My students are used to working in response groups and they understand the value of this, but again it is often their impatience, their desire to get their work in the mail, that keeps them from seeking the advice they need from other readers. To ameliorate this situation, I try to always provide students who request it time within the class period for them to present their work to their response groups or to the entire class if they wish. I consider such time well spent. This not only promotes better writing and more revision by the writer, but it also encourages other students to tackle their own publishing projects, and it improves their own writing skills as they work as editors.

Once a piece is in the mail, I can offer only empathy to students who fret over the time it takes to hear from an editor.

"I know," I tell them. "I've had stories returned to me after such a long time that I'd forgotten I'd sent them out!"

This understanding does little to soothe some of them, but swiftness is not the way of the publishing world, and that is a reality writers need to get used to. Seniors whom I have in a Creative Writing class are often amazed when I tell them that they will most likely not receive a response from an editor on their final publication project until long after they are settled in their college dorms or post-high school apartments, but I make them promise to contact me if their work is accepted for publication. They are savvy. There is always one student who asks, "And if it is, will you change the grade *you* gave me?"

To be sure, classroom conditions are not perfect for nurturing long-term writing goals. Each term a grade has to be recorded, and so, throughout the term, writing must be produced on some sort of schedule, revised under some sort of time constraints, and eventually graded. Even those students whose reveries I applaud have to stop staring into space and put their words on paper. On the positive side this exigency parallels the reality a writer faces if he intends to make writing a career. Each writer has to work hard, stay focused, and adhere to deadlines, imposed either by an editor or by one's own self, if any writing is ever to be finished. Moreover, the professional writer ultimately faces someone, generally an editor or an editorial board, who judges his writing just as I must judge my students' work. The standards a writing teacher establishes and the discipline she enforces in her classroom are not that far removed from what a professional writer encounters in the "real" world, and this is something I make very clear to my students.

Unfortunately, however, the time a student spends in one teacher's classroom, especially on the high school level, is very short. My Creative Writing class, for example, meets for only one semester, the second semester of the students' senior year, hardly a time known for constructive work. By the time my students have experimented with prewriting techniques, established productive response groups, and learned to feel comfortable when faced with the blank page, much of the semester has gone by. Though they all are working toward a final piece to submit somewhere for publication, there is very little time for truly long-term projects—a well-developed short story, for example, or a children's picture book. Certainly there isn't time to let a manuscript linger in a drawer growing better (or worse) with age.

The constraints of a school schedule then often work against some of what I try to teach young writers. For that reason, I encourage them to think beyond—and work beyond—those parameters. I want them to continue as writers when they leave my classroom, and what better way to promote that than to have them engaged in a writing project even as the semester or the year ends. I'm happy to have students send me copies of the pieces they are working on over the summer or bring them to my classroom when the new school year begins, and I enjoy responding to their work. Sometimes I try to pair a writer up with another enthusiastic student whose work is at a similar level so that they can serve as readers/peer editors for each other outside of the classroom. I tell them to be on the lookout for other astute readers, sometimes an older sibling, a neighbor, even a parent, who can offer both continued support and constructive criticism on the writer's work. And I remind them that all writers struggle with the loneliness of writing, the need to find a way to share both the joy of writing and the frustration of it.

This past Christmas I took a very long walk with Marcy, a young woman, now a college senior, who sat in my classroom during her senior year in high school. She was easily one of the most wonderful students I have ever had, a talented writer with a thirst for writing and a zest for life that delighted me. That winter she began a somewhat autobiographical story that dealt with the pain of prejudice and the special intensity of that pain when you encounter it head-on at seventeen. The story was poignant and passionate and contained a very sophisticated metaphor in its focus on blood ties.

Marcy wrestled with that story throughout the semester. I encouraged her heartily because I thought she had something very important to say, and I knew she had the ability to say it well. The story never got finished, partly because of the pressures and distractions of the end of senior year, but partly, as I realize now, because Marcy wasn't really ready to finish it. She wasn't ready to see all sides, to face her own feelings about the prejudice she had faced. But in these last four years, that story has never been far from Marcy's mind, and each time we talk, we speak of it. Sometimes it's sitting in her desk drawer; sometimes she takes it out and rewrites a few lines. This year, as we walked along a snowy street, Marcy told me the direction her story is now taking. No longer quite so autobiographical, it is now a story that reveals the pain of the perpetrator as well as that of the victim. It is now a story of incredible depth and real maturity. I am sure I will see that story in print some day. More than four years have passed since that story's inception; another four may pass before that story lands on an editor's desk. Marcy is not impatient. She has grown with her story, both as a writer and as a woman. She understands the beauty of a long-term goal.

Part Two

Once a teacher has assessed the risks and rewards of taking her students down the path to publication, then she has to consider the nuts and bolts of marketing a piece of writing. The next section of this chapter discusses concerns about selecting a market and preparing a manuscript.

Choosing a Market

For a young writer, choosing a market can seem as easy as opening a market guide and picking a title. Such a choice should not, however, be made lightly. When a piece is accepted for publication, it is not only a reflection of the quality of the work, but also the choice of an appropriate market. There are many things a writer needs to consider when he chooses a potential market for his work, and there are particular things he needs to be cautious about. There are, then, certain questions that the writer needs to ask himself before he puts an address on an envelope.

Is this a legitimate publication/contest?

In encouraging student writers to submit their work to publications, this question is one of my most immediate and serious concerns.

Most market guides preface their listings with a statement regarding the integrity of the listings. The editors of such guides do their best to investigate the publications and contests they list, but, considering the rapid appearance, disappearance, and change of publications, they cannot possibly guarantee the accuracy of every listing. In fact, many market guides come to depend on information from reader-writers in order to update their listings.

Generally, however, one can assume that if a publication or contest is listed in a guide like *Writer's Market* (which is published annually by Writer's Digest Books and is supplemented with other more specific guides like the *Novel & Short Story Writer's Market*), it is likely to be a legitimate market. By legitimate, I mean that the publications and contests it lists are offered in good faith and that a writer's work will be read in a timely fashion and then either returned to the writer, held temporarily for possible later publication with the permission of the writer, or immediately accepted for publication to be rewarded with payment as described in the listing. Certainly this process is not often as swift as a writer might like, and, as was noted earlier, young writers need to be accepting of the inevitable delays that are part of the publishing process.

What young writers should not, however, ever be accepting of are publications, and particularly contests, that seem to prey on adolescents' naiveté and desire to be published. Such markets might, for example, guarantee publication in return for a fee—either an extremely high entry fee or the purchase of a book in which all such eager young authors are published. I tell my students there is no honor in paying for publication, and I warn them to avoid such situations.

Despite my warnings, however, students do fall victim to such propositions. Usually they find such "markets" advertised in the back of a magazine or newspaper, where a headline shouts to them to be part of some impressive national collection of prose or poetry. Frequently there is no initial entry fee, and it isn't until later, when their work has been "accepted," that writers find that they must purchase a copy of this very expensive volume if they are ever to see their words in print. Sadly, it's all too often the enthusiastic but not especially talented student who gets involved in this scheme. It's heartbreaking when such a student runs into class beaming with pride and holding out an "acceptance" letter from some such venture. I hate having to disillusion a young writer about the "honor," but so too do I hate having him or her give any support to such a scheme. My best advice, then, is to offer a red alert to students about such opportunities long before they begin to send work out and to be on the watch for any similar duplicitous enterprises.

Is there an entry fee?

An entry fee is certainly not always a sign of a dubious publication. Some highly respected publications for students find it necessary to require a nominal entry fee in order to offset their own costs of production, payment to writers, etc. The key word here is nominal. *Merlyn's Pen,* for example, requests a postage/handling fee of $2.00 if a writer's school subscribes to the magazine; $5.00 if the school does not (and it is worth noting that editors do critique each manuscript). *ByLine* generally has a $1.00 entry fee for its monthly student contests. For many students, particularly high school age students, such fees are manageable, but for those students who have financial constraints or who simply want to submit to many publications, there are student publications that charge a young writer nothing, other than postage, for submissions.

Usually commercial markets open to writers of all ages require no fees, though some smaller literary journals do demand that those who submit work be subscribers to the journal. A careful reading of any market listing will inform the writer of any such costs and/or requirements.

Contests, however, both those for students and those open to all writers, frequently do have entry fees. Sometimes these fees can be quite high, up to $25.00 per manuscript, though $10.00 is an average rate for contests geared to adult writers. I try to steer my students away from expensive contests, especially those where the competition is stiff because practiced adult writers, even published writers, are likely to enter. But there are students who have the money and the inclination to enter such competitions, and, as long as I know they understand the costs and the slim odds of winning, I recognize that the decision to enter is theirs. Sometimes there are benefits that offset the entry fee, a written critique of the writer's work, for example, or a subscription to the publication sponsoring the contest. The important thing is that students learn to be careful consumers and to examine any publication opportunity carefully before they invest money—or time—in it.

What about contests for student writers? Should I enter?

Contests are exciting; there's no denying that. When a glossy poster arrives from Scholastic, Inc., bearing a full-color picture of Tracy Chapman and the promise of an in-school concert for the winner of this year's song lyrics contest, my students are filled with energy and immediately start scribbling song lines in their notebooks. When I find an envelope in my mailbox from the Skirball Institute on American Values touting the question "Will One of Your Students Win $5000?", I admit I'm eager to open the envelope.

Contests, with the lure of big prizes and the glitz of advertising that accompanies them, are often excellent motivators for students, partly because they make it seem so easy to win. Of course, it's not that easy, and it's the teacher's responsibility to make sure students understand that. But the truth is, it's not at all easy to be published in any publication, and so I tell my students that the decision about sending work to a contest or a magazine should not focus on the chances of publication. Rather, I tell them, you need to decide if you want to do the kind of writing the contest requires, or if you have that kind of writing tucked away in a drawer or notebook ready to be pulled out and revised.

Scholastic's "Write Lyrics" songwriting contest, for example, offered a rare and welcome opportunity for the musicians in my classroom who have virtually no outlet for the songs they love to write. Though some of these students have turned their songs into poems and submitted them to poetry markets, most of this group of writers simply pen their songs and put them away, imagining the day when they will be "discovered." This contest gave them a perfect opportunity to share their work with a panel of judges and perhaps win an award, not to mention a visit by Tracy Chapman!

On the other hand, my enthusiasm about this year's Skirball Institute Essay Contest on American Values was not mirrored by my students. This year's essay was based on the question "What does U.S. History Teach Us About the Role of Immigration in the Creation of American Society?" The question is certainly an interesting and timely one, but it was not one which my students in this particular year felt knowledgeable about.

Had this been an issue they had studied in depth in a social studies class, I suspect there would have been students who would have tackled the essay eagerly.

As a quick look at the Contest List in the Appendix indicates, there is a wide variety of contests open exclusively to student writers, most of which have no entry fee. Some stress the creativity and imagination central to the writing of poetry and fiction; others are looking for a more academic approach seen through research and essay writing. Not surprisingly, student writers tend to prefer the former, but I have had students seize on the opportunities presented by the latter. Recently I read an announcement from the American Zinc Association regarding an essay contest on the properties and uses of zinc. In truth there was probably a bit less enthusiasm in my voice than when I described the songwriting contest, for example, and I didn't imagine a room full of students fighting over the copy of the guidelines. But suddenly, one young woman looked up with a bright smile on her face.

"I just wrote a research paper on zinc," she said. "Can I see those guidelines?"

The fact is, there is probably a contest for everyone!

And that's the point. Writing contests exist because they focus on particular interests. Through their specific requirements, they encourage certain writing styles, topics, and themes, and so they provide students with opportunities to try something new or to find a perfect niche for the writing they already do.

I particularly encourage two disparate groups of writers to peruse the contest information regularly. One is the group that struggles to find something to write about. Contests often provide specific subjects and ideas that give the writer the first push onto the paper. When the International Rivers Network sponsors a poetry contest whose theme is "Watersheds," a young writer whose interests have been more scientific than literary suddenly sees an opportunity to indulge both pursuits. On his own, however, I doubt he would have ever thought that his ecological concerns were material for poetry.

The other is the group that has notebooks full of writing, some completed pieces, some works-in-progress. These students can often find a "home" for a particular piece in a writing contest. Shawn, who has been writing plays since September, is overjoyed to learn that next year, when he's a junior, he can enter the Princeton University Secondary School Ten-Minute Play Contest, open only to eleventh graders. I've told him that gives him plenty of time for revision! But, I remind him, you have to remember to follow through, to actually get your entry in the mail.

I'm candid with my students about this aspect of any writing contest designed exclusively for students: getting your entry in is half the battle! Any time I announce an interesting contest, one that features a flashy prize or one that offers an appealing writing challenge, almost all the students in the room are caught up in the excitement and assure me that they are going to enter. I know the reality is that maybe one or two will enter any given contest, but I encourage all of them, never knowing who will be the one or two this time. When the postmark deadline rolls around, I ask who in class entered. One or two hands go up, and twenty-plus pairs of sheepish eyes go down.

My point is not to shame those who didn't follow through, but rather to give them a vivid picture of what I know is happening in classrooms all over America. When a major contest is announced, every student wants to enter. Yet when it comes to doing the work by a certain date, the field of entrants narrows dramatically. I want my students to understand that you can't win unless you enter, and that simply by entering you have put your words into the world and given them a chance to shine. That in itself is an accomplishment to be proud of.

I'm happy when students are interested in writing contests. I'm happy to see them inspired to write and pleased that they are learning how to follow specific guidelines and meet absolute deadlines. And on some level I share their excitement about the prospect of "winning." But I am always reminding them that writing is work and that the real prize is the accomplishment a writer feels when he knows that a piece of writing "works," when it says what he wants it to say and means what he wants it to mean. Then that piece of writing has meaning and importance that extends beyond any contest requirements.

The market listing says "Query." What does that mean?

When a publication is seeking nonfiction work—particularly articles, feature stories, how-to pieces, and interviews—it will often ask the writer to query first. A query letter is written in order to interest an editor in a manuscript on a certain subject. Like a cover letter, it is short and to the point, preferably no more than a page long. In it, the writer gives a brief but detailed description of the article she has written or plans to write, explaining the structure of the piece, the central facts, the interviews involved if applicable, and also her own particular qualifications for writing the piece. The aim is to pique the editor's interest so that he offers the writer the opportunity to submit the article for consideration.

Certainly writing a compelling query letter is not a simple task, and as a writer I have sometimes found writing a query letter more daunting than writing the article itself! For that reason, and because often quite a bit of time passes before a response to a query is received, I try to steer students away from markets that require a query, preferring that they focus their energy on the piece itself. However, on occasion, a student really wants to pursue an article for which a query is required. One boy, an ardent student of karate for many years, wanted very much to write a first-person piece for *Inside Karate* about how karate had shaped his growing up. He struggled with the query letter, and, though it did not evoke a positive response from the editor, he realized that writing it did help him in the development of the piece, which he ultimately wrote anyway simply because the topic was so important to him.

There are, however, many markets for nonfiction, particularly in student-written publications, that do not require a query letter, and I encourage students to try those markets first if they are appropriate for their work.

Is there a deadline for submissions?

Students often balk at due dates, frequently begging for just one more day to complete an assignment. Deadlines, I tell them, are adult versions of due dates, and deadlines are firm and fast. Writers who choose to submit to contests and/or publications that have specific deadlines must adhere to them, and with experience they learn to do so. More than once I've had a student dash breathlessly into my classroom after school in search of my signature on an entry form so she can get her manuscript in the mail with the day's postmark!

Deadlines teach students discipline, and that's clearly a good thing. Moreover, when deadlines are imposed by an outside source, rather than by a teacher, they frequently carry more weight. No "let-me-explain-why-this-is late" story, whether fiction or fact, will earn a writer extra time in a writing contest, and that awareness often makes a writer work more steadily on a piece in order to meet a deadline. My second-semester seniors, caught in the throes of senioritis, often appreciate contest or publication deadlines because such deadlines inspire them to finish pieces that otherwise might linger forever not "quite" done.

Some pieces of writing, however, need time to mature. It may take a semester, a school year, or even longer for a piece to develop into a polished work. In such an instance a mid-November deadline, for example, would only be detrimental, causing an author to hurry the piece and send it out long before it's ready for serious evaluation. A piece of writing isn't finished because a deadline arrives. A piece of writing is finished only when its author, in his own honest appraisal and aided by the advice of trusted readers, determines that it is his best work.

Although contests do impose deadlines, most publications do not. Some publications, however, especially those geared to student writers, read work only during the school year, and submissions must be received during those months. Small journals also often have specified reading periods during which manuscripts must be submitted. This information can usually be found in the market listing.

What is this particular publication really *like?*

Market listings as well as Writer's Guidelines supplied by a publication are extremely helpful in describing a publication. However, the best way to know if a magazine/journal might accept one's own style of work is to read the magazine itself and, even better, to read more than one issue.

For some magazines that's easy. I doubt there's a middle or high school classroom in America where some student isn't hiding a copy of *Seventeen* in the covers of her notebook! Magazines that students are very well acquainted with need no further study. But there are a vast number of lesser-known publications students would likely have more success publishing in, if they knew of their existence and understood the particular slant and style of work generally accepted by each.

Even the smaller magazines/literary journals are sometimes available for perusal at public or college libraries. Sometimes they can be purchased at local bookstores. But often these publications are readily available only to subscribers, which makes studying a number of them a very expensive proposition.

The best bet for an interested writer, then, is a sample copy, which is usually offered at a reduced rate. Often market listings will make a notation regarding the cost of a sample copy, and requests can be sent to the same address as submissions. A sample copy can be an invaluable investment, and I would encourage teachers to seek them out, particularly those publications devoted solely to student work. Not only are such publications very appreciative of and very worthy of financial support, but also they frequently offer specific writing suggestions and guidelines for student submissions. The quality of student publications varies greatly too, and I like having an array of such publications available to my students so that they can decide for themselves where they would most like to send their work.

It is an equally good idea to study the magazines/journals open to adult writers, but even at a minimal price, the cost of a collection of sample copies can become prohibitive and well beyond the means of most students—or even teachers. Aspiring writers, then, need to be selective, reading the market listing carefully to see if a publication does, in fact, seem to be a potential market before investing in a copy of it. I try my best to keep my collection of publications growing and up-to-date, and if a student does decide to send for a sample copy, I encourage her to share it with her classmates, even those who are not interested in it as a possible market, simply because the examination of any literary publication contributes to their growth as enthusiastic writers and readers.

Is my work right for this publication?

On one level, this is an easy question to answer. If a market listing says that a certain publication accepts only poetry and a writer submits his best short story, that short story is never going to be published, regardless of its quality. Students need to understand that when a market listing lists *Needs* or *Publishes,* that is quite literally what a publication needs, and editors are not going to be interested in anything that does not fall into the categories described.

I understand why one of my students would like to see his fictional account of being lost in the wild published in *Outdoor Life,* but if the magazine does not publish fiction, then that is not a viable market for the story and he needs to look elsewhere. Even if a magazine does publish fiction, perhaps it's looking for a particular kind of fiction—sci-fi, maybe, or humor—in which case an adventure story still isn't going to be received with interest.

Students must then examine the needs of each publication in terms of genre, style, and length and be very aware of the "No's": *No how-to's . . . No fiction with explicit language . . . No why I like* _____ *articles.* Some of this is merely a matter of reading a listing closely and following directions, and so, on that level, deciding if a work is right for a publication is relatively easy. But even if a piece of writing seems to fit the expressed needs of a publication, it still may not be exactly right for the publication.

There are subtleties involved here. Adult readers are generally cognizant of the fact that all magazines have a certain slant. Sometimes it is as obvious as a left- or right-wing leaning to all their nonfiction; sometimes it's as subtle as a particular voice in all their fiction. The slant is often a reflection of the audience which comes to expect a certain quality to the magazine's content.

It is difficult to explain this elusive characteristic to young writers. My older students can recognize the difference between *New Yorker* fiction and *Yankee* fiction, for example, but I know that younger readers would be hard pressed to grasp that difference, and I'm sure even the older ones would find it difficult to see the finer distinctions in some of the literary journals. In order to explain the concept, I try to offer them examples more within their ken, having them bring in a variety of teenage magazines and asking them to explain how the magazines differ from one another in terms of their portrayal of the teenage world. I also ask them to tell which magazine they like best, and while there are definitely majority favorites, there are usually one or two that are defended passionately by certain students who like the slant they offer.

The truth is it's often next-to-impossible to know the perfect place to send your work. If we could determine it more accurately, no doubt more of us would be published! But it still should be a consideration for young writers. If nothing else, such careful study of literary publications can only make them more astute readers.

Should I tailor my writing to fit a particular publication?

Young writers often experiment with voices and styles. They adopt and abandon certain styles in much the same way they don and discard fashions or change their hair from blonde to blue to green. Such experimentation is positive in that it helps them grow and discover who they are as writers and what writing style they are most comfortable with. A publication that requires pieces on a certain theme, in a certain voice, or of a certain length can provide an impetus for students to try something a little different and to perhaps discover a new talent.

I have one student who recently happened upon a sonnet writing contest on the Internet, scrolled through sample sonnets, and then came to me intrigued by the form and wanting to know how to write her own. Rarely have I had students begging to write sonnets, but this contest triggered a new writing interest, and one for which she showed real ability.

Certainly, too, writing can be tailored in minor ways to produce major results. If a magazine wants stories of fifteen hundred words or fewer and a writer's story is 1650 words, then some careful revision and editing can create a story that fits the publication and is very likely a tighter and better story as a result. Or perhaps a student's essay about a hunting experience in his hometown could, with some minimal adaptations and additions, be made into a first-person essay for a regional column in a hunting magazine. Changes of this sort do not tamper with the heart of a piece, but simply alter its size and shape so that it better fits the publishing world.

What I caution students against, however, is sacrificing sincerity for a sale. When Jim, a frequent patron of the local McDonald's, spots an issue of *How On Earth!*, a quarterly published by the Vegetarian Network, on the bulletin board and tells me he's going to write a piece in praise of a vegan diet for the "Living Vegetarian" column, I can't help but ask if he's made a radical change in his diet.

"Nah," he says, "but I know a bunch of kids who don't eat meat. I can make it up. It'll be easy."

That's not tailoring; that's fictionalizing, and it's probably not a good idea unless you're writing a short story. I firmly believe students should write about what matters to them and I believe too that, if they do so, there will be a market for their work. I suggest to Jim that his essay might focus on what it's like to be a meat-eater in a vegetarian crowd, and he gives me a look that says he'll think about it. I want my students to be proud of the words they put in print. I want them to own the thoughts and ideas they struggle to express. They argue sometimes that professional writers have been known to sacrifice their literary integrity for the sake of a quick sale, maybe in the form of a steamy romance novel published under a pseudonym, and I can't dispute that. But, I ask them, at sixteen do you really want to sell your writing soul?

Preparing a Manuscript

I've chosen a market. Now what?

On a given day in my English class two students approach me. Jen clutches pages of yellow lined paper torn from a legal pad and a copy of submission guidelines taken from the bulletin board in the back of the room. Andy holds a market guide with sheets of his manuscript poking from its pages. Both have worked long and hard on their respective pieces, rewriting and revising until they feel satisfied with their work. Both have scoured the market listings, searching for the best place to send their work. Both are eager to send their work out, and they have come to me for help. But both know they are still a long way from a final product, a piece put in proper manuscript form, ready to be read by an editor. Although I tell each of my classes as a group the how-to's of preparing a manuscript for publication, I know it is only at this point—the moment when a student is ready to put his work in the mail—that he will really understand and absorb the details of manuscript preparation. I know I will answer the questions Jen and Andy are asking over and over again as other students reach that moment, and that's O.K. because it is through these questions and answers that students turn into real writers.

What is *proper manuscript format?*

Although certain contests and publications may require specific variations in manuscript formats, there is one standard format that marks the writer as a professional, and unless guidelines specify a variation, a writer should adhere to this basic format. I am adamant that my students do so when they submit work for publication. Even the students who are not generally concerned about details understand why. You have to look the part. If you want an editor to think you're a writer, maybe even an adult, professional writer, then your manuscript had better look like the work of a professional. No fancy paper, no handwritten scrawls, no cross-outs, no decorations, no lovingly constructed manuscript covers. The content of the piece is where the writer makes his own mark. In format he should look like every other professional writer.

Sample pages for prose and poetry manuscripts are included in the Appendix. They are presented according to the following basic rules of manuscript preparation:

1. All manuscripts must be typewritten. Typing may be done on a typewriter, a computer, or a word processor. Print should be black. Use pica type or a standard computer font such as Courier or Times.

2. Use twenty-pound white bond paper, 8 ½ x 11 inches. Do not use erasable paper, because of its tendency to smudge.

3. Make margins of 1-1 ½ inches on all sides of the page. It is best not to justify the print.

4. Prose should be double-spaced. Poetry should be typed as you want it to appear on the page.

5. Manuscripts should be typed on one side of the paper only. Each poem should be typed on a separate page. Each poem should include a heading as described below.

6. Use a paper clip, not staples, to keep pages together. Generally a title page or cover sheet should not be used.

7. Heading—Page one of the manuscript should include a heading. In the upper left corner, using single spacing, type your complete legal name, your address, and your telephone number with area code. Beneath that, type your social security number, which a publisher must have in order to pay a writer for his or her work.

8. Word count—In the upper right corner across from your name, indicate the number of words in the manuscript. If necessary, you can estimate (twenty-six lines of type per page generally averages 250 words per page), but most word processing programs can give the exact word count. Poets should indicate the number of lines in a poem rather than the number of words.

9. Title and Author—Approximately one-third of the way down the first page, center the title of the work in capital letters. Double-space and center the word "by," and then double-space and center again and type your name or pseudonym as you would want it to appear on the work.

10. Double-space twice, indent, and begin the body of the work.

11. Page two and on—The author's name and the page number must be indicated on each subsequent page. A key word from the title is optional. Some variation in format is possible, but a simple format is to put the last name, a dash, and the page number in the upper right corner (e.g., Rubenstein-2).

12. At the end of the manuscript, double-space, and type the words THE END.

13. Make a copy of the manuscript. Although a reputable publication will always do its best to return a manuscript in the self-addressed stamped envelope provided by the writer (see below), mistakes can happen or mail can get lost. The writer should always retain a copy of the work.

One reminder: sometimes a contest or publication will have unique rules for submissions, perhaps, for example, requesting a cover sheet with name and address, in order to make the submission itself anonymous to judges. A writer should always study the submission guidelines carefully and follow them exactly.

Do I really need a cover letter?

Yes, I tell Jen and Andy and every other student who comes to me with this question and a perfectly prepared manuscript in hand. They're generally not pleased with my answer, seeing the cover letter as just one more formality and a useless one at that. "I don't have anything to say," they complain. "What's the point?"

The point is that a cover letter, like a properly prepared manuscript, is a mark of a professional writer who is inviting an editor to read his work. It's true that, unlike published writers, most adolescents don't have publishing credits that they can showcase in their letters, nor do they generally have any professional experience relevant to the piece they're submitting that they wish to make an editor aware of. But that doesn't mean that they shouldn't write a courteous, concise cover letter that presents them as serious writers. (Nor, though I don't tell my students this, does it mean I should miss this perfect opportunity to teach them about business-letter format!)

A cover letter (see sample letter in the Appendix) is simply a business letter, stating in a clear, businesslike manner the relevant information. Written in proper business-letter format, it should be typed single-spaced with a space between paragraphs and should include a heading (the writer's address and phone number, and the date) and an inside address (name and address of the publication that the manuscript is being sent to). The salutation should include the name of the editor (e.g., *Dear Mr.* or *Dear Ms.* followed by the last name) which usually can be found in the market listing or the masthead of the magazine. The body of the letter should be polite, succinct, and direct, including only pertinent information. Sometimes, when a publication makes particular mention of its interest in young writers, I suggest that students mention their age. Otherwise, no personal information need be included unless a brief biography is required. Sometimes submission guidelines, particularly for student publications, will request other information, and a cover letter is the place for that material.

Does anything else go in the envelope?

Occasionally a publication or contest will require an entry form and/or a release form, guaranteeing that the work is the original work of the author. In some instances, the form will require a parent, guardian, or teacher signature if the writer is under eighteen. When any such forms are required, the writer should fill them out carefully and completely and attach them to the manuscript.

What about envelopes and postage?

Students, especially younger ones, generally do not have much experience with correspondence by mail, and the evolution of e-mail seems sure to exacerbate that situation. For that reason, they often find the "packaging" of their manuscript something of a challenge.

The first thing I tell my students is always to include a self-addressed stamped envelope (SASE) with sufficient postage (the same amount that goes on the mailing envelope) to ensure return of the manuscript. The only exception is in those cases when the submission guidelines specifically state that a manuscript will not be returned. The SASE is another mark of a professional writer, and generally editors will not even read a manuscript that does not come with an SASE. The writer's name and address should be typed or neatly printed on the envelope.

A manuscript of three or fewer pages plus cover letter can be folded in thirds and mailed in a standard-size white business envelope. The trick, for my students, tends to be how to fit that same size self-addressed, stamped envelope inside! There's usually someone who is completely baffled by the task until a classmate demonstrates folding the envelope also in thirds.

A manuscript of such length can also be sent folded in half in a 6" x 9" envelope.

A longer manuscript of five pages or more should be sent unfolded in a manila envelope, usually 9" x 12". The SASE should be of the same size, folded in half and enclosed.

Envelopes should be addressed carefully and, whenever possible, should include the editor's complete name. Naming an editor helps to ensure that the manuscript will reach an editor quickly, and also indicates that the writer has taken the time to find out who the appropriate editor is. Manuscripts that are not directed to a particular person are apt to be relegated to the very bottom of the slush pile. If a market listing or magazine masthead does not include an editor's name, the writer can call the publication and ask for the current editor's name. At the very least the writer should note "Fiction Editor," "Poetry Editor," etc. on the envelope. The envelope should always include the writer's return address.

A thirty-two-cent stamp will pay for first-class postage for a manuscript of up to one ounce, usually two to three pages plus SASE. Each additional ounce requires twenty-three cents postage. There is also an assessment for oversized mail. It is best to take a long manuscript to the post office to determine the correct postage since any envelope with insufficient postage will be returned to sender. Certainly in these days of rising postal rates, attempting to publish can become quite costly, and young writers need to be guided in making wise choices of potential markets so that the endeavor does not become a financial burden. Some student-written publications will accept one envelope of student submissions sent in by a teacher to reduce individual costs.

So is it best for the teacher to send a packet of class submissions to a magazine?

Generally I believe it's best for students to send their submissions individually unless a publication specifically states that it is willing to receive the work of an entire class. *Merlyn's Pen,* for example, notes on its cover sheet that teachers can send the work of several students in one large envelope, including one cover sheet and the required two dollars fee per student. *Stoneflower Literary Journal* and *Writes of Passage* are two other publications that will accept submissions through a teacher.

Most publications, however, are understandably not eager to take on the role of teacher/corrector and prefer to see only the best work of individual students. They are, moreover, not likely to publish a number of pieces similar in subject, so if a class assignment is submitted, it is reasonable to assume that only the very best pieces on a particular topic might be chosen for publication. It would seem wiser for students to send their work to different places.

I also believe that older students ought to approach publishing in the same way adult writers do and that they deserve to be treated as adult writers. Unless there are special circumstances, I believe a teenage writer should take individual responsibility for his or her work and learn how to present and submit it as a professional writer would. As noted above, I do not encourage my students to include their age in their cover letters unless a publication geared to young writers requests it or unless a publication states that it is especially interested in the work of young writers. High school age writers should, I feel, enter the competition on an adult level. If a piece of writing is good enough for publication, there is no way an editor can—or need—determine whether it is the work of a fifteen-year-old or a fifty-year-old. The piece should stand on its own, separate from its author.

Can I send my manuscript to more than one place at a time?

The question of simultaneous submissions (the practice of sending the same manuscript to more than one publication at the same time) is a tricky one, both for student and adult writers.

It used to be absolutely verboten to send a manuscript to more than one publication at a time. To do so marked one as unprofessional, if not out-and-out disreputable. That notion has changed somewhat, however, as editors recognize that a great amount of time generally elapses from the time a writer puts his work in the mail to when the editor sends out a response to it. Many publications take three to six months to respond to a manuscript, which means that a writer is fortunate if he can send his piece out three times in the course of a year!

To ameliorate this situation, many publications now state "Simultaneous submissions O.K." in their market listings, giving the writer the freedom to submit his work to more than one market. However, I caution students not to pepper the markets with any one piece but rather to choose potential markets carefully and submit to perhaps three at the most and only to those that designate their willingness to accept simultaneous submissions. Also, students should know that if a writer is lucky enough to have his work accepted by one of the publications, he must immediately inform the others and withdraw his submission.

If a market listing states that the publication does not accept simultaneous submissions—and that is often the case with student-written publications that do try to respond quickly to submissions—under no circumstances should a writer send his work to more than one place. Instead, as I tell my students, he should work on revising and polishing other pieces of writing so that he'll have plenty of pieces to submit to a variety of markets.

My manuscript is in the mail. Now what?

The truth is, now you wait. Some days you wait with hope in your heart, eager to go home and check your mail, sure that there's going to be an acceptance letter in it. Other days all you can think about are the things you didn't like about your manuscript—that second-to-last line that just didn't click, that paragraph of description you should have cut even more—and you dread opening the mailbox because you're positive your big brown envelope will be there waiting.

All writers suffer such ambivalent feelings, and, though I admit I don't always heed my own good advice, the best solution is to immerse yourself in another writing project. For students that might be another class assignment or maybe another contest. Writers are people who write, not people who wait around until someone tells them they're writers.

I also advise students to keep careful records of their submissions. Some keep this list in their writing class folder; others keep a list at home. Even though student writers are not as prolific as their adult counterparts and generally don't have more than a couple of pieces out in the world at any given time, it's still a good idea to keep a written record of each piece, noting where it was sent and when. When a decision is reached on a manuscript, the writer can record that information as well, and I defy any writer, young or old, not to savor every second of the time it takes to pen the word "Accepted"!

If a manuscript is rejected, I encourage students to take a few days to reconsider the piece, particularly if there are editorial comments that could help in revision. But if the writer feels no changes are in order, then he should get it back in the mail right away. Nothing takes away the sting of rejection as much as renewed hope.

Occasionally a student will send out a manuscript, wait patiently even beyond the response time stated in the market listing, and yet hear nothing. When that happens, I suggest the student send a polite letter with a SASE inquiring about the status of his manuscript, another excellent occasion for a business letter. It may be that an editorial staff has simply gotten behind in its reading or that the manuscript is being held for final consideration, but in some instances a manuscript has been lost in the mail or a magazine has suspended publication, and a writer who doesn't inquire about the situation will find himself waiting forever.

Certainly there are risks involved in the attempt to publish. But for me, and for my students, the rewards far outweigh these risks. Young writers who understand both the risks and the rewards and who are taught to present their work as professionals do can go forward into the publishing world with courage and confidence, knowing they and their work are ready.

III The Creation of a Community

When students are actively and honestly engaged in writing and in the attempt to publish, they leave the confines of the classroom and become members of a community, a writing community. This is one of the most positive and natural outcomes of the approach to writing described in the previous chapters. This community of writers who appreciate, encourage, and advance each other's efforts is very different from a classroom of students who often see themselves in competition with one another. Within a writing community, teacher and students share roles, and all are encouraged to demonstrate their particular talents—be it as thinker, listener, writer, editor, or critic—and to take on the challenge of improving themselves in all the varied roles writers assume.

Chapter 5, "Evaluating Student Writing," explains how even the process of grading/evaluating student work becomes a cooperative project in a writing community. The chapter describes three processes— peer evaluation, self-evaluation, and teacher evaluation—which all work together to improve the skills of young writers and to encourage more and better writing.

The final chapter, "A Community of Writers," discusses the five principles upon which a classroom-turned-writing–community is based and illustrates how vividly the community differs from the classroom. These principles challenge the teacher to give her students the freedom and opportunity to become "real writers," who write from the heart and who are ready to share their words with the world.

5 Evaluating Student Writing

In a perfect world, every student would leave my class having published a piece of writing. They would leave knowing they were writers. I would watch them go, knowing I had helped give them the skills and confidence to continue writing.

But of course it is not a perfect world. Though I have many success stories to tell, it is certainly true that in any given class only a tiny fraction of the group will see their words in print. Another fraction will try to publish and will grow as writers for their efforts. But some students still won't be ready to tackle the publishing world or just won't be interested in it. Yet I am responsible for all these students, for encouraging their efforts, tracking their progress, and measuring their achievement. Ultimately, I am responsible for putting a letter grade on a piece of paper and judging their worth as writers.

I do not like this task. Tell me to grade a vocabulary test or a reading quiz on a short story, and I do it with ease and a light heart. Tell me to grade a personal essay about the death of Ellen's little sister, and I am almost paralyzed by the weight of the task. Far easier to be the editor who accepts or rejects Ellen's essay; he doesn't have to justify his decision nor does he have to look into Ellen's eyes when he returns the piece to her. I have to do both. I have to explain why a piece that clearly tears at Ellen's heart is a B- piece of writing, and I have to see the sadness in her eyes which I know comes not only from the grade but from the moments she relived in her writing.

Evaluating student writing, the writing that comes from their hearts, is, for me, one of the most difficult aspects of a teacher's job. I can red-pen the spelling, the errors in grammar, the misplaced comma, but that's editing and easy and a task that touches neither the writer nor the reader. A computer can do most of that these days. It is when I have to evaluate the content of their work that I grow uneasy.

I am candid with my classes about this dilemma. Early on in each class, when I discuss my expectations for the course, I discuss with the students the difficulties I face in evaluating their writing. I describe to them three particular ways in which my methods of evaluating their work are likely to differ from those they are used to.

First, I tell them, please be aware that I am not your audience. That one simple sentence usually evokes a look of surprise on the faces of most students. Isn't the teacher always the audience? Isn't she the one with the red pen? Isn't she the one you have to please? And if the teacher isn't the audience, who is?

I tell them to look around the room, at the faces of their friends and acquaintances, the peers who will people the response groups we will soon form. Those people are your audience, I say, and you need to please them. And they serve simply as representatives of a larger audience composed of readers outside this classroom, outside this school, in fact, an audience of strangers who have never met you but who may read your work. You have to please them too.

They blink, disquieted. It's hard enough to please one teacher, but a world of strangers? Won't their opinions differ? What if one reader likes what another reader hates? What if some readers don't *like* dog stories, or rhyming poems, or essays about childhood? How can you please them all?

I let them wrestle with these questions for a few minutes, and then I offer them the only answer I have. You can't please them all; you can please only yourself. Ultimately as a writer you are the final judge of your work, and though you need to listen to the praise and the criticism of as many readers as are willing to give you feedback on your work, the final decisions about that piece are yours alone.

But, they (savvy veterans of the grading game) say, "You *are* still going to give us a grade, aren't you?"

"Well," I tell them, "you're going to get a grade on your work. But I'm not going to give it to you. We're going to figure it out together."

And that is the second way my evaluation methods differ from those many of my students are used to. I ask my students to be not only writers but also critics and commentators on their work, responsible both for creating the work and for assessing its quality. I promise to show them a variety of ways to do this assessment. I can predict the response I will get. Inevitably there are students who groan and roll their eyes. "Just grade it," they say. "It's easier that way."

I shake my head. "That's the point," I say. "Writing is not supposed to be easy." This does little to comfort them, so I offer my third evaluation technique.

In my classroom a student's work is viewed as a body of work, not as a series of individual papers. My intent is to measure a student's growth as a writer. Works do not stand alone but rather as pieces in a process of development and maturation. I am far less concerned about the quality of any one piece than I am about what it shows about the student's growth (or lack of it!) as he or she develops as a writer. Integral to this is the idea that students do not "compete" against their classmates for the high grades or the high praise; they compete only against themselves and their own previous efforts.

I have no doubt that there are teachers who would question this approach, who believe that the teacher should set the standard for quality and be the sole judge of how well the work meets this standard, awarding A's to those papers that come close and D's to those that do not. If there were an absolute standard, I might agree with their approach, and, in fact, if one judges writing on how well it adheres to the rules of grammar, spelling, and mechanics, then perhaps the standard seems obvious. But I know most teachers today recognize that good writing is not simply correct writing. If it were, computers would be earning our students A's daily! Good writing is far more difficult to define and highly subjective. We might agree that good writing is interesting, or that good writing takes a fresh approach to its subject, or that good writing moves the reader. But what's "interesting" or "fresh" or "moving?" I refuse to let my students believe that my definition of any such term is the right one. I want them to find their own definitions and apply them to their own work. What I can do is guide them in their search for a meaningful definition through two important processes—peer evaluation and self-evaluation. It is only in conjunction with those two processes that I can do my work of teacher evaluation.

This chapter describes these three categories for the evaluation of student writing. No one method of evaluation is enough. Peer evaluation, self-evaluation, and teacher evaluation are all integral to the writer's growth.

Peer Evaluation

I believe that students should evaluate student work. This idea is certainly not revolutionary, and in many writing classrooms it is common practice. But it is a practice that many students and teachers continue to struggle with because it demands of the student evaluators certain skills and responsibilities which traditionally have been accorded to the teacher. Students need to be taught to be effective evaluators and, equally important, they need to be trusted in that position. The skills, a teacher can teach; the trust grows out of the camaraderie and collegiality of the classroom.

In my classroom, response groups are the primary means of student evaluation. Choosing to use response groups is a serious commitment to a teaching style, and the use of such groups determines the ambience of the class. Most of this section will deal with response groups. However, at the end of the section, I will discuss other techniques to successfully generate student response to student work.

Response Groups

Response groups have been a staple of writing classrooms for many years and as such need little introduction. Teachers who use response groups with their students generally take the basic model of a small group of students working together to experience each other's writing and adapt that model to suit their own teaching styles and the needs of their class. The suggestions I offer here for the design of response groups are simply that, suggestions. Teachers should experiment to find the modifications that work best in their classrooms.

For me, response groups have a three-fold purpose: 1) to encourage students to take their writing seriously and to take responsibility for their work; 2) to offer a microcosm of the wider audience that students who want to publish will write for; and 3) to promote a spirit of community within the writing classroom. I want the experience of working in a response group to be a positive one for students. I want them to enjoy working with fellow writers, and I want them to develop both the confidence and the skills necessary to be good writers and good critics. For these reasons I am careful in the way I organize groups.

I think it is important for every student to have the opportunity to include what I call a "security blanket friend" in her response group. This is the person who represents the "perfect reader" that every writer imagines she is writing for. This is the reader who knows exactly what the writer is trying to say, even when she doesn't say it very well! In the writing classroom, this is often a student's close friend, someone who has known her for a long time, who understands the stories she's trying to tell, and who instinctively knows when to cheer and when to criticize. Now, this friend may not be the best critic or editor, but that is not his purpose. He's the one whose presence makes it possible for the writer to put her words on the line.

Because of the way classes are scheduled, particularly in secondary schools, not all students are fortunate enough to have such a soulmate in their English class, but most students could name one other person in the class whom they would like to see sitting in their response-group circle. I honor these requests, scrawled on small slips of paper, when I put together these groups of four or five or six, knowing that writers need first to feel comfortable in a group if they are to take the risks as writers and responders that may lead to some discomfort.

So, too, do I try to honor the request of a student who feels she simply cannot work with another student in the class—and not surprisingly the request generally comes from both sides. Although of course I would like all my students to work together harmoniously, I am realistic enough to know that adolescents carry a lot of history with them as well as a very adult sense of whom they trust as readers. Certainly as a writer I have turned down opportunities to work in particular writing groups simply because I'm not comfortable with certain participants. I believe my students deserve the same freedom, and in a class of twenty to thirty students, it is not impossible to make congenial groupings that students have a voice in.

I do not, however, allow students to form their own groups. This is partly because it inevitably leads to someone being left out, but more important because I want students to experience the opinions of responders whom they don't know very well and who might have views different from those they are used to. As any teacher knows, teenagers are by nature pack animals, traveling in groups with those whom they most resemble. As long as there is no strong personal animosity between particular students, mixing up the masses—the freaks and the jocks, the scholars and the slackers, the poets and the pragmatists—is an exciting venture and one that can lead to some amazing results. I love to watch the interplay between the class clown, the one whose work is a series of one-liners, and the philosopher, whose work is so thick with meaning that sometimes he gets lost in it. Their ideas and their opinions of good writing constantly collide, but force both of them to recognize that there is no one way to speak the truth. If all the philosophers were in one group, they might enjoy the discourse and debate just as five clowns might enjoy a lot of laughter, but as writers none of them would grow.

My students also know that the response groups we form early in the year are not necessarily static. Changes may occur as the year goes on, initiated either by me or by the group itself. Sometimes a group simply finds it has no energy, no spark. This is not the fault of the individual participants, but rather the result of bad chemistry. Groups need a leader, a person to get the action going, and, if all participants are passive, nothing happens. On the other hand, groups don't need four leaders, and if I see a group spending too many weeks working out the group dynamics, I'm apt to make some changes. So too do I intervene when I find that a group has become a social club, more concerned with gossip and the weekend's activities than the works-in-progress. A little socializing is reasonable and even good in that it creates bonds among group members, but too much is time wasted.

A more problematic issue in the formation of groups involves the idea of "good" writers versus "not-so-good" writers. Should the two levels be mixed so the better writers can help those less skilled, or should good work with good, and bad with bad, so as not to hinder the growth of the talented or intimidate those who are not? It's a tough question to answer, as certainly the continuing debates over homogeneous versus heterogeneous groupings in education indicate. In terms of response groups, however, I find the question seems often more significant on paper than it is in the writing classroom. In a group of four to six students, there is almost always a wide range of writing ability, particularly when the work is varied and close to their hearts. Even the slowest students become master storytellers when asked to write of their childhood, for example. They may not have the language of their more articulate peers, but sometimes their writing is all the more powerful for its simple, uncluttered honesty. Or perhaps they are not great writers themselves, but they surely know a dull story when they hear it, and so they make excellent critics, able to tell the writer just where in the story their interest flagged and what would have kept it going. And sometimes these students who have never been called writers by their teachers manage to cut through a lot of the pretense. Unimpressed by tricks their peers have learned to make teachers happy, they offer writing that is real and risky and wrenching—and encourage others in the group to do the same.

The fact is, I have never had a student come to me and say, "Change my response group. They're not good enough writers for me," but I have had students say, "I don't think I'm good enough for the group." I take that concern seriously, never wanting any writer to feel that he is pulling down a group or failing to make a contribution to it. Often, then, to protect the student's anonymity, I'll ask all the students in the class to write a reflection about their own group, discussing how each participant, including themselves, contributes to it. The student who voiced the original concern generally learns what a valued member of the group he is and recognizes strengths he never knew he possessed.

The formation of the groups is only one concern a teacher needs to consider. Students who have not participated in response groups also need training if the groups are to be worthwhile. Before students work in their individual groups, I model a very large response group using the entire class as the group. I act as the writer and the students are the responders. I also give the students a hand-out describing the process that will go on within the group.

As the writer, I open the response session by introducing my paper to the group. I begin with a very brief description of the work, my purpose in writing it, and the stage it is now at. I also ask my listeners to cue in to certain specific areas which I have questions/concerns about. In this way I direct their listening and make it easier for them to focus on the parts of the paper that may need the most work. An example of my introduction might go like this:

"This is a poem I'm working on for this class, and I'm thinking of maybe sending it to *Rosebud*. They're looking for writing about relationships, and this poem is about mothers and daughters. This is the third draft of the poem. I'm still not happy with the way it ends, and I'm not sure if the physical description of the daughter works."

Following this introduction I read the poem aloud. It is important that the writer hear her work, because often in the listening she can hear where a piece falters. Students sometimes find it difficult at first to read their work aloud to the group, and if so I give them the option of having another member of the group read it. The important thing is that all the group members—responders and writer—hear the work.

In an ideal writing classroom, one equipped with a copier machine, all group members would also have a copy of the piece to read on their own and perhaps note comments on. Although I like listening to writers read, I know I am a more astute critic when I can also see the work on paper. In this age of word-processed writing, my students frequently print multiple copies of their work which they can hand out to their response-group members. Without photocopied or word-processed copies, however, the best approach is to pass the piece around the group, giving all the responders a chance to read the entire work or specific sections after the work has been read aloud.

When the piece has been heard/read by all the group members, there is almost invariably a pause which for the writer seems to be very long. I tell my students I know how interminable those seconds can seem to a writer who suddenly is sure her work must be just awful, since it appears to have rendered her group speechless! In fact those seconds of silence are very natural and are generally no indication of the quality of the piece. Responders need time to absorb what they have heard, formulate their reactions to it, and find the words to express their opinions. Moreover, responders are frequently beset with insecurities similar to those of the writer. A responder fears speaking first in case his opinions are wrong!

When the silence is broken, however, I suggest that it be broken by praise, with each responder telling the writer something he liked about the piece. Sometimes my students balk at this. "You want us to lie?" they say. "What if it's really terrible?"

My response is this: in all my years of reading student papers, I have always been able to find something good in every one. Maybe it's the topic, maybe it's the opening line, maybe it's one tiny detail buried in the third paragraph. The point is, unless a paper was written in the corridor on the way to class (and it is rare that a student has the nerve to read such a paper to his peers!), it is likely to have some redeeming feature, and the first responsibility of a response group is to emphasize the good.

There's a reason for this. All writers, and especially young writers, are vulnerable. Putting your heart into words and offering those words to a group is a very difficult thing to do, particularly when that group's task is to critique your words. I tell my students the praise they give inflates the writer's ego like air added to a not-yet-to-bursting balloon. Inevitably will come the pinpricks of criticism, and a little of that air will leak out. But when the student leaves class that day, I want his head and heart to be the size they were when he entered. I want his confidence in himself and his words to be intact, not shriveled and unsalvageable. So the praise we give a writer is a way to ensure that his faith in his work is safe.

Sincere praise has another important purpose. Beginning writers sometimes have a hard time distinguishing the good from the bad. It's not uncommon for a student who relies on only his own judgment when making revisions to revise away the good parts, leaving the awkward areas unchanged. Writers need to hear from their peers exactly what it is in their pieces that works. What are the vivid details, the great lines, the perfect words? Why is the opening exactly right the way it is? Which are the lines of dialogue that reveal the character? When response-group members comment on and often agree in their assessment of the strengths of a piece, a writer can feel quite certain that those parts of the piece should stay.

After responders have offered praise, their next task is to tell the writer what they see as the central point of the piece. This may seem rudimentary, but it is an important part of the response process. When young writers write about what is very close to their hearts, they often assume that others will understand exactly what they are trying to say, even when it isn't said very clearly. I listen in on a group discussing Nick's story about being ostracized on his first day in a new school for wearing the wrong kind of clothes.

Tom: I guess the point was you were a geek then.

I watch Nick blink. A look of surprise mixed with some distress crosses his face.

Kate: No, I think he was just trying to say how different things were in Tennessee than here. It was like that for me when I moved here.

Adam: I agree with Tom. It says right here, "I wasn't like the rest of the kids in my new class." So he was a geek.

The three of them look at Nick expectantly. He's shuffling through the pages of his rough draft, and I can see he's trying to find evidence of the point he meant to make.

Kate: So, Nick, what are you trying to say?

Nick: That the kids in that school were mean, at least to me they were. That's what I'm trying to say. But (he looks sadly at the papers strewn on his desk), *I guess you didn't get it.*

Tom: That's because you didn't say it.

All of them, even Nick, laugh, but Tom moves beyond ribbing with his next comment.

Tom: You can fix it, though. Write down some other mean things they did. Did they make fun of your accent too?

And the group is quickly engaged in helping Nick find those details that make the reader understand the point he means to make.

Sometimes, as in Nick's case, the process of establishing the focus leads naturally into a critical commentary of the piece, but frequently it's not that easy to generate constructive criticism. When a class first begins working in response groups, it's not uncommon for me to notice that a session has concluded with remarkable speed. In fact, the whole session has taken not much longer than it would take for the participants just to read their pieces.

When I wander over and inquire as to how the session went, there is generally an enthusiastic nodding of heads.

"Good," the students say.

"And the pieces?" I ask. "How were they?"

There is more nodding of heads. "Good," they say. "They were good."

Good. I'm leery of the word *good* when used too eagerly and widely by writing students. Sometimes the statement, "His paper was good," simply translates into, "I'm too lazy to think about his paper," but more often it means, "I just don't know how to respond."

Students need to be taught both how to be critics and how to express critical opinions in a sensitive and productive manner. Neither task is easy, but students generally find the latter the more difficult. I understand that. Even as a teacher with many years of "diplomatic training," I find it easier to write my criticisms on a student paper than to say them to a student in a writing conference. Yet I also know that my spoken comments are much more meaningful and have a greater impact on the writer and his or her work.

In response groups, then, I don't want students simply scribbling comments on the piece or writing answers to a worksheet full of questions like "Do you like the opening? Why/why not?" I want the writer and the responders to discuss the piece and share in a discussion of its strengths and weaknesses.

To model that activity, I continue to use the whole class as a large response group with me as writer of a piece. After they have offered praise and discussed what they consider to be the central point of the piece, I then ask them to talk about the problems they see in the piece, reminding them to comment particularly on the areas that I mentioned, in my introduction to the piece, as having questions and concerns about.

That opens a door for the responders. If, as the writer, I can, for example, say, "I'm not happy with the lines that describe the mother. I think they're too vague," I have in effect given permission to the responders to criticize my work, and that permission makes the responders more comfortable. It also reminds them that the writer is ultimately responsible for the piece, and that as writers they need to continually look at their own work with a critical and honest eye.

Of course not all problems in a paper are immediately visible to the writer, and so it is the response group's responsibility to bring these problems to the writer's attention. But what if they don't see the problems either? That is a common situation when students first begin to evaluate each other's work.

I have a technique to counteract this dilemma, but it is one that I am loath to admit I use, and were it not for its effectiveness, I wouldn't use it at all! It is a technique that employs the concept of grades, a focus I like to avoid as much as possible. But the reality is that students "understand" grades. They understand the quality of work an A represents, and they understand the gradations of difference between an A and B+.

So, in this model response group, when students hesitate to criticize the piece I have read and offer as their sole critique the classic line, "It's good," I ask them to jot down on a piece of paper the grade they would give it. Then, with a show of hands, we take a tally of the grades and usually find that there is close consensus, give or take a plus or minus, and that rarely does the paper earn that magical straight A.

"O.K.," I say, "so it's not an A paper. Then imagine you're the teacher and you have to explain to me, the student, why you didn't give me an A."

I admit I love that moment when suddenly they are in my shoes, struggling to find a way to put into concrete terms why the piece just doesn't work perfectly. This exercise is valuable for two reasons. First, it makes students see just how subjective and difficult the grading process is in terms of student writing. I think this builds empathy for me, the person with the red pen and grade book, and perhaps eliminates some of the controversy over grades that is a part of every classroom.

More important, though, this activity forces students to pinpoint problems in a piece of writing and to offer specific suggestions for improvement. They understand then it's not enough to say, "The ending's bad, and I don't like the way you wrote the piece, so I'm giving you a B-." They understand because they would never let me get away with grading one of their papers in such a vague manner. They would want to know why the ending is bad and how it could be made better. They would want to know what I meant by "how you wrote the piece," and they would want guidance in changing the voice or style. Although I do not want my students to be obsessed with the grades they receive on their writing, I'm realistic enough to know that, at least in the beginning, the idea of a grade and its variable worth gives them something familiar to hang onto when they are trying to judge the quality of a piece of writing.

Some students, perhaps in an attempt to take the easy way out, direct their criticism to the mechanical errors in the piece, errors like a misplaced comma, a misspelled word, a misused modifier. It's far easier to tell a writer how to punctuate a sentence than it is to tell her how to describe the feeling of the wind, for example. Though final drafts—those we hang up on the wall, publish in a class anthology, or send out into the world—need to be absolutely correct in terms of grammar, spelling, and punctuation, those areas are not primary concerns when writers begin their drafts. I expect response-group members to serve as line editors only when the content of the piece is in its final form. Prior to that, criticism should focus on larger issues—organization, the need for detail, the use of dialogue, awkward phrasing, openings and endings, and the like—and so those are the areas we discuss in model response groups.

In classes where some of the students have had previous experience with response groups, one modeling session is enough to send them on their way in their own groups. Other classes, however, need even more experience with "practice pieces" before they feel comfortable dealing with each other's work.

In those instances, I ask students to meet in their newly established response groups, and I give them each a piece of writing that is not that of any other class member. I tell them to pretend the paper is the work of one member of the group, to introduce it and read it as such, and then to let the group praise it, discuss its central point, and criticize it. This exercise allows students to practice all the techniques integral to a good response session while alleviating some of the stress involved in presenting one's own work. Because the fear of hurting the writer's feelings is eliminated, it is especially effective in helping students learn to be critical about a piece.

At some point, of course, the practice ends and the real game begins. When students first begin to meet in their groups and present their own work, I make it a point to visit the groups, to listen in on the reading and to encourage the response. My visits, however, are brief, and only when a group seems truly lost as to how to proceed do I sit down with the group and become part of it. I believe every response group needs to find its own way, and that it is the members of the group, not the teacher, who should carve out that path. Group dynamics being what they are, some groups will take longer than others to gel and to become productive, but often it is the group that struggles the most to find its way that in the end is most effective and most connected.

It is not unusual for students to take on particular roles within the group, and that discovery of individual strengths is another positive aspect of response-group work. Before the days of computerized spellcheckers, it was common for one student in each group to become the human spellchecker, the person who saved my red pen by applying his own. Often another student is the one with a gift for organization, the person who can take a rambling piece and find a way to sort it out so that it reads clearly. Another student may be the one who can always offer suggestions for stronger openings and endings. Another may be the cheerleader, the one who offers the writer the kind of encouragement he needs to go on with his work. And sometimes there is a student, the consummate critic, who knows instinctively how to go to the heart and guts of a piece and make it better.

In my classroom the good critic is as valued as the good writer, and frequently the two talents are quite distinct. Often I have students who struggle with their own writing, finding it difficult to start from scratch and create a compelling and coherent piece. But these same students may have an uncanny ability to read another writer's finished piece, see the problems with it, and offer solutions. They have an editing ability that goes beyond the areas of grammar, spelling, and mechanics. Perhaps they will become editors, or teachers, or other problem-solvers in our world. The point is, just as no professional writer could function without a good editor, so too do the members of a writing classroom need students with such talents. Sometimes when I chat with groups and discuss how their work is going, I'll ask whom the group members see as their most valuable critic. Generally there is consensus; one name emerges from each group. I want that person to be aware of his talents and to recognize how valuable a member of the group he is.

Working in response groups takes time. It takes time to form the groups, time to train them in response techniques, time to let them find their own methods. But I can think of no better way to spend time in a writing classroom. In these groups students build a sense of community and a sense of shared purpose. It is cooperative learning at its best with students engaged in the challenge of improving their own work as well as the work of their peers.

I remind my students that professional writers work in similar sorts of writing groups. The task of writing is essentially a lonely one, and it is only through such group endeavors that writers find the connections they need to inspire them and move them forward in their work. I try to emphasize this by bringing in articles in which writers talk about their writing groups. I want my students to understand that the process of writing is very much the same whether you are an amateur or a professional.

Using Response-Group Feedback

The work does not end when the response-group session concludes. The teacher needs to be aware that no matter how productive the groups seemed during class time, the real effect of the group happens outside of the class—when the writer revises.

This, too, is something students need to be taught. It is easy for students to compartmentalize their work, to see the meeting of the response group as a class activity and the writing of their paper as homework, without ever really understanding how the two connect. Students need to learn how to take the discussion of the group and use it in the revision of their work.

When students first start meeting in response groups, I will often ask them to end the session with each student telling the group at least two things she is going to change as a result of what she has heard said about her work. She then writes these two things on a piece of paper and attaches them to her draft. Verbalizing to the group the planned revisions clarifies the plans and ensures that the writer heard accurately what the responders said. Putting the plans in writing serves as a memo to the writer so that when she sits down in front of the computer, which may not be for a couple of days, she remembers exactly what parts of the piece she wants to work with. It also serves as a kind of contract between the writer and her peers, guaranteeing that she will tackle these revisions however challenging they may be and not simply opt for simpler changes.

Although I have students who on their own continue to write messages to themselves to guide their plans for revision, most students eventually outgrow this need. No matter what approach students choose for themselves, I do request that their drafts, the ones they read in response groups, show the efforts of the group by the scrawls and scribbles the writer puts on them.

By that I mean that every draft should indicate that it is a work-in-progress, a piece with cross-outs and corrections, arrows and alterations. I tell them quite seriously that though I expect them to hand in every draft that contributed to the final piece, I sincerely hope I am unable to read the drafts because they are so marked up and messy that they are rendered illegible. One of the worst "crimes" a writer in my class can commit is to pass in a number of drafts with the final one indistinguishable from the roughs because they all are neat and unmarked. Drafts should look like drafts and should bear the stains (sometimes quite literally) of sweat and effort. Some of my more technologically advanced students object, maintaining that their early efforts are swallowed up by the delete button on their computer. I appreciate that—and am grateful too that some of my own worst writing has never gone beyond the screen stage. But, I remind them, you need hard copies of your work to read to your response group, and these should show the notes you made from the group's response, the plans for revisions in the piece.

I believe that hard copies of a piece are necessary to the writer too. When a writer is engaged in the process of writing, not all problems are immediately evident to him. Furthermore, a passage may look fine on the screen at a particular moment, but a hard copy reread a day or two later may reveal flaws in that passage. Though the writer will make the actual changes on the screen, I hope he will note his concerns on the draft itself.

Students are funny, though, about handing in these so-called scribbles and scrawls. Sometimes I fear we have taught them too well. They have a sense that what pleases the teacher is a final product that is slick and sanitized, one that bears no indication of the "dirty work" that went into its creation. Students apologize as they hand me a pile of rumpled papers, marked and muddled with ragged edges and creased corners, the final draft—pristine and polished—placed carefully on the top. "My drafts are really messy," they say. "Are you sure you want me to staple everything together?" Clearly we have taught too many young people that the product is far more important than the process, which I suspect most teachers would vehemently deny. The work students do in response groups as they struggle with revision is a way to counteract that mindset.

Although this is the standard and most significant way in which response groups are used in my classroom, they do have other functions. Sometimes a student is "stuck," caught in that purgatory writers dread when they simply can't come up with an idea for a piece. When that happens, I suggest he sit down with his response group and share his dilemma with them.

Jesse, for example, is trying to write a piece about his very early childhood, the years before he went to school, and he is simply blocked, sure that he has absolutely no memories of that time. His group members ply him with questions: "Do you remember your birthdays then? Did you go to daycare? Were you scared of anything? I got my first guinea pig when I was four. Did you have any pets?"

Jesse shakes his head glumly, seeming more and more discouraged until suddenly Kate pipes up with, "Well, your brother is only a year younger than you. What was it like when he was born?"

Suddenly a light goes on in Jesse's head. He remembers Jason screaming to get out of his crib, and Jesse, the big brother at three, going to "help" him and . . . . Suddenly he's off on a story, a story complemented by a photograph he brings in the next day to share with his response group, little brother next to big, both peering into an enormous fish tank, another story waiting to be told.

A response group, then, can serve as a sounding board, a group of students who share a special empathy with the writer, not only because they are often involved in similar writing dilemmas but because they often share backgrounds and histories, knowing more about each other than the teacher ever could.

If a response group can help a writer give birth to an idea, so too can it help the writer in the final stages of a work's development. I am adamant that when a piece is ready for possible publication—be it on the classroom wall or in the pages of *Teen Voices*—it must be error-free. A final draft is precisely that—the writer's final chance to get it right and to produce a piece of work that he is proud to put his name on. Response groups can serve as the final proofreaders of a finished piece. Though it is true that word processors correct many mechanical errors these days, there is still a definite need for a human eye, one that will catch the *an* that's meant to be an *in* or the missing quotation marks at the end of a line of dialogue. Having four student proofreaders plus one teacher proofreader is infinitely preferable to that one set of eyes alone, and many times students catch errors that slip by me. With the help of response groups, a writer can feel quite confident that the work he sends out into the world is free of errors.

A response group can also help the writer decide where he is going to send that work. I enjoy watching students get together to talk about markets. Their comments are frequently insightful and absolutely honest.

"Don't send it there," a senior girl will say, disdain dripping from her voice. She holds up a publication with young children's drawings, a publication that some of my younger students would kill to be published in. But at seventeen it is, as Melissa tells us, "for babies."

Other students have had experience trying to market their work to certain publications and can offer "inside information." "They said it took six weeks to get a response, but I heard in a month, and they sent comments too." Or "A girl I know got a poem accepted there and they paid her fifteen dollars, but they still haven't published it."

This kind of dialogue is exactly the sort of conversation that goes on in adult writing groups, and though some of the "someone I know said" information might best be taken with a grain of salt, it is the sharing of ideas and the collegiality as writers that is important. With that in mind, I sometimes suggest that students who are choosing markets break out of their established response groups and meet occasionally with students who are doing similar sorts of writing and looking for similar sorts of markets.

Justin, for example, is a sci-fi freak. He reads every science fiction story he can get his hands on and subscribes to a number of magazines that publish science fiction material. He is a valuable resource in my classroom because my knowledge of the genre is limited. What I do know about science fiction I have learned from students like Justin. So when one of my students is working on a story about space-age technology in the year 2050 and wants to know about markets, I can send him to Justin, knowing that he will get solid, up-to-date information.

In much the same way do I match up students who are working on similar sorts of writing projects. Together they can pool information and ideas, and sometimes they will even decide to collaborate on a piece of writing. Sometimes they need my assistance to find a particular market, a magazine looking for articles about teen service projects, for example, or a publication that accepts haiku. It is often effective for me to meet with small groups of student writers who are working on similar sorts of writing in order to help them research these very specific markets. This kind of shared group activity does much to build a strong community of writers who appreciate each others' efforts. And when one of these writers is published, the group of students who worked most closely with him share in the success.

Other Techniques to Generate Student Response

As I noted in the beginning of this chapter, there are other techniques that I use to generate peer response to student work. Some of these techniques are described below. None, however, takes the place of response groups. Over the years I grow increasingly more committed to this approach, as I see students who participate in these groups improve dramatically as writers. Sometimes, however, another method is better suited to a particular assignment, and sometimes there is simply a need for some variety in the classroom routine. In those instances, one of the following techniques might be most effective.

Pass the Paper

Students love to read other students' work. Give them a choice between reading a story by a famous author or reading a story by one of their classmates, and they will almost always choose the latter. For this reason— and because I know that students learn much about writing from sharing their work with one another—I try to find ways to promote classroom-wide reading even when time constraints are a factor.

One quick, easy method is the "pass-the-paper plan." Students sit in a big circle—or two circles if the group is large enough to warrant it— and at the word "Go!" pass their own pieces of writing to the left. As time-keeper I watch the clock, allowing a certain number of minutes, depending on the length of the pieces, for the reading. Generally I give students less time than it might take to read the entire piece, but enough time to get a good general impression of it. When the allotted time is up, I say "Pass!" and the papers go again to the left, unless a reader is holding a paper which she particularly likes. Then she may hold that piece as long as she likes, until she finds one she likes even better. Papers continue to be passed for as long as time allows. The only rule of the game is that no reader may hold on to more than one paper at a time. Then, about ten to fifteen minutes before the period ends, I ask those readers who are holding papers they like to read the pieces aloud and tell the group why they enjoyed them.

This activity has a number of positive features. First, it engages all students, allowing them to read many pieces in a relatively short time and to see how their peers are tackling certain writing tasks and assignments. Second, it motivates readers to compare pieces of writing, to make decisions about quality and to determine what makes one piece better than another. Finally, it gives real positive feedback to those students whose work is read aloud, and the enthusiasm of the group precludes any negative feelings of competition.

This method is particularly effective when students are in the beginning stages of a writing activity and are trying out ideas and approaches. Reading their peers' early attempts stimulates ideas and discussion and allows students to leave class with a clearer sense of the direction their own pieces can take. When all emphasis is placed on the positive and no critical comments are voiced, students also feel free to take risks in their work, to try styles and voices they may have never before experimented with. "Pass the Paper" is a nonthreatening group activity whose success seems to rise from the sheer pleasure students take in their classmates' work.

In a variation on this activity, one which makes it more focused and formalized, I have students sit in their response groups, but they do not read the work of the group's members. Instead, a person in each group collects the pieces of writing and passes them on to the next group, whose job it is to read the four or five pieces and select, as a group, the one which they like the best. They must also come up with a clear statement of the reasons for their choice. When they have completed the task with one set of papers, they repeat it with another set of papers from another response group. This process is repeated until each response group has read all the papers in the class, except for those of their own group. Then, as a class, we discuss the choices the groups have made, noting particularly those papers that were selected as "best" by more than one group. We note the reasons for the choices, and from the class comments about what makes a piece work, try to come up with some sort of rubric to guide all the writers as they work on revision.

Classroom Swap

Capitalizing on the pleasure students take in reading each others' work, I sometimes have students from different classes share their writing. This works particularly well when two classes are working on similar assignments.

For example, two of my classes were working on character sketches with each student creating a fictional character whom he might later incorporate in a story. Students worked on many drafts of the sketch and also completed a characterization sheet listing every bit of information they could about their invented characters, from the way they looked to the foods they liked to eat, from their superstitions to their political beliefs. Much of this activity went on in response groups and through informal sharing with other class members. By the time all this work was finished and students were at the final draft stage, they knew their characters—as well as the characters created by their response group members—inside out, and more than one student expressed a bit of boredom with the characters. They needed a fresh view of their work.

New eyes came from students in another class. The two groups swapped copies of their work and read them in response groups, sending a marked-up manuscript as well as a written group evaluation back to each writer. Writing the evaluation was a challenge in itself, as each group took on the task of an editor who takes the time to comment on the manuscript she receives. Responders had to struggle to put their comments, both positive and negative, into clear, concise language, something they don't always do when they are able to verbalize their reactions to a piece. I also encouraged them to serve as line editors since the sketches were at the final draft stage. Without the writer there to explain his or her intended meaning, it was often a difficult task for the responders to know whether a comma should go or stay, or a modifier move.

The activity definitely builds empathy for editors who read many, many manuscripts daily, and it also demonstrates dramatically to young writers how important it is that the final manuscript be well written and free of errors. They suddenly understand that the manuscript will stand alone on the editor's desk with no writer there to argue or explain its merits.

For the writers the return of their manuscripts was a bit like seeing that brown envelope in the mail, but with the bonus of editorial comments and not just a generic rejection slip. Students took their evaluations seriously, perhaps because they knew the responders were writers too, people who understood the challenge of the work. They shared the evaluations with their own response groups, who sometimes concurred with the criticisms and suggestions, surprised that they hadn't seen these flaws themselves, or who sometimes heartily disagreed with the comments. I'm unperturbed by diverse opinions on a piece of writing, seeing it as a vivid parallel to the way work is regarded by different editors, but my students are not so unflappable. They want to know which view is right and what they should do to make their paper work. I have to constantly remind them that ultimately each writer is his own harshest critic, and having taken all outside opinions into serious account, he must finally write the piece so that it pleases himself.

Occasionally I have had classes take this activity one step further to more completely replicate the publishing world. Then I ask each class to choose the one piece they would want to publish. To accomplish this in an efficient fashion, I ask each response group to choose the one sketch they feel is most worthy of publication, and I tell them that that sketch will be submitted to the final editorial board. This board will be composed of one student from each response group, and I ask that each group elect its own member, basing its choice on the one group member with the best editorial skills. This rewards the student who is perhaps not the best writer but whose responding skills are very worthy of praise.

The editorial board, made up of five or six students (depending on the number of response groups in the class), then meets and reads the five or six chosen papers in order to decide which one will be published. It is usually a very difficult decision to make because at this stage all of the papers are quite good. Even if the board can dismiss two or three as not quite as good, the remaining pieces are generally of similar quality. The board discovers then that its final decision may end up being based on very minor aspects of a piece, or sometimes even on which "editor's" voice is loudest!

Once again this is a vivid and eye-opening dramatization of what goes on in the publishing world. Through this process young writers come to truly understand that rejection does not necessarily imply that a piece does not have merit. Competition is the name of the game, whether it takes place in Room 224 or in the editorial offices of *Stone Soup*. Difficult choices have to be made, and all a writer can do is submit her very best work, work of a quality the publication demands, and then hope for the best. And if the piece comes back to her, she needs to reassess its strengths and weaknesses, make any necessary revisions, put it in another envelope, and get right back in the game.

A Step Beyond

Not all evaluation has to happen within the classroom. In fact, as I tell my students, sometimes the best way to determine the readability—and salability—of a piece is to offer it to a reader who can see it with completely fresh eyes and whose view of it has not been "tainted" by all of the planning and discussion of the piece that goes on in the classroom. That sort of "outside reader" is the one who will best represent the editor of a magazine or its typical reader.

So, in order to get this kind of objective response, I often ask students to give their piece to a serious reader who is willing to give the writer both positive and negative feedback. Sometimes students appeal to friends outside of the class, sometimes to parents, and sometimes to another teacher, a coach, or a boss. One student, who had participated in a local writing workshop months earlier, took the initiative of sending her piece to the mystery writer who had facilitated her particular group, and was delighted when he wrote her a long and detailed letter, full of excellent commentary to aid her in revision. I do ask my students to get some sort of written statement, either actually penned by the reader or summarized by the student herself following their conversation about the piece. This is their "proof" of having done the assignment, but more important it is the reminder of what might stay and what might be changed when they begin to revise.

This activity is obviously a form of mini-publication in and of itself, and students realize that. For that reason, approaching an outside reader with their work is somewhat intimidating to them, and so this is not an activity I use until I know students have confidence in their writing. I am careful to remind them too that one reader's opinion is only that—one reader's opinion—and I generally use this method only in conjunction with other forms of response.

This sort of "outside response" can also be done in a less structured, more ongoing manner throughout the year. Frequently I have my students display their writing on the bulletin boards and walls of the classroom. It's not unusual for students to peruse the walls before each class begins, reading the pieces and sometimes commenting on them. My seniors this year, for example, took quite an interest in the "I Was, I Am, I Will Be" poems penned and illustrated by my sophomores. When a student seems particularly taken by a piece, I ask him to write a short note to the author, expressing his interest and noting what he especially liked about the piece. Younger students are flattered by the compliments they receive from the juniors and seniors, and the older students thrive on the admiration their work generates from those a little less practiced. This positive reinforcement clearly has a profound effect on student writers, but even more important, it demonstrates to them how powerful their words are in the world and how publishing, even in the small world of the classroom walls, is a gratifying experience.

Self-evaluation

Certainly peer evaluation is an effective and productive process to use with young writers. There is no question but that they learn much about writing and improve as writers through the comments, both positive and negative, which they receive about their work from reader-responders. But we are doing student writers a disservice if we allow them to become completely dependent on outside response. As any writer will tell you, writing is essentially a solitary activity, and in the process of writing any piece, whatever its length, the writer must constantly make decisions about her work. Should she use this word or that? Are her ideas developed in a logical sequence? Does this concept need further clarification? What about the tone?

At some point before they attempt publication, most writers do bring their work—and their worries—to trusted readers for feedback and guidance, but prior to this point they act as their own editors and evaluate their work word by word. Students need to be taught to be self-evaluators as well if they are to develop into autonomous writers and learners. Teaching them to take on this role is a difficult and demanding task and one that I approach in very small steps, well aware that I am unlikely to see tremendous growth, but trusting that the habits I hope to instill in them will remain long after the course ends.

Student writers are not naturally critical of their own work. Yes, they are known for prefacing an oral reading of their piece with a line like, "This is really bad but . . ." but that sort of disclaimer is more an adolescent convention than an honest opinion of their writing.

I believe there are two reasons why students are not naturally drawn to self-evaluation of their work, and they reflect two ends of a spectrum. On one end are the lazy writers, students like Pete who sit in my sixth-period class and routinely produce work that will earn them a grade with which they are comfortable, usually something in the B-/C+ range. For these students, work of this quality takes relatively little time or effort, and that's the way they like it. But their work has the potential to be much better than this, and if their response-group members and I poke and prod and provoke them enough, they may be persuaded to make those revisions that will boost their grade a bit. But left on their own, neither Pete nor any of his classroom copies would ever take the time to examine their work critically to try to find the places where the writing falters and revisions are necessary. For these writers, their work is "good enough" and they are loath to struggle to make it better.

On the other end of the spectrum are the students who do put time and effort into their work, and who feel when a piece is "done" that it is absolutely done and that nothing they can do will make it better. Paula is one such writer. "This is my best work," she tells me, holding her paper against her like armor. "How can you expect me to do anything more?" Writers like Paula are not necessarily egotists; they simply have a strong sense of ownership about their work, and sometimes even when their response group makes suggestions for revision, these writers refuse to consider any changes. For them, their work is not good enough; it is "good."

I think the Petes and Paulas of the classroom can be approached in the same way and can be taught similar techniques to encourage them in self-evaluation. These techniques also serve all the students in the middle, the ones who might make more revisions if only they knew how to judge their work, if only they knew the questions to ask themselves about their own writing.

I believe in questions, not a checklist of criteria for the writer to march through—topic sentences, concluding paragraph, use of sensory detail—but rather serious questions that force the writer to really think about the piece and the process that created it. It's easy to put a check next to the phrase *topic sentences* whether you have them or not. There's no easy way, however, to respond to a question like "Where did you grow most frustrated writing this piece, and how did you move beyond the frustration?"

Those are the sorts of questions I ask my students to respond to when they hand in drafts of a piece. Generally I give each student a list of three questions, and I vary the questions from assignment to assignment though the questions share a similar slant. One asks the student to write about a positive aspect of the paper; another asks him to consider a weakness in the paper, and the third asks him to reflect on the process involved in the writing. (At the end of this section is a list of representative questions.)

I ask the students to respond in writing to these questions, and usually I give them class time for this purpose. This assures me that they are taking the questions seriously and putting time into their responses. Even Pete and his cohorts are motivated to answer the questions simply because all around them their classmates' pens are scratching. And yes, Paula will undoubtedly say, "I can't do Question 2. There's nothing I'd change in my paper," but I give her one of my rarely used teacher looks and tell her she's got to come up with an answer. The first few times we do these questions she's stubborn and sure that her paper is perfect; by the third or fourth she's decided it's easier to find a minor flaw in her work than to argue; by the fifth she's begun to believe those flaws might be real and even revisable.

Students staple their answers to their drafts, recognizing that their responses are a part of the commentary and grade they will ultimately receive on their work. When I read their work, I wait to read their responses until I have read the piece itself, not wanting my view to be influenced by their own. Yet time and time again, the two of us agree. The part of the paper that I single out for the most praise is almost always what the writer has noted is its strongest feature, and the part that I feel is weak and most in need of revision is usually the part he is still struggling with. I enjoy reading the students' accounts of their writing process. I find that their comments frequently help me to structure assignments to make them more valuable for students. I also like to know how the writing process differs from student to student so that I can make my teaching more focused on the individual. I can now watch Liz sit at the word processor for a forty-five minute period and produce only a short paragraph without wondering if she is wasting time. Her descriptions of her writing process make me understand that Liz is a writer who must get every word right before she moves on to the next. She is a word-by-word reviser, and though that method might be less than efficient and certainly not productive for everyone, she is comfortable with that process and the quality of her final drafts indicates it works for her.

I would be less than honest if I made it seem that student responses to my questions are always intelligent and insightful and show thoughtful consideration of their work. I have students who explain that a particular line in their paper is the best "because it's good," and those who maintain that the most critical revision they have made since the previous draft is the spelling. Students, being students, will frequently look for an easy way out and will in effect "test" the teacher to find out how serious she is about a particular practice. My students find out quite quickly that I am serious about this form of self-evaluation. They realize it because I am fixed in my habit of doing it, because I give them class time in which to do it, and because I base part of my evaluation on their responses. Also, and perhaps most happily, they realize it because together as writer to writer we enter into a dialogue that is initiated by their comments. Frequently their responses are the starting point for my written and verbal reactions to their work. When I write comments on their papers, I begin by scrawling rejoinders to the points they raise. When we conference about their work, I use one of their comments as a jumping-off place. "You weren't happy with the way the paper ended?" I say, pointing to the response to Question 2—"What are you still dissatisfied with in your piece?" So the conversation, in written or spoken words, begins with something that matters to the writer, not simply to the teacher. With such a start there is a very good chance the whole conversation will be productive.

Questions for Consideration

What's the best line in this piece? Why?

What pleases you most about your piece?

What detail in the piece is *exactly* right? Why?

What's the most memorable part of this paper? Why?

What's the biggest positive change you've made in the piece from the previous draft to this one?

If you could change or improve only one thing in the next draft, what should it be?

Where could you include more specific detail?

What's one thing you'd like to do to improve the piece, if you only knew how to do it?

After reading your piece, what question(s) might a reader still have?

In writing this piece, what did you discover about your subject that you didn't realize before?

In writing this piece, what did you discover about yourself as a writer? As a person?

Tell me about the process you went through to write this piece. Be as specific as you can.

What parts of this piece seemed to "write themselves," and which parts caused you to feel frustrated? Why do you think that was?

Once students have grown accustomed to answering questions about their writing, they become more self-directed evaluators of their own work. At this point I ask students to hand in drafts covered with their own comments scrawled in the margins, a draft that looks much like my own working drafts when I am involved in a piece of writing. I encourage them, through their comments, to reflect on what they see as both the positive and negative aspects of a piece, because the ability to see both the good and the bad is part of the critical process.

This technique serves a number of purposes. First, it forces young writers to read and reread their work with an eye toward evaluation. They cannot simply finish a draft, figure it's "good enough," and hand it in. When they must go back and comment on each part of the piece, they come face-to-face with the parts that could be better. Many times students will make revisions right then, for sometimes it's just as easy to fix a problem as it is to explain what's wrong! Other times a writer is aware of a flaw in his work—a weak ending perhaps, or a paragraph of description that is wordy—but he doesn't know how to improve it. Now he can scribble his cry for help right in the spot he needs it most, and I can direct special attention to that problem.

This makes the teacher's job a little bit easier. I will not deny that the process of reading and commenting on multiple drafts of a piece is time-consuming and sometimes tedious, but it is a highly effective method of improving student writing. As much as I value response groups, I know that teacher intervention is also necessary. Not only do students benefit from the teacher's expertise, but they also relish the attention a teacher gives to their work. I am happy to provide both, but only if the writer himself is part of the process. I want to know that the writer is as concerned about his piece as I am. I want him to have given it at least as much attention as I do. So when students fill the margins of their pieces with their comments, their questions, the things they'd like to say about their piece if only there were time every day for a one-on-one conference, I feel they are truly involved in the development of the work. I can focus my comments on their concerns and address the areas of the paper that they are struggling with, knowing that my suggestions for revisions will be put to good use and that the next draft will be a stronger one.

Students frequently ask me how many drafts they need (they come to my class already aware that one is never enough; they hope two is!). The question is a difficult one to answer. Of course I could arbitrarily decide that three is a magic number and demand that every final draft come with two rough drafts stapled to it—and I confess I have made such a requirement more than once, particularly in classes peopled by students like Paula who don't quite believe in revision. But that is an arbitrary demand and one that I as a writer would not want to feel shackled by. Each writer is different, as is each piece the writer struggles with. Some pieces are painful to produce and take more drafts than the writer wants to count; others seem to almost tell themselves and the revisions are so minor that the changed work barely seems a draft. Sometimes, in fact, students want to know what qualifies as a draft. If you start a piece about the fight you and your mother had about your nose ring, and then decide that's not the story you want to tell at all—you're going to write about the day your dad left home—well, does that paragraph about your mother yelling count?

I don't know the answer to that—which is one reason why I try not to prescribe a required number of drafts. What I do demand is that students prove to me they have been writing and revising and rewriting some more. The writing they hand in to me, be it a completed piece or a section of a piece, needs to show the mark of its maker in the comments and questions and answers to questions that accompany it. And when the final draft—the one that's ready for the world—is done, it should be a "perfect" piece with all the imperfect pieces that preceded it attached. *This* is what I mean by process, and my students understand it is just as important as product.

When students are actively involved in self-evaluation, they are able to chart another process: their growth as writers. As exciting as it is to see a piece of writing develop, it is even more thrilling to see the writer herself grow. A writer grows not simply in proportion to the amount of writing she does, but also in proportion to the understanding and insight she brings to her work. When a young writer develops the ability to find the flaws in her work, then she can move forward to a new level of writing. I tell my students that the more they write, the better their writing will be only if they refrain from repeating the same mistakes.

Christina was a writer who struggled for months with the concept of "show, don't tell." I penned that phrase in its many variations on every piece she handed in. I suggested lines that would give her papers the description they sorely lacked. I listened to her response group beg her for more detail and offer her examples to add to her pieces. Throughout it all Christina didn't get it. She wasn't a lazy or stubborn writer; she just didn't understand what was wrong with a line like "It was fun," or "He was cool."

Then one day I returned a draft to her unmarked.

"Christina," I told her, "there are at least five lines in here that tell instead of show. Find them."

She did.

"O.K.," I said, more than a little amazed by the ease with which this was happening. "Now fix three of them."

She didn't. She fixed all five, and though the revisions were not pieces of masterful description, they were lines that were bright and alive and that gave the piece substance. Why at that particular moment was Christina able to grasp a concept that had seemingly eluded her for months? I don't know. Maybe it was just a teachable moment, or maybe, finally, all that I had tried to teach her had sunk in. Or maybe it was because Christina discovered that she could no longer depend on me or her peers to find and fix her writing problems. I'm convinced that until students feel they own their papers—their topics, their words, the revisions they make—they will never feel like writers. I believe teachers must give them that sense of ownership through the skills, like those of self-evaluation, they teach them.

Teacher Evaluation

There's no getting around it. No matter how much a teacher implements peer evaluation and self-evaluation of a student's work, at some point she is responsible for putting a grade, be it in letters, numbers, or words, on that piece of work. And, though the teacher may strive to diminish the power of her red (or blue or green) pen, the truth is that most students take the teacher's words as gospel and measure their success or failure as writers by the grade she puts on the page.

Of course every teacher has his or her own grading process and the decision of how to grade writing is an individual one. It is also a very difficult one. At a certain level good writing is subjective. As someone who is repelled by violence, I may have to grit my teeth to get through Nate's graphic description of the murder of a woman, but I know that it's good writing, and the product not of a troubled mind but of a creative one. I can guide and encourage and hope that Nate will find another outlet for his considerable writing talent, but if he doesn't, I still have to grade his work with a clear, unbiased mind.

So too when Caitlin appears with a twenty-two page science fiction story must I ignore my own literary likes and dislikes (sci-fi being one of the latter!) and give her work the fair reading it deserves. In many ways, the job of the writing teacher mimics that of the book reviewer. Whether either likes the subject he is reading about is irrelevant; the issue is how well the writer communicated what he had to say.

Another important issue is reflected in the continuing debate among English teachers about the weight given to content as opposed to that given to mechanics. If the content of a piece is excellent but the spelling atrocious, should the writer lose credit? If so, how much? What about the paper that is a model of mechanical perfection—and boring beyond belief? Should the writer be rewarded for the extraordinary editorial effort he put into the work?

Every teacher has to make a decision about grading that both he and his students can live with. Though the advent of process writing has put the emphasis on process over product, teachers are justifiably unwilling to abandon the standards of good grammar, spelling, and mechanics—though sometimes, in the name of good writing, those standards need to be relaxed. I tell my students that in my classroom the once sacred standard established by Warriner's grammar doesn't hold, that my standard for good English is the standard accepted by the literary community as demonstrated in publications like the *New Yorker* or the *Atlantic*. So I let them use fragments, run-on sentences, and lines beginning with "and." Does it sound like I'm letting them off easy, relaxing the standards of good English to such an extent that they won't know wrong from right? I don't think so. Justifying your stylistic decisions on the basis of a literary standard demands that you fully understand what that standard is, and that knowledge, gleaned from careful reading and study of contemporary prose, serves my students well. Moreover, when a young writer in my classroom purposely defies the conventions of standard English, he has to have a reason, just as does the writer of a piece of *New Yorker* fiction. When a sentence fragment appears in Meg's essay and it doesn't work stylistically, isn't there for a purpose, or actually obscures her meaning, then, like a line editor, I tell her the sentence must be revised.

The point is that good writing does not always play by the rules, and any writing teacher could name a favorite author or two whose work is marked by stylistic eccentricities that could be red-penned if one were so inclined. Writing is an art, like painting or dance, and like any art form it demands both an understanding of an underlying structure and an expression of individual freedom.

"So," my students sometimes say, heady with this new-found freedom, "we can write anything any way, and as long as we have a reason for what we write it's O.K.?"

"Sure," I tell them, "when you're writing in your journal or in your diary or on a scrap of paper meant for you alone. But when you're writing for the world—me, your response group, your public—there is one rule you cannot break."

They groan, sure that it is some rule of grammar they have yet to master.

"When you're writing for an audience, no matter how big or small, you must communicate clearly. You must work with your words until your message is heard."

So where does this leave the writing teacher, the one who is struggling with a stack of papers, a red pen, and a grade book filled with empty spaces? I can only return to my earlier comment: how to grade student writing is an individual decision, and one that the teacher must be comfortable with in order for him or her to function as an effective writing teacher. Tell me that I have to take off five points for every spelling error on a final draft, and I'll become as paralyzed as many student writers. I'll want to encourage them to write less so that what they write will be correct, so that I can "save" their points for the content! Yet I have colleagues, highly successful writing teachers, who do in fact impose such a rubric, and though we debate the practice endlessly, I understand that this method works for them and presumably for their students. The important point is that the teacher must make very clear to his students just what his standards for grading are. Students are remarkably adaptable. They can go from my class to that of the strictest grammarian in the English department and succeed, but they need to understand what each teacher expects. I tell them it is a bit like working with different editors or writing for different magazines. There is no one way to do it right, but you need to be clear about the guidelines.

For some teachers the solution to the content versus mechanics dilemma is to offer two grades, one for content, the other for mechanics. Though I understand the rationale behind this, I don't think it truly resolves the problem, for inevitably students want to know which grade counts more. Are the two averaged together? How many spelling mistakes equal a B-? Other teachers design a strict point rubric, like the spelling rule mentioned above, and grade the mechanical end of the paper accordingly, figuring it to be a certain percentage of the entire grade. My technique is to grade almost entirely on content, and though I know that is a controversial practice, I honestly believe that my students make no more nor no fewer mechanical mistakes than do students in other classrooms.

I feel strongly that content-based grading is justifiable for a number of reasons. First and foremost, what my students say is of utmost importance to me. I go back to an earlier point regarding students' fear of doing it wrong. When students feel pressured by perfection—every comma in place, every verb tense correct—they frequently decide that the safest thing to do is as little as possible. Better to write two paragraphs perfectly, they think, than four marred by errors. I don't agree. I want them to write what they have to say without counting the points they could lose.

But, I can hear the naysayers cry, if students are going through a number of drafts (as I have stated mine do), then shouldn't the final product, having been viewed by teacher and other students, be letter perfect? Yes, it should, if adolescents were even more free from careless errors than their adult counterparts. But they're not, and so a final paper might have an error or two, an *it's* that should be *its,* a *was* that should be *were,* simply because no one caught it, not even me when I was reading that messy but marvelous third draft. The truth is, though, that any student who has approached his work as I hope he has, who seeks out many readers and incorporates their responses into his writing, often does produce a final paper virtually free of mechanical errors. Certainly were I to catch an error in a final draft, I would red-pen it and tell the student to fix it before the paper went public, but to deduct two points or to refuse to give a final grade to the paper until it is absolutely perfect seems excessive to me. I tell my students that, as a teacher, I have been given a red pen, and part of my job is to use it. Any error I see in their work, at the rough draft or at the final draft stage, I correct, and I expect my students to note the correction and learn from it, but I do not generally penalize them for such errors.

There is that qualifier—*generally*. My students do lose credit for mechanical errors when such errors make it impossible for me, or any other reader, to comprehend the content of the work. Many years of teaching English have made me quite a pro at deciphering words like *mabye* and *alot,* and I am not easily confused by a misplaced semicolon. But if a paper comes in riddled with errors that obscure the meaning of the piece, I have to give it a lower grade, not because I'm counting errors but because I can't understand or appreciate the content. That is the point I want my students to understand: the rules of grammar, spelling, and punctuation exist not to confound students but to give our language a structure that allows us to communicate clearly.

There is another reality here which even the most stalwart grammar teachers recognize, and that is that in the world of published writing, writers are routinely aided in their quest for error-free writing. They have editors whose responsibility it is to proofread every word, to ensure that it is not only correct but apt. A talented writer may be a miserable speller, someone who uses a dash too often, or a person who's never sure whether to use *lie* or *lay.* His editor will fix his mistakes, and the reader will never know his weakness.

Students do not come equipped with editors, but the computer is a close substitute. Technology has freed our students from much error making. I watch my students run through spellcheckers with an ease that astounds me, and I'm delighted that I rarely any more find myself writing *receive* above the misspelled *recieve.* But not all students have school systems, or parents, who can afford to buy word processors or the latest computer programs to aid their children in writing, and it seems unfair to penalize those students who don't have easy access to such wonderful tools. If Jamie has a spellchecker, it's unlikely her work will have spelling errors (though I am constantly reminding my students that only the most sophisticated programs can tell a *there* from a *their*!), but for Melissa, who labors earnestly but with a dictionary as her only tool, the proofreading process is much harder and more open to error.

So, when I approach a pile of student writing, I am concerned almost entirely with content. Not that it makes my grading job any easier; in fact, sometimes I wish I could just focus on mechanics, the obvious rights and wrongs, and grade accordingly. For me, correcting means commenting, and I'm hard pressed to understand how it could be any different for any writing teacher.

But commenting on what? And when? And by whom? What should be graded? Drafts as well as final papers? Process over product? Growth? Risk? Effort? Should every assignment earn a grade? Should students choose the work they want evaluated? What about portfolios? And when should grades be given? Steadily throughout the term? Weekly assignments, each one for a grade? When a student decides a piece is done? For a magnum opus, the portfolio? And who should give the grade? The teacher alone? The student? The members of his or her response group? A combination of all three?

These are questions each individual writing teacher must answer for himself. My approach is not likely one that would work for every teacher, nor perhaps is it as student-centered as I myself would like. But decisions about grading are not based solely on one's philosophy of teaching; they are also necessarily influenced by the realities of one's teaching schedule. If I were teaching two classes, say fifty students, I would be a passionate proponent of the portfolio approach in its most elaborate form for every one of my students. I would cherish it as a means of encouraging and documenting individual student growth as learners and particularly as writers. A portfolio that is not simply a repository of student work, but rather a working folder of works-in-progress, shared frequently and in depth by teacher and student, is enormously effective in facilitating the development of a young writer. I can think of no better way to motivate a young writer than to sit down with him periodically throughout a term to peruse his papers—from those that are finished products to those that are simply scraps of ideas—in order to encourage his efforts and to point him in new directions. And I would love for that student and me to take the time together at the end of the term to evaluate his growth, assess his effort, and agree on a grade that represents fairly the work he has done.

That's what I would do if I were teaching two classes; that is what I try to do, with some variation, with my two Creative Writing courses. But the reality is that I, like most English/language arts teachers, teach five courses and upwards of 120 students. Though I fervently believe in the portfolio approach, I simply cannot figure out how to implement it effectively under the constraints of a typical teaching load and schedule. I admit, I'm terrified of the specter of 120 portfolios piled on my desk the week before Term 2 ends. Every one of those portfolios should be bulging with writing, and I don't see how I can give each author the attention he and his work deserve in such a short time span. I understand that

I will have been reading this work throughout the term, that the pieces will not be new to me, that I should be able to skim and survey the work, and in conference with the student, make a good assessment of his growth.

But, for me, that doesn't happen. For me, every piece of revised student writing is new, no matter how many times I have read it before, and so no piece goes quickly through my hands. I can't quite control my highlighter (my students learn quickly that lines highlighted in yellow mean "I like this a lot!") or my pen, nor do I especially want to. I always have too much to say, so much so that I sometimes imagine recording my comments on tape, if only I had some guarantee that my students would insert that tape into their Walkmans! So, considering my student load and the amount of writing I want my students to do, the only approach that works is to grade assignments as they are completed, with some sort of relatively flexible due date established for each.

Therefore I read drafts as students complete them, adding to the comments they themselves and their response groups make. I pay special attention to the questions and concerns the writer has noted, but I respond to the whole work. Students generally do drafts when they should, not because I assign a due date, but because we are using them in class in response groups and they want their moment in the spotlight, not to mention the help of their peers. I try to conference with students around response-group time, using the minutes when one group has finished and another has not, to work individually with students, discussing their concerns about their work, the direction it is taking, and possible plans for future publication. I tell students to hold on to every one of their drafts, even that scribbled beginning that didn't quite work and has since been abandoned, so that both of us can see, when the final draft is done, all the thought and effort and decision-making that went into creating the finished product.

When that finished product is handed in to me, it comes with all the drafts and the writer's own commentary on the work. My grade, for I do put a grade on that bundle of writing, is an assessment of both the final piece and of its development. A writer in my class can earn an A on a piece, not because it's the most brilliant in the class, but because the pile of drafts that accompany it show that the writer labored hard and long on the piece, not settling for a good first effort, but rather forcing himself to re-see and revise and rewrite, proving himself a true writer.

Jon is a true writer. He is imaginative, perceptive, and bold, and he understands the importance of painstaking revision. Jon worked long and hard on every piece he did for my Creative Writing class. What follows at the end of this chapter are two drafts of an autobiographical essay he wrote. I offer them to illustrate some of the methods of evaluation that work for me.

Draft A is an early draft. I can't call it a "first draft" because I don't know how many starts—and perhaps false starts—Jon did before this piece, and in this age of computer technology there are not even crumpled balls of paper to mark a writer's first efforts! This draft, however, is the first that Jon handed in to me, the first that he wanted my input on. Different students want different things when they ask me to read a draft. Some are looking for major editorial help; they are counting on my pen to "fix" their papers. Some tell me not to bother correcting a certain aspect of the paper, spelling for example. They know the errors are there; they simply haven't gotten to the spellchecker stage. Sometimes they are looking for help with style. They have learned the importance of "show, don't tell," but they are not sure where in their papers more detail is needed. Or maybe they know the organization of the story is poor, but no one in the response group knows quite how to improve it. Either through conversation or their own written comments, students generally tell me what I should be focusing my attention as reader on, and though I don't limit my response to that, I do make sure I address their concerns.

Jon was concerned about the ending of his paper, feeling that perhaps he should extend it. He also wondered if he needed more detail in the story. And, like many writers, he was eager for editing help.

So I began to read Jon's paper. I always read the paper through once—no pen in hand—simply as a reader, someone who enjoys writing. I need that overall sense of a story before I can begin to make suggestions about it. I loved Jon's story, and my comment at the very end, describing how sad it made me, was my simple, gut-level response, a response every writer deserves. From there, I could pick up my yellow highlighter and green pen and begin to concentrate on the concerns both Jon and I had about the piece.

The simple ones first: the corrections. Certainly Jon needed to make a number of mechanical corrections, many of which he would have found on his own, when he reached the final editing/proofreading stage of a later draft. But I find that when students *request* this help at an early draft stage, it is valuable to give it to them. I believe too that this help should be true correction—a period after *head* and a capital *I* on *It*—not just a check at the end of the first line indicating to the student that there is an error there somewhere and he or she better find it! I justify my approach, which some might call coddling, because I believe it works. My students learn from my corrections, perhaps because they grow weary of green scribbles and scrawls but more likely because they quickly see how valuable just a little editing can be. Corrections in grammar, spelling, and punctuation improve the readability of the paper so that the writer can then concentrate on the important content revisions.

As my comments on the paper indicate, I thought the content of Jon's paper was excellent. He did a fine job of capturing a moment when innocence is lost. We see him bright and beaming with the joy of Christmas, and we feel it all go dark in that moment of humiliation on the stage. His details were wonderful, from the cans of Hi-C punch so evocative of childhood to the tinsel around his neck. I love the connections he made— the blood in his head glowing "like a bright red Christmas tree light," the candy cane he yearns to use as a weapon. He knew too when to summarize and when to dramatize—a few quick sentences describing his Christmas preparations and a slow, second-by-second description of those agonizing moments on stage. I liked his ending too, and told him so. That doesn't mean he couldn't change it in the next draft, for as I always tell my students, their work should please themselves first, but I want Jon to know that the ending worked for me and that the picture of this boy with his head buried in his lap stayed with me long after I finished reading the piece. One of Jon's greatest strengths as a writer is his willingness to put his feelings on the line in his work. Other adolescents might hesitate to write a piece like this, fearing it might make them look vulnerable and "uncool." Jon is a courageous writer, and his honesty makes his work powerful. I am careful to consistently praise that aspect of his work, because it is a quality I don't want him to lose.

It is very important to praise a writer for all he does right, particularly in early drafts. Many young writers are unaware of their strengths, of the things they do well and that set their work apart from that of their peers. I write a lot on student papers, and usually my praise outweighs my criticism. I believe students learn as much, if not more, from these positive comments. Certainly they gain confidence in themselves as writers, but they also learn what things "work" in a piece, what techniques and talents they might use in later pieces. Young writers need a great deal of positive reinforcement, and what my pen can't give them, my highlighter does. I highlight words, lines, and paragraphs that I think work well, sometimes adding comments, sometimes not. It's not uncommon for me to hear a student say to a friend, "I got a lot of yellow. She liked it!"

And what about the things I don't like? I tell them that too, but usually I couch my criticism in the form of questions, especially on early drafts. This is not simply a "trick," a way to make criticism less stinging. It is rather a sincere reader response. My questions are honest ones: *I don't understand this . . . Did you really mean that . . . Could you add a little more detail about . . . .* My criticism has one goal: to improve the clarity of the paper, ensuring that the words on the page express the ideas in the writer's mind. In Jon's story, many of the problems came within the first three paragraphs, where there was some confusion in time and place. That's not uncommon for a writer who begins to tell a story that is vivid in his mind, forgetting that he has to set the scene clearly for the reader who was not there to experience it. As Jon's revised draft indicates, he understood my concerns and was able to make some good revisions that make the story clearer.

Students don't always agree with my suggestions, nor do I expect them to. Like each of the members of their response group, I am but one reader with my own individual likes and dislikes. I might suggest that more description is needed here or dialogue there, or that a paragraph could be deleted or perhaps moved to a different part of the paper, and I hope and expect that my students will take my suggestions seriously and consider them. But ultimately the decision about content revision is theirs alone. A writer has to live with his words, and so they must be ones *he* has chosen.

The words Jon finally chose are those in the Revised Draft B, which he now titled "'Tis the Season." This is the draft which was ready for grading. He handed it in to me with all of his previous drafts, marked with my response and comments from his response group, stapled to it. Also attached were the three self-evaluation questions that I asked my students to do for this particular piece. (The questions and Jon's answers appear after the revised draft.) These types of questions are important in helping students become thoughtful evaluators of their own work. The responses help me, too, in my evaluation, and ultimately allow us to work as two writers together, joined in an effort to improve the writing.

I approach the revised, to-be-graded draft in much the same way as I do the earlier drafts. I am realistic enough to know there are still likely to be a few mechanical errors, and until the piece is ready for actual publication—when it should be error-free—I can accept that, continuing to make corrections. I am eager to comment on the parts of the paper I especially like, even if I have offered this same praise on previous drafts. It never hurts a writer to hear he has done something well. But I pay special attention to the revisions, flipping back and forth between drafts to see the improvements and making sure to comment on them. I continue to highlight sections I like, perhaps partially because my students would be devastated by a paper devoid of yellow, no matter how good the grade! And of course I comment on those aspects of the piece that could still be improved. I do this not only to justify the grade I give, but also to offer further possibilities for revision should the writer want to continue to rework the piece, maybe for future publication.

It is Jon himself who points out what could be a significant improvement in the paper, and one which neither of us had focused on in the previous drafts. He suggests the idea of adding dialogue, and I concur, feeling that it might be effective to hear the conversation between Jon and the Student Council member. I am always glad when students complete a paper, do it well, and yet still see that it could be even better. That is an important lesson for young writers to learn. No piece is ever done. Because each piece is a reflection of its author, as the writer grows and changes, so too may the words he puts on the page.

But, at this point, for this assignment, the paper is complete—and waiting for a grade. Jon's paper earns him an A-. I feel it is a fine piece. It says something important in a way that is both interesting and moving. The details are excellent and the scenes come to life. And the piece has voice. Were I to pick it out of a pile of anonymously written student papers, I would know it was Jon's. Jon has worked hard on the piece, making a variety of revisions throughout the various drafts, and his work shows. The only part of the piece that still seems weak to me is the opening, and that is what keeps the paper from earning a straight A.

The grade I put on the paper goes in my gradebook. It is put there in pen; it is not carved in stone. If a student feels the grade is unjust, I want him to come to me; I want to discuss the piece, and the work put into it, to see if I've missed something. Sometimes I have; sometimes a response group has truly delighted in a piece and recognized positive qualities in it that I did not. I'm happy to listen and to rethink my grade because, as I tell my students, I am not the official audience. I cannot represent all readers, nor do I want my students writing only for me. To give that declaration more than lip service, I have to be open to the judgment of other readers and willing to consider their opinions as worthy as my own.

Students are also very welcome to rework any piece throughout the term. I do think young writers, especially those who are not particularly eager writers, need a time frame in which to work. If I allowed my sophomores the luxury of turning in five pieces before the end of the term, I suspect many of them would find themselves completing five stories the night before the term ends. That's clearly not the way to get good writing done, and so I believe in making assignments complete with due dates throughout the term. But students who are not happy with the work they hand in, or who later in the term, having suddenly had an idea for revision, want to rework a piece, are more than welcome to rewrite—and I will re-grade. No piece is ever completely finished; no writer is ever completely satisfied. Revision is what writers do. My students read Raymond Carver's "The Bath" and his later version, "A Small, Good Thing," and marvel at a man who regarded a published story as just another draft.

At the end of every semester I ask my students to write a piece in which they assess their growth as writers. This piece takes the form of a letter, a letter to me. I tell them to first spend time with their writing folders, rereading all the writing they have done throughout the semester. They are usually impressed by the sheer quantity of work they have done, and so too are they impressed by the quality. The writing that students do in January sometimes bears little resemblance to that which they did in September. By June, their first works seem to have been done by a different hand.

Once they have carefully considered their work, I ask them to meet in response groups and talk to each other about the growth they perceive. This is an important step, and one that goes back to the practice of peer evaluation. Sometimes it's hard to see how much you've developed as a writer. When you live with your work each day, it's hard to see its maturation. You need a bit of distance, and response-group members, like the grandmother you see only a few times a year, are often the best able to note, "My, how you've grown."

Armed with their own evaluation of their work and the conversations they have shared with their peers, my students sit down and write their letters to me. I offer them the following series of questions to consider, although I don't require them to respond to each and every one. Some students do, using the questions as guidelines and answering each quite methodically, but in truth those are generally not the best letters, either in style or in content. The most powerful letters come from those students who have grown the most as writers, and who use their new-found skills and confidence to offer positive proof of their growth. For me these letters serve as a mini-portfolio for each student, and though they too spill across my desk during the final countdown to the grades-due deadline, I find reading them a relatively effortless task, and one that is highly rewarding.

a) Which one of your papers is, in your opinion, the most effective, and which is the least effective? Give a brief rationale for what you see as the good and bad aspects of each, and explain what you learned by doing these two assignments.

b) Discuss what you have learned about writing in general during this course. Make connections with various assignments/activities to illustrate your growth as a writer.

c) How would you describe the writing process that works best for you? Be specific! Use detail. Has it changed as a result of this course? If so, explain how.

d) How would you describe your writing voice? How does it differ from that of other students in the class whose work you have read?

e) What are your major strengths as a member of a writing community?

These letters, though they themselves are not graded, assist me in the decisions I have to make about final grades. Although I have before me a series of grades on a series of writing assignments which students have completed (as well as the many other grades English/language arts teachers accumulate on vocabulary work, reading quizzes, etc.), the grade a student receives is not a strict mathematical calculation. When you're dealing with writing, it can't be. If a story earns a B+, is that an 87 or an 88 or an 89? And what's the difference in quality between each point? Points, product, process . . . there are no absolutes. I can only do my best as I judge each student's writing and the effort he put into it.

Is this the best approach to teacher evaluation? For me it is, though every writing teacher has his or her own techniques, and perhaps only pieces of my approach would work for other teachers. The important thing is that teacher response and evaluation must serve not only to correct the work of young writers but also to create it, to offer the kind of inspiration and encouragement that sends the writer eagerly onward in his work. I want my response to the writing my students do to be clear and fair and honest. And if I am to err on either side, too kind or too cruel in my response, I hope I am too kind. In my experience, young writers who are told their work is good, struggle on to make it even better. But tell them that their work is bad and they rarely write again. My intent is to keep my students writing, with joy and enthusiasm and a desire to improve, just the way all writers write.

DRAFT A

The bells rang in my head. It
was the day before Christmas
vacation and I was ready to
celebrate. Ever since birth I
had loved school parties. The
homemade cupcakes, large cans of
Hi-C punch, movies, and the
overwhelming ~~amount~~ number of shiny
happy faces. In grade school the
Christmas parties were perfect,
in ~~6th~~ sixth grade they were familiar,
but by the second year of middle
school (~~7th~~ seventh grade), ~~it was~~ they were an
absolute nightmare.

~~It had been asked of~~ The
students were asked to dress up in holiday
attire on the day before break.
I thought that sounded like a
fun idea and spent an hour going
through my closet. I searched
for anything and everything that
could fit on my body and that
was a part of Christmas. Finally
I had gotten everything together
but lay awake all night, too
excited to sleep. In the morning
I easily got up at the terribly
early hour of____ and carefully got
into my garb. I was decked out
in green sweatpants, a red
sweatshirt, a Santa Claus hat,
tinsel around my neck, and

(margin notes)

This opening needs some work.

Nice details

This line sounds funny since at birth you knew nothing about school parties. Can you rework it?

What time did you get up?

seven
~~7~~ holiday pins all over my body.
I got ready in a rush, *and* then set
out ~~the door~~ into the harsh
bitter cold that nipped at my
rosy red cheeks.

When I got to *S*~~S~~chool I was
disappointed *to find.* ~~by finding~~ hardly
anyone ~~who~~ dressed up. I started
feeling paranoid as many criti-
cal eyes *Awkward phrase* were laid upon me. But
I was not going to let them get
in the way, for I was charged
with [*word choice* undefeatable] joy of Christmas. The smirks and stares con-
tinued at lunch, but I found that
others were getting the same
treatment. One girl ~~had~~ *wore* a complete elf costume ~~on~~, shoes and
everything, bless her heart! As
I got up to throw my tray away,
I bumped into a member of *S*tu-
dent *C*ouncil. She asked me
rather enthusiastically if I
wanted to take part in a competition for best Christmas costume. The best dressed girl and
boy would each get $10.00. I was
quite flattered and quickly
agreed.

Near the end of lunch all of
the "chosen" were asked to stand
on stage. There were ~~about~~ *six* 6 of
us, *two* 2 boys, including me, and *four* 4
girls. The other boy was in
jeans, shirt, and a Santa Claus

(margin note, rotated) Which others? How about a more descriptive line here, like "who were in holiday dress". -or something more clever?

hat. Not much competition. The thing was, he was popular, and in middle school that could cause a problem. The Student Council members announced that the lucky winner would be determined by applause. After hearing this I got nervous as I saw the other boy's good friend run to all the tables saying something I couldn't make out. I knew it wasn't a fair way to judge, and I began to sweat as fear rushed through my body.

Suddenly they started down the line, each person stepping forward and being clapped for. Some were getting more applause than the others, but still all got ~~getting~~ a fair amount. I started thinking that it wasn't that bad and told myself just to have fun. I mean it was Christmas. Then came my name. (The letters seemed to drip slowly from the announcer's lips) Excellent Line! as I breathlessly waited to hear the response. I stepped forward and smiled. I looked out at the whole seventh ~~7th~~ grade and there was silence. Everyone just emptily stared back at me as the unbearable silence grew. My knees began to shake and all my blood just shot right up to my head

What a perfect comparison!

as (it glowed like a bright red Christmas tree light.) I felt as if I was standing at my execution ready to get shot, and I surely was. I was hit so hard ~~and~~ that the spirit inside of me was dying. I quickly hung my head down ~~real~~ low and took a step back trying to hide in the shadows.

This is heartbreaking, Jon. It brings back to me all those terrible momments in childhood when cruelty masquerades as "coolness." You write this so well. You make me feel *your sadness.*

The other boy was next, wearing ~~more than just~~ *not only* his spiteful hat but a huge disgusting grin that stretched for miles. Before he even stepped forward, the cafeteria filled with chants and cheers as the twerp (hotly) danced around the stage. As much as I wanted to take a candy cane and jab it ~~throw~~ *through* the kid's eyes incessantly, I was too depressed to even move.

word choice?

Great line! 'Tis the season, right?!

Finally this hideous contest was over. I dreaded coming face to face with the hundreds of eyes that had coldly stared me down. I wanted to be alone so much at that very moment. Some people even gave me (apathetic) looks and words which meant nothing to me. The same Student Council member who had asked me to take part in this act *of* public humiliation came up to me. She told me she felt bad and that I

Do you mean sympathetic? Apathetic means without feeling, indifferent.

should have won. I told her it
wasn't her problem as I smiled,
and at the same time a tear
rolled down my cheek. It wasn't
that I lost that bugged me. It
was the feeling that no one
cared that haunted me. That I
had stood in front of my whole
class and no more than ~~10~~ ten hands
clapped for me. I knew I wasn't
popular and didn't care to be,
but I was not prepared for the
cruelty and coldness middle
school had to offer.

Excellent Line

When I arrived home I felt
safe at last, but the heavy sor-
row still hung tightly to my
back. My mom was not expect-
ing this change of attitude,
for I usually was jumping up
and down on the start of vacation. She was worried and so
was I. I felt like so much was
taken away from me that day: my
innocence, my self-esteem, and my
belief that everyone has something nice about them. All
these dark ideas, were ~~quickly~~
scrambled ~~through~~ in my mind as I
sat in the family room next to
the Christmas tree with my head
covered in my lap.

I love this line

This paper moved me very much. It made me so sad. It's well written and completely honest. I hate that this happened to you, but you certainly turned the experience into a strong piece of writing.

I like this ending. What more could you possibly say?

Jonathan Foss

REVISED DRAFT B

'Tis the Season *Good title!*

The bells rang in my head. It was the day before Christmas vacation and I was ready to celebrate. Not only did I love Christmas, but I was born loving school parties—the homemade cupcakes, large cans of Hi-C punch, movies, and the overwhelming number of shiny happy faces. Before Christmas parties were perfect, but in ~~the~~ my second year of middle school (seventh grade), ~~it~~ the party was an absolute nightmare.

Good revision!

Before what?

The students were asked to dress up in holiday attire on the day before break. I thought that sounded like a fun idea and spent an hour going through my closet. I searched for anything and everything that could fit on my body and that was a part of Christmas. Finally I had everything together, but I lay awake all night, too excited to sleep. In the morning I easily got up at the terribly early hour of 5:30 and carefully got into my garb. I was decked out in green sweatpants, a red

sweatshirt, a Santa Claus hat,
tinsel around my neck, and
seven holiday pins all over my
body. I got ready in a rush,and
then set out into the harsh,
bitter cold that nipped at my
rosy red cheeks.

When I got to school, I was
disappointed to find hardly
anyone dressed up. I started
feeling paranoid as many
Good revision
critical eyes scanned my out-
fit. But I was not going to let
them get in the way, for I was
charged with the joy of Christmas. The smirks and stares continued at lunch, but I found
that others who cared enough to
dress up were getting the same
treatment. One girl wore a complete elf costume with shoes
and everything, bless her
heart! As I got up to throw my
tray away, I bumped into a member of the Student Council. She
asked me rather enthusiastically if I wanted to take part
in a competition for best
Christmas costume. The best
dressed girl and boy would each
get $10.00. I was quite flat-
tered and quickly agreed.

Near the end of lunch all of
the "chosen" were asked to stand
on stage. There were six of us,

two boys, including me, and four girls. The other boy was in jeans, shirt, and a Santa Claus hat. Not much competition. The thing was, he was popular, and in middle school that could cause a problem. The Student Council members announced that the lucky winner would be determined by applause. After hearing this I got nervous as I saw the other boy's good friend run to all the tables saying something I couldn't make out. I knew it wasn't a fair way to judge, and I began to sweat as fear rushed through my body.

Suddenly they started down the line, each person stepping forward and being applauded. Some were getting more applause than the others, but still all got a fair amount. I started thinking that it wasn't that bad and told myself just to have fun. I mean, it was Christmas. Then came my name. The letters *I do love this line!* seemed to drip slowly from the announcer's lips as I breath-lessly waited to hear the re-sponse. I stepped forward and smiled. I looked out at the whole seventh grade and there was silence. Everyone just emp-tily stared back at me as the

Again, this is an <u>excellent</u> section It really <u>shows</u> your pain unbearable silence grew. My knees began to shake and all my blood just shot right up to my head as it glowed like a bright red Christmas tree light. I felt as if I was standing at my execution ready to get shot, and I surely was. I was hit so hard ~~and~~ that the spirit inside of me was dying. I quickly hung my head down low and took a step back trying to hide in the shadows.

The other boy was next, wearing not only his spiteful hat but a huge disgusting grin that stretched for miles. Before he even stepped forward, the cafeteria filled with chants and cheers as the twerp proudly pranced around the stage. As much as I wanted to take a candy cane and jab it through the kid's eyes incessantly, I was too depressed to even move.

Good revision!
Great verb

Finally this hideous contest was over. I dreaded coming face to face with the hundreds of eyes that had coldly stared me down. I wanted to be alone so much at that very moment. Some people even gave me sympathetic looks and words—which meant nothing to me. The same Student Council member who had asked me to take

part in this act of public humiliation came up to me. [She told me
she felt bad and that I should
have won. I told her it wasn't
her problem as I smiled,] and at
the same time a tear rolled down
my cheek. It wasn't that I lost
that bugged me. It was the feeling that no one cared that haunted me. That I had stood in front
of my whole class and no more
than ~~10~~ ten hands clapped for me. I
knew I wasn't popular and didn't
care to be, but I was not prepared for the cruelty and coldness middle school had to offer.

When I arrived home I felt
safe at last, but the heavy sor-
row still hung tightly to my
back. My mom was not expect-
ing this change of attitude,
for I usually was jumping up and
down on the start of vacation.
She was worried and so was I.
I felt like so much was taken
away from me that day: my innocence, my self-esteem, and my
belief that everyone has something nice about them. All these
dark ideas were scrambled in my
mind as I sat in the family room
next to the Christmas tree with
my head covered in my lap.

Jonathan Foss

Handwritten margin notes:

Yes, you're right. This would be a good place for dialogue.

Excellent line

This, to me, is a perfect ending.

SELF-EVALUATION QUESTIONS

a) What's the best line in this paper? Why?

Yes, I like that line too.

"I felt as if I was standing at my execution ready to get shot, and I surely was." I think this line sums up what was going through my mind at that moment. It expresses the fear, anger, and utter shock I was feeling.

b) What's one thing you would do to improve this paper—if you only knew how?

I would add some dialogue. I know I always say that, but I feel it would make it more interesting, but I don't know if it would take away from the detail.

Yes, I think you could include dialogue, maybe at the end where the Student Council member speaks to you. It would be effective there.

c) Tell me about the process you went through to write this paper.

You've done a great job of recapturing those feelings on paper.

I had thought about writing about this topic shortly after I had passed in the last piece. I had almost forgotten it had happened, but once I remembered it, all the feelings came back to me that I had had that day. It was tricky getting started,

but it was much easier as I went
along. One of the drafts I had
corrected on the computer contained some good ideas for revisions, but the revised version
didn't save. I tried doing it
over but I didn't catch everything I revised the last time I
wrote.

O.K. I understand!
Sometimes the wonders
of technology
aren't so wonderful!

(A-) I really like this paper, Jon. I like the vivid
description of the whole experience, the way you truly
SHOW your humiliation, sadness and pain.
I like too how you move beyond this one
awful experience to show how it represents
that inevitable loss of innocence.
Nice work, Jon!

6 A Community of Writers

Throughout this book I have frequently used the phase "a community of writers." It is a phrase that comes easily to me and one that seems particularly right when describing the intense alliance that grows among writers who are engaged in the pursuit of words. In fact, I write these words from a dormitory room at Colgate University, where I am, for one week, part of a group of forty-seven writers. We are the Chenango Valley Writers' Conference, but I suspect that last word could be changed to Community, for in five short days that is truly what we have become, a community of writers who are consumed by words. I don't know what the man across from me at dinner does to earn his living, but I know the story he is writing. I don't know whether the blonde woman in my workshop has children, but I know she has a genius for dialogue. And I don't know how many pages of this manuscript I'll write before I have to pack my car and head for home, but I know that every word I've written has come more easily than it does at home because I am in a world where I breathe words.

It is that kind of world that I dream of creating for my students and one that I hope many of them will find again after they leave my classroom. Writing is hard, hard work. I know. I watched the digital clock beside me count off eighteen minutes as I labored over the seven sentences in the paragraph above, and I'm sure many more minutes will go by as I revise and rewrite that paragraph, putting it into final form. To stick with such hard work, you have to love the labor, yet so many of our students come to us feeling nothing close to love. Writing for them is a school subject, an impossible task, something the teacher knows how to do and they don't. When they were small, they could cover a refrigerator with the stories from their souls. Now as adolescents they stare woefully at blank paper and blank screens. Nothing to say, nothing to say. Somewhere along the way the fervor little children feel for the stories they invent has faltered, and they forget how to put what's in their hearts into words.

For me the goal of the writing community is to provide a safe, encouraging, and productive environment in which young writers can find the words they've lost, the words that mean something to them, the words that define who they are and how they see the world. Buoyed by the spirit of the writing community, these writers can, I hope, find the courage to go one step farther to share their words and their visions with a wide world of readers.

Though the focus of this book has been on publishing, the backbone of that endeavor is the writing community, and even when the quest for publication fails, the community continues, allowing the writing to do the same. A community of writers is very different from a classroom of students. It looks different. It sounds different. It feels different. And in every way it is better.

Look in the door of a writing community. Some writers are sitting in a circle on the floor; others are sifting through a pile of magazines; one is staring out the window. There is a thrum of activity: the shuffling of papers, the rhythm of a writer's voice, the clatter of computer keys. And there is a spirit of caring and connection—eyes that meet across a circle, high-five hands in the air, a burst of applause. Somewhere in this room you'll find a teacher. She's probably not at her desk. She might be sitting in that circle, listening to a writer's words. She might be thumbing through *Poets & Writers*, helping someone find a market. Or maybe she is watching that writer who is staring out the window, loving the attention he is giving to his thoughts, wondering what his words will be.

How does such a community happen? What must a teacher do to turn a classroom into a community? Though there is no magical formula, there is magic simply in the teacher's desire to promote such a community. Any teacher willing to remove herself from the center of the class and fill the void with the words of her students is already partway there. Believing in the possibility and efficacy of a writing community is the crucial part of the creation. Implementing and executing it is much easier.

Each time I greet a classroom of students, I am already seeing them as a community of writers. I believe that vision is critical to the success of the undertaking. Part of that vision for me is a belief in five principles that underscore it.

1. A writing community supports the writer.

Notice that the key word is writer, not writing. Clearly the writing is important. It is, after all, the goal; good writing is what we are all struggling to achieve. But when you are working with a group of young people, I do not believe you can ever, for a minute, put the writing before the writer. If you do, you may find that the writing, certainly the good, strong, from-the-heart writing, may cease to exist.

There are those who argue, those who say that one should not put the feelings of the writer above the quality of the work. If the writing community were composed of adult writers, experienced writers, I would agree. I have been part of writing groups where the feelings of the writers have been sacrificed for a harsh but honest assessment of the work. But in those groups, the writers have come seeking just such a critical approach. The writers were all confident enough in their abilities to survive the "attack," and in fact they recognized the necessity of such callous criticism if they were to compete with other published writers.

The young writers we encounter in our classrooms are not so tough, nor should they be. They are learning to be writers. They are learning to trust their voices and their visions, and in the process they must take many risks and likely suffer a number of failures. In order for them to survive such failures with their faith in themselves as writers intact, they need the unequivocal support of the community. This does not mean they will not hear criticism; obviously one important function of the response group is to offer solid and specific criticism. But the criticism will always be of the writing, never of the writer. A particular piece of writing may be boring for a variety of reasons (and a good response group will offer suggestions to give life to the piece), but that is not a comment on the writer nor on the potential his work has. I ask my students to remember the Wicked Witch of the West, reduced to a mere puddle on the floor. None of my students should ever find themselves in such a metaphorical state. In the time they spend as part of a writing community within the walls of my classroom, they should always see themselves as writers. They may—and should—question the strength of a piece, but they should never question their own potential to grow and improve as writers.

2. The writing community respects the writing.

Each piece of writing that a writer offers to the community— whether it be in first draft form or polished for publication—deserves attention and respect. Anyone who writes understands the enormous amount of effort involved in such work. Good writers agonize over every word. Good writers revise and rewrite and revise again. Good writers always wonder, "Could I have said it better?"

When an entire group of students is involved in such work, there is a strong appreciation for that effort, as there should be. That is one reason why it is so important for every student to be writing. It is not enough to be the editor, to be the audience. You have to be personally engaged in the struggle to put your heart and your mind on the page to understand just how hard a task it is. Only when you yourself are struggling too can you understand why it isn't okay to say, "I didn't like your story," or "That was dumb." It is okay to say, "I didn't like your story because you left the ending hanging without any resolution," or "That was dumb because in real life people don't act like your main character does." Those latter comments show an appreciation of the effort put into the writing and a desire to help the piece succeed.

That's what it means to respect the writing: to see in it the potential for success. In a writing community, all the participants are working to help improve each piece. Some pieces are clearly going to need more help than others—and on occasion a piece may best be abandoned entirely—but every piece is worthy of a serious review and response from the community.

3. A writing community values the process.

No writing is ever wasted. Every attempt to put words on paper teaches the writer something he can use the next time. The piece mentioned above that is abandoned entirely is not a useless effort. In doing it, and in deciding that it did not work, the writer learned something. Perhaps he learned that too much description is tiresome or that weak verbs weaken an entire piece. Maybe he discovered that he needs to practice writing dialogue or that he needs to take the time to write outlines of his plots. The point is that every moment spent writing is part of the learning process, and the skills and knowledge gained in those accumulated moments are far more valuable than any one polished piece.

As teachers we are too easily pleased by the product, a perfect paper that convinces us that our students have learned what we believe we should teach them. Perhaps we value that product because we see it so rarely. Students are by definition learners, engaged in the process of developing certain skills and abilities. No matter what the subject matter, the process involved in mastering it is not often straightforward or linear. What students seem to understand one day, they are just as apt to forget the next. They are likely to stumble often, and sometimes they jump two steps ahead only to have to go backwards to fill the spaces in between.

This is precisely what happens when students are learning to write. A student who produces a wonderful piece one day may hand in a dreadful piece the next. His words may be fluent and effective on Tuesday and stalled and stagnant on Thursday. In a writing community such seemingly erratic growth is accepted and in fact applauded. The members of a writing community—and that definitely includes the teacher—understand that though the writer's goal is publication, the process involved in attaining that goal is equally important. It is only when young writers feel free to experiment with words that they grow comfortable with language—and with the blank page. It is only after much experimentation and practice that they can begin to communicate clearly all that they have to say.

And that leads to another important point: does anyone ever truly learn to write? Writing is not like riding the proverbial bicycle; when you've done that once, you never forget how. Nor is it like reading or doing math equations or hitting a baseball. Those are skills we learn and master and generally know how to do forever more. Writing isn't like that. You don't struggle and strive and then one day say, "There! Now I know how to write," feeling certain that from that moment on you can sit at your word processor and write with ease. Those who write know that writing well is a constant challenge. Some days the words come freely, and sometimes they just don't come at all. A writer understands that and recognizes that not only the work but also the writer is always, to some extent, "in process," working to be better. A writing community values the process that leads to that growth.

4. A writing community appreciates the strengths of its members.

It is certainly true that writing as a skill is at the center of the writing community. Of course I wish that every one of my students in my classroom-turned-writing community could become an excellent writer, and I do believe that every one of them can improve. But I am honest enough to realize that some young people do not possess an interest, a talent, or an instinct for writing, and, though with effort they will improve as writers, writing will never be one of their strengths.

A writing community, however, recognizes that other abilities and skills, besides that of writing itself, are important to the community. If there were no community members with these strengths—the ability to edit, to proofread, to offer substantive criticism, even simply to listen well—the community as a whole would falter. If twenty-five students wrote with eagerness and alacrity, but there was no one there to respond critically to their work—to offer not only suggestions on content but also to explain such things as how to use a colon—not one of these writers would grow.

It isn't easy to get students to develop an appreciation for these "supporting roles" in the community. The talented writer seems to be the "star"; the talented proofreader appears to be little more than a walk-on. But this proofreader, like the person who instinctively knows how to draw a story out of a writer or the one who can bring a sense of organization to a disjointed piece, makes an important and necessary contribution to the work—the writing—of the community. It is the teacher's job to call attention to the many and varied abilities her students possess, not only to create an appreciation within the community for such skills but to reinforce and reward these strengths in the individuals who possess them. Many of these abilities are ones which will serve students well long after they leave any classroom. For example, the skills required to be a good editor—attention to detail, insight, and a clear sense of organization—are ones that will bring a person success in a variety of careers. A teacher must nurture these abilities, just as she nurtures the creative bent of a talented young writer. The truth is, very few of our students will achieve great glory as writers, and though the ability to communicate effectively is an extremely valuable skill, there are other skills young people learn in a writing community that will be important to them throughout their lives.

Any teacher who supports the idea of a classroom-turned-writing-community probably has little trouble embracing these four principles. It is the fifth and final principle which is perhaps the biggest stumbling block, partly because of the way many of us have been trained as teachers and partly because of the way most schools are structured. In my own classrooms-turned-communities, I find myself constantly struggling with this, never achieving the maybe idealized vision I believe would ultimately bring most success to my students. Too often I settle for something less, but I never give up believing in the principle.

The fifth principle is this: *A writing community is a democratic community.*

In a democratic community all members have an equal voice. That one line is no doubt enough to explain why this is a stumbling block for many teachers in many schools. Traditionally, the teacher has stood at the center of the classroom. It is her voice which is heard above all others. Many would argue this is the way it should be, that she certainly knows better than her students what they should learn and how they should learn it. Maybe she does; I'm not sure. But what I am sure of is that in an ideal world, even if she does possess this knowledge before her students do, they will be better off if she can give them the freedom and space to discover it on their own.

So, in an ideal world, I would like to hand my students a blank pad of paper at the start of the year and let them find their own way as writers. I'd like them to tell me what they want to write about, how they want to share their work, and how they can best hone their skills. I would like them to decide together to form a community that nurtures each of its members.

I truly believe that given enough time my students could achieve these things without my guidance. There would be false starts and futile efforts, but eventually they would each find their own way as writers and be better writers, more committed writers, than they are now. But the fact is, there is rarely enough time for this sort of exploration. The demands of the school calendar, especially with that one day marked "Grades Due," make it impractical if not impossible for a teacher to give her students complete control of their learning. There are schedules to adhere to that force the teacher to structure some sort of timetable for her students to follow.

Most students, too, have spent most of their school years in classrooms that are teacher-centered. Though they may balk at being told what to do and how to do it, they are used to such control. The freedom of suddenly being part of a democratic classroom can be overwhelming and can result in a temporary, but nevertheless frustrating, deterioration in positive behavior. Like first-year students in college who find themselves quite free of the restraints of home and high school and often in response go a little bit wild, younger students who are given unaccustomed control of their learning may fail to use their power responsibly. Again, with time, all this can be worked out and can contribute much to the students' maturation process, but the time demands, as well as the emotional demands, are formidable, and many teachers justifiably feel they cannot commit themselves to a totally democratic classroom.

There are, however, compromises that can be made, ones that ensure that young writers are taking ownership of their work and of the community as a whole. The most important thing a teacher can do is to dispel the image her students have of her as The One Who Knows—who knows what to write, how to write it, whether it is good, and how to publish it. Through the practices described in earlier chapters, particularly that of the response group, the teacher can give her students the responsibility for all those things. In doing so, they develop the skills and the confidence to become independent writers and independent learners, people who recognize the value of advice and support from others but who trust in their own instincts and abilities and who understand that success depends on their own efforts.

As mentioned earlier, I meet every class of students believing it will become a community of writers. With these principles firm in my mind, I go forward, sometimes with varying degrees of success.

One year I had two Creative Writing classes—Period 4 and Period 8—two different (and different is the operative word!) groups of twenty-two juniors and seniors who had presumably elected to take the course because they liked to write. Although I love the challenge of trying to turn non-writers and not-so-sure-writers into real writers, it seems a wonderful gift when students come to me with a built-in love for words. Though not all of the students knew each other or each other's work, they seemed, by their shared interest in writing, to be members of a writing community already, and I relished the thought of working with them. The semester seemed golden.

I designed the classes in a similar fashion. Though certain adjustments and alterations must always be made to any course to accommodate the needs of a particular group of students, I had one basic course design for Creative Writing. The course would run as a writing workshop with student work, supplemented by models from established writers, generating the principal content. We would start with autobiographical writing, exploring the possibilities of the personal essay. We would then move into fiction techniques, and finally to poetry. Writers would, of course, have the freedom to move back and forth between genres, discovering their own subjects, style, and voice. We would rely heavily on response groups, and we would learn to be both peer- and self-evaluators. Together we would examine possible markets for our work, and always the idea of publication would stand as an ultimate goal. I had taught the course many times before, but I had new ideas and new energy. I was ready.

Had the school day ended after Period 4, I would have gone home each day happy, exulting in my abilities as a writing teacher. Within a week, the students in that class were transformed into a community of writers. Eager to write and to share their work with one another, they formed response groups epitomizing the model. Though the students were generally soft-spoken, they read their work with passion and seriousness of purpose, supplying, without my importuning, copies of their pieces for one another, and then offering insights on the work that allowed me to put my pen away. They understood the power and the practice of revision, and, though they welcomed my opinion, they relied equally on each others' ideas, as it should be. They were eager to enter contests; they gathered around the writing board daily; they sought passes for the Computer Lab so they could put their work in proper manuscript form. And the writing they did was extraordinary. Finally, when two of the writers found publishing success, one as the winner of a local poetry contest, the other in a commercial anthology of young peoples' writing, the entire class clapped loud and long.

None of this was just my hopeful imagination. Partway through the course, I bumped into a parent of one young writer who gushed, "My daughter loves your class! She says it's so relaxed, but she's getting all this wonderful writing done. And she just loves her response group! You're doing everything right!"

If I'd had no Period 8 class, I might have accepted her compliments and let her stroke my ego. But instead what I wanted to say to her was, "I love your daughter's class. *They're* doing everything right. And it can't be because of me. Just look at Period 8!"

Period 8 was a problem. I felt it the very first day as one burly boy after another entered the doorway to the hoots and jeers of his buddies who had already taken seats. For a minute I thought it was a mistake. A Guidance error perhaps, or maybe I was in the wrong room, or worse, if this *was* my class, maybe they had all taken it believing it was a gut course.

None of that was true. These twenty-two students, mostly loud, large, and male, were my students—and they were writers. It took only a couple of classes for me to discover that. What took a lot longer—and what I never felt I completely achieved—was for me to turn them into a community.

The guidelines listed above became my mantras. Before the class would even start, I found myself repeating, "The writing community supports the writer." I did support—and like—them, these crazy kids bursting with energy and ideas but seemingly incapable of focusing either. "The writing community values the writing." I liked their work, colorful and creative as it was, but I wished just once I could get them to take it seriously, to give it the attention it deserved. "Writing isn't a series of one-liners," I'd tell them time and time again, and always someone would have a comeback. "It is if you write for Letterman!"

This wasn't exactly a discipline problem. They did their work. They worried about their grades. They genuinely liked me and one another. They were a funny, happy group—but they fought against being a community of writers. When they met in response groups, their assessment of each other's work was often facile and ineffectual. I heard a lot of "It's good" from this group. Not surprisingly the revisions that they made were relatively insubstantial. A paper in third-draft stage was strikingly similar to the earlier drafts. The topics they chose for each assignment were repetitious. They depended too much on easy humor, for, not having worked to establish trust with one another, they didn't have the courage to take emotional risks. Publication didn't interest them much (though imagined grandiose rewards did!), and when I passed around a flyer for this opportunity or that, it was just as likely as not, partway around the room, to flutter to the floor.

It sounds as if I'm blaming them. I don't mean it to sound that way, and in fact, if any blame is to be placed, then it should be placed on me for not having found a way to subdue the clamorous energy of such a group without killing their creative spirit. I tried. I made those adjustments and accommodations designed to improve the sense of community. I rearranged response groups; I redesigned assignments; I reinforced positive behaviors. And things got better. When, at the end of the semester, the seniors, whose school year ended early, wrote me their letters assessing their growth as writers, I realized that they *had* grown. Josh told me he now understood what it meant to bring characters to life. Greg said he felt pretty good because he was the one in his group who could fix opening lines. And Anne, who seemed to be spending too much time socializing, convinced me that her chatter with her peers had unearthed some interesting stories she could now write. So, for these seniors, the semester wasn't wasted. But I never felt we'd done enough. Period 8 was a classroom; it wasn't a community—and I didn't expect it would ever be.

When the seniors graduated, a kind of ragtag group of juniors, eight in all, remained. Some of them were the quietest students, likely intimidated the entire semester by the boisterous older students, but not all of them were quiet. A couple were among the most colorful of the whole class of twenty-two. We settled in for three more weeks of school, and though I imagined things would be calmer, I didn't expect any enormous changes in the commitment of the group or in the quality of their work.

I was wrong. Within a matter of days, this little remnant group formed a close-knit community and began to produce work that stunned me. Kelly, whose previous work had been good but glib, wrote an essay about her mother's alcoholism that was one of the most powerful and wrenching pieces I've ever read. Mark, who all semester had floundered, never feeling he was writing anything worthwhile, suddenly found his story and wrote it in a burst of brilliance. And Chris, one of the most flamboyant students in the class, grew quiet and spent whole periods combing *Writer's Market* for places to send his medieval fantasy story. Ultimately he couldn't control his excitement and sent it out to four.

Not only did they seem to care more about their own writing, but they also began to show a real concern for each other's work. When we'd work in the Computer Lab, they'd huddle around the computers, reading the screens and offering solid suggestions for revision to one another. Kelly took Jason under her wing and guided him in his final project— the preparation of a manuscript for submission. Sure where she was sending her work, she helped him assess the possibilities for his own essay, and he finally settled happily on *Young Voices.* And when all the projects were complete, they were eager to read all the final pieces, and I heard them say to one another, "I think yours will get published." The final, wonderful irony was that Kelly's piece did. When I bumped into her over the summer, she was beaming.

"I'm going to be published," she said. "*360° Magazine* wants my essay. The editor even called me! I just had to make a couple of revisions."

Why did this happen? Why did this group of students suddenly form a community when they had struggled mightily against doing so throughout the whole semester? I don't know. Perhaps it was simply a function of numbers. When there are only eight students, they seem to fall more naturally into a community model because they are all very aware of each other's work. Certainly as any English teacher knows, amazing things happen in a small class that are rarely duplicated in a large one.

But Period 4 was a large class and it was a community, so why did it take so long to happen in Period 8? All I can say is maybe those students needed time to grow into an understanding of the concept of community. Perhaps they had spent all of their academic lives in classrooms where a teacher told them what to do and how to do it and then decided whether they had done it right. A writing community is an enormous responsibility, not only for the teacher but also for the students. Students, though they may complain about it, are very used to being told what to do. It may be irksome, but it's easy. When you have to make your own decisions and take charge of your own growth, as well as assist others who seek your guidance, it's much more difficult. For many of those students in that Period 8 class, this new responsibility was, I think, overwhelming, and they responded by resisting. They had the talent of writers but had not yet developed the temperament. They were not ready to own their words. That's a serious commitment, and, in their refusal to be serious about the content of their work or its development, I think they were telling me they just weren't ready.

I tell this story not to discourage teachers from seeking to turn their classrooms into writing communities. In fact, my intent is quite the opposite. I want teachers to understand that not all attempts to establish a writing community will go smoothly, with students like those in Period 4, flourishing as writers and loving every minute of it. Sometimes, a group will be like my infamous Period 8, and it will seem far easier for the teacher to take charge, direct the work, measure its quality, and demand improvement, all the while using her power as teacher to "encourage" growth. Maybe it is easier—it certainly tempted me on those days when the room buzzed with activity that was neither productive nor connected to the work—but it isn't better, and it simply perpetuates the problem. Until students are given, and perhaps forced, to take responsibility for their work, they will never become real writers. They will always be only students who write.

In this discussion of the writing community perhaps it seems as if I have abandoned the focus on publishing. I have not. The idea of publishing is never far from my mind, nor, I believe, is it ever far from my students' minds. From the day they enter my classroom, as we begin to shape ourselves into a writing community, I talk of publishing, not of the glory or of the gains, but of the power of putting one's words in the world.

"Go public!" I tell them, and though at first they shake their heads, shy and unsure or maybe simply surprised that I would think their words matter, I know that eventually they will begin to nod in agreement instead. Nurtured by the writing community and given responsibility for their own words, they will become real writers, and real writers, by nature and need, want to publish.

Of course, not every student will publish widely, but every student writer can—and should—have his moment in the spotlight, reading his work to his peers or displaying it on the classroom wall. That is publishing, and no teacher, however strongly she embraces the idea of marketing student work, should forget that. When a young writer shares his work with an audience, he is publishing, and no matter how small the audience may be, that takes tremendous courage. In fact, it sometimes seems less risky to be a writer in a big world where no one knows your name than in the confines of a classroom where everyone can see your face.

And once a young writer has experienced the thrill of knowing his words have had an impact on a reader, even if it is just the boy in the next row, he will not want to stop writing or publishing. A myriad of opportunities await him. He may write a letter to the editor or to a long-forgotten friend. He may write a script to be performed by his classmates or a children's book to be read by the younger students down the hall. He may send his poetry to *Skylark* or his essay on steroid use in high school sports to *The 21st Century*. And maybe he'll even give it a shot and send that piece about kayaking in Maine to *Outdoor Action* or his sci-fi story to *Analog Science Fiction & Fact*. The important thing is that each of these pieces will be good. They will be strong, powerful, polished pieces of writing because this young writer will care about the work. When he types his name on the piece, he will do it proudly, not for the teacher, not for the grade, but for himself, the Writer. And he will be ready to call himself that.

Appendixes

Appendix A
Publishing Opportunities: The Market and Contest Lists

The following pages list a number of publishing opportunities, most of which are particularly appropriate for and/or limited to student writers. Teachers and students are reminded that there are many, many other opportunities open to young writers if they are willing to compete with adult writers. These opportunities are best discovered through a careful study of *Writer's Market* or other such reference books. (A listing of such resources follows later in the Appendix.) Some of these books divide the markets into very specific categories (e.g., "Automotive and Motorcycle," "Regional," "Science Fiction, Fantasy and Horror," "Sports," etc.) and thus provide easy access to information on markets for writing that has a focused audience. In the following Market and Contest Lists, those opportunities which are open to adult writers as well are starred with an asterisk (*). Otherwise, teachers and students can assume that only young writers, ages as specified, can submit their work. Care has been taken to determine that each publication and contest is a current and legitimate one; however, young writers are advised to contact the publication/contest before submitting work in order to ensure that it continues to exist and maintains the same guidelines, deadlines, etc.

The Market List

The Market List is an alphabetical listing of magazines, journals, newspapers, newsletters, and book publishers. Each listing begins with the name, address, phone and fax number (when available) of the publication, the name of the present editor, the publication schedule, and the subscription and sample copy rate. This is followed by a section called "Needs" which states the type of material the market is interested in receiving. "Submission Guidelines" describes the particular format required for submissions. Young writers should pay special attention to this section and submit only work that meets the guidelines. The next section lists "Payment" when applicable. The optional section "Comments" gives additional information which may be helpful to teachers and young writers. Any material that appears in quotation marks comes directly from the publication and/or its submission guidelines. Some publications are listed in both the Market and Contest Lists because they offer two different publishing opportunities.

THE ACORN, 1530 7th Street, Rock Island, IL 61201. Published five times a year. Subscription $10, sample copy $2.

    Needs: Fiction and poetry, from writers grades K–12.

    Submission Guidelines: Fiction up to 500 words. Poetry up to 35 lines. Include name, address, age or grade on each manuscript. If submitting more than one manuscript, send them all in one envelope with separate SASEs.

    Comments: "We do not use manuscripts with the killing of humans or animals in them."

*AIM—AMERICA'S INTERCULTURAL MAGAZINE, 7308 S. Eberhart Ave., Chicago, IL 60620-0554. 312-874-6184. Editor: Myron Apilado. Published quarterly. Subscription $10, sample $4.

    Needs: Fiction to 1,500 words, essays and articles to 800 words, poetry to 30 lines that deal with social issues. No religious material.

    Submission Guidelines: Use standard format.

    Payment: Fiction and nonfiction, $25–$35. Poetry, $3–$5.

    Comments: Seeks "to purge racism from the human bloodstream." *Aim* also sponsors a Short Story Contest. See Contest Listings.

*ANALOG SCIENCE FICTION & FACT, 1270 Avenue of the Americas, New York, NY 10020. 212-698-1313. Editor: Dr. Stanley Schmidt. Published 11 times a year. Sample $4.

    Needs: Fiction of 2,000–80,000 words based on some aspect of future science or technology.

    Submission Guidelines: Use standard format. Include SASE.

    Payment: $.06–$.08 per word for stories under 7,500 words. $450–$500 for longer stories.

    Comments: *Analog* is a competitive market but is interested in working with new/unpublished writers.

THE APPRENTICE WRITER, c/o Gary Fincke, Writers' Institute Director, Box GG, Susquehanna University, Selinsgrove, PA 17870-1001. 717-372-4164. Editor: Gary Fincke. Published annually in September. 11,000 copies sent to 3,400 schools in Middle Atlantic Region and nearby states.

    Needs: Writing by high school students from the Middle Atlantic Region and nearby states. Categories for submissions are 1) fiction, 2) poetry, 3) drama, 4) essay, 5) journalism—features/interviews.

    Submission Guidelines: No restrictions on style, subject matter, or length. Manuscripts must be typed and double-spaced on 8½" x 11" pages. Include writer's name, address, and name of appropriate teacher on each page. Manuscripts are not returned. Submission deadline: March 15. Acceptance announcements in May.

Payment: Payment in copies to writers and their teachers.

Comments: Susquehanna University also sponsors a Summer Writers' Workshop for High School Students with classes in Fiction, Poetry, Magazine Writing, and Oral Interpretation. Contact Gary Fincke at above address for more information.

BLUE JEAN MAGAZINE—*for Teen Girls Who Dare,* P.O. Box 90856, Rochester, NY 14609. 716-654-5070. Fax: 716-654-6785. E-mail: BlueJeanMg@aol.com. Published six times a year. Subscription $39, sample $8.

Needs: Fiction, essays, articles, and poetry from teenage girls ages 13–19 across the United States.

Submission Guidelines: Fiction and poetry of no specified length. Essays and articles in various categories including 1) Cover Story to 2,500 words, 2) Nothin' but the Earth—community environmental action stories to 600 words, 3) Community Challenges—essays on experiences with community charities and non-profit groups 500–1,500 words, 4) Daring Feats—articles on teenage adventurers 750–1,500 words, 5) Personal Stories 750–1,000 words. Type and double-space all manuscripts. Include name, address, phone number, and age on each submission. Include a recent photo of yourself.

Payment: Cover story, $100. Fiction and nonfiction, $50 plus two complimentary issues. Poetry, two complimentary issues.

Comments: *"Blue Jean Magazine* is multiracial, multicultural and advertising free. We are devoted to publishing what teen girls are thinking, saying and doing. . . No dieting tips, make-up copy, or supermodels in this magazine."* Writers are encouraged to send relevant photographs and artwork to accompany manuscripts. Students can also apply for the Teen Editorial Board by contacting the above address.

*BOYS' LIFE, P.O. Box 152079, 1325 W. Walnut Hill Lane, Irving, TX 75015-2079. 214-580-2366. Editor: Scott Stuckey. Fiction Editor: Shannon Lowry. Published monthly. Sample $2.50.

Needs: Fiction, nonfiction, and column fillers of interest to boys ages 8–18 with a special emphasis on Boy Scout activities.

Submission Guidelines: Fiction in all genres from 500–1,500 words. For nonfiction, query first. Articles 750–1,000 words. Columns include Sports, Pets, Science, Music, History from 400–600 words. Type, double-space, and number all pages. If using a word processor, submit manuscript on 3.5" floppy disk also.

Payment: Fiction and major articles, $500 and up. Columns, $150–$350.

Comments: *Boys' Life* prefers to work with established writers but does work with a small number of new/unpublished writers each year. This is a potential market only for the best of young writers.

*BOYS' QUEST, 103 N. Main Street, P.O. Box 227, Bluffton, OH 45817. 419-358-4610. Editor: Marilyn Edwards. Sample $3.

Needs: Fiction, nonfiction, and poems for boys ages 5–12.

Submission Guidelines: Fiction and nonfiction from 300–700 words, poetry 10–30 lines. Include cover letter and one-page bio.

Payment: $.05 per word for fiction and nonfiction. $10–$15 per poem.

*CALLIOPE, The World History Magazine for Young People, Cobblestone Publishing, Inc., 7 School Street, Peterborough, NH 03458-1454. 603-924-7209. Fax: 603-924-7380. Published five times a year. Sample $4.50 with 7" x 10" or larger SASE.

Needs: Fiction, nonfiction, and poetry RELATED TO THE THEME OF A SPECIFIC UPCOMING ISSUE. *Calliope* covers world history (East/West) for readers ages 8–14. Previous themes include "The Phoenicians," "Doges of Venice," and "Islam."

Submission Guidelines: Send SASE for upcoming themes and deadlines. Query with cover letter, outline, bibliography, writing sample, and SASE. Nonfiction 300–800 words. Fiction to 800 words. Poetry, serious and light verse, to 100 lines.

Payment: Fiction and nonfiction, $.20–$.25 per printed word. Poetry pays on an individual basis.

Comments: "Historical accuracy . . . and lively, original approaches to the subject are the primary concern of the editors in choosing material."

*CAMPUS LIFE, 465 Gunderson Drive, Carol Stream, IL 60188. 630-260-6200. Fax: 630-260-0114. Manuscript Editor: Christopher Lutes. Published bimonthly. Sample $2 and 9½" x 11" envelope.

Needs: Fiction, articles, humor, and poetry for late high school and early college age students. Work should represent a Christian worldview.

Submission Guidelines: No unsolicited manuscripts. Query with one-page typed synopsis, published samples, and SASE. Fiction to 2,000 words.

Payment: Generally $.15–$.20 per word.

*CHILDREN'S DIGEST, 1100 Waterway Blvd. P.O. Box 567, Indianapolis, IN 46206. 317-636-8881. Editor: Layne Cameron. Published 8 times a year. Subscription $16.95, sample $1.25.

Needs: Fiction, poetry, jokes and riddles for children ages 10–12.

Submission Guidelines: Fiction up to 700 words. Type manuscripts and include name, address, age, and school.

Comments: The above guidelines refer specifically to submissions by readers ages 10–12. Older writers may want to submit work as adult writers would. Send SASE for further guidelines.

THE CLAREMONT REVIEW, The International Magazine of Young Adult Writers, 4980 Wesley Road, Victoria, British Columbia, Canada, V8Y 1Y9. 604-658-5221. Fax: 604-658-5387. Editor: Terence Young. Published biannually. Subscription $12, sample $6 with 6" x 9" envelope and $2 Canadian postage.

Needs: Fiction and poetry by writers ages 13–19 or those in grades 8–12.

Submission Guidelines: Fiction, 1,500–5,000 words, and poetry, "anything from traditional to post modern, but with a preference for works that reveal something of the human condition." Type and double-space all manuscripts and include the author's name at the top of each page. Include a brief biography and SASE. Note: submissions from the United States require International Reply Coupons (IRC). Often comments on rejected manuscripts.

Payment: One contributor's copy (a copy of the issue of the magazine in which the writer's work appears). Cash payment possible.

Comments: *The Claremont Review* also sponsors various contests, subject to change from year to year. Contact the above address for current information.

*COBBLESTONE, The History Magazine for Young People, Cobblestone Publishing, Inc., 7 School Street, Peterborough, NH 03458-1454. 603-924-7209. Fax: 603-924-7380. Editor: Margaret Chorlian. Published ten times a year, September–June. Sample $4.50 with 7 ½" x 10" or larger SASE.

Needs: Fiction, nonfiction, and poetry RELATED TO THE THEME OF A SPECIFIC UPCOMING ISSUE. *Cobblestone* covers American history for readers ages 8–14. Previous themes have included "Elections in America," "Anne Hutchinson and the Puritans," and "Geronimo and the Apache Indians."

Submission Guidelines: Send SASE for upcoming themes and deadlines. Query with cover letter, outline, bibliography, writing sample, and SASE. Nonfiction 300–800 words. Fiction to 800 words. Poetry, serious and light verse, to 100 lines.

Payment: Fiction and nonfiction, $.20–$.25 per printed word. Poetry pays on an individual basis.

COMING OF AGE, P.O. Box 700637-WGT, San Jose, CA 95170. E-mail: comingofage@earthlink.net. Editor: Margaret Pevec. Published quarterly.

Needs: Writing by young people ages 15–25 that informs parent readers about "youth oppression, the special challenges young people face in this time, and their perspectives and dreams."

Submission Guidelines: Articles 100–3,000 words, fiction, and poetry. Include name, address, phone, e-mail address, and one-paragraph biography. Send SASE for guidelines.

Payment: Free one-year subscription and three contributor's copies. No cash payment for first four issues, but future payment likely.

Comments: Request "Writer's Guidelines for Teens and Young Adults" for detailed information and description of magazine's philosophy. The editor is also willing to communicate with teachers and students by e-mail.

*COMPOST, P.O. Box 226, Jamaica Plain, MA 02130. 617-524-1456. Editorial collaborative. Contact: Meg Bezucha. Published biannually. $5 per copy.

Needs: Fiction and poetry. Also especially interested in "literature in translation as a way of sharing cultures."

Submission Guidelines: Standard manuscript format.

Comments: Although *Compost* is not a student-written journal, its editors are very interested in reading student work.

THE CONCORD REVIEW, P.O. Box 661, Concord, MA 01742. 800-331-5007. Internet: fitzhugh@tcr.org. Web: http://www.tcr.org. Editor: Will Fitzhugh. Published quarterly. Subscription $35, sample copies available free of charge to school libraries or History departments.

Needs: Essays on any historical topic by high school students.

Submission Guidelines: Essays should be about 4,000–6,000 words and include endnotes. Submissions should be typed or printed on a word processor or submitted on a Macintosh disk. They must be accompanied by the "Form to Accompany Essays" which can be requested at the above number.

Payment: One contributor's copy of the issue and twelve reprints of the published essay.

CREATIVE KIDS, P.O. Box 8813, Waco, TX 76714-8813. 800-998-2208. Published four times a year. Subscription $19.95, sample $3.

Needs: Fiction, essays, plays, poetry, editorials, songs by students ages 8–14.

Submission Guidelines: Stories between 800 and 900 words. No specified length for other categories. Manuscripts must be typed on 8½" x 11" white paper. Include author's name, address, age, date of birth, school name and address, grade, and statement of originality signed by parent or teacher. No more than one submission per envelope. Include SASE and cover letter with each entry. No multiple submissions.

Payment: One contributor's copy.

Comments: *Creative Kids* does not want to receive school assignments. Work must be submitted by the author, not a teacher or parent.

*CREATIVE WITH WORDS PUBLICATIONS, P.O. Box 223226, Carmel, CA 93922. Fax: 408-655-8627. Editor: Brigitta Geltrich. Published ten to twelve times per year. Subscription $60, single issues $9–12, sample of back issues $6.

Needs: Prose, especially folkloristic tales, and poetry by both children and adults according to themes set twice a year. Previous themes have included "Nature—Seasons," "Life's Important Things," "Humor," and "Pets." (Send SASE for upcoming themes.)

Submission Guidelines: Prose to 1,200 words. Poetry to twenty lines. Shorter works have a better chance of publication. Include a cover letter stating the issue to which the submission is directed. Include name, address, and age, and officially verify authenticity of the writing (by a principal, teacher, or notary) on the first page. No multiple submissions.

Payment: Published writers receive a 20 percent discount on every copy purchased of the issue containing their work.

*EMPOWERED, P.O. Box 40998, Phoenix, AZ 85274. 888-TEENMAG. E-mail: eyf@eyf.com. Web: http://www.eyf.com.

Needs: Personal essays and articles about topics, issues, and people of interest to young female readers. Particularly interested in articles about what is unique about where the writer lives and how she spends her time.

Submission Guidelines: For articles of more than 200 words, send both hard copy and disk. Include name and address on every page. No manuscripts returned. Writers may work together to create a combined photo and article layout.

Payment: Writers are paid for all work accepted for publication.

Comments: *empowered* is about "the strength, intelligence, spirit and power that girls have to offer." More than 70 percent of the magazine is created by teenage girls.

*FACES, The Magazine About People, Cobblestone Publishing, Inc., 7 School Street, Peterborough, NH 03458. 603-924-7209. Fax: 603-924-7380. Published nine times a year, September–May. Sample $4.50 with 7½" x 10½" or larger SASE.

Needs: Fiction, nonfiction, and poetry RELATED TO THE THEME OF A SPECIFIC UPCOMING ISSUE. *Faces* is an anthropological magazine for readers ages 8–14. Previous themes have included "Communication: Talking Drums to Computers," "Early Settlers to the Americas," and "Divination: Looking into the Future."

　　Submission Guidelines: Send SASE for upcoming themes and deadlines. Query with cover letter, outline, bibliography, writing sample, and SASE. Nonfiction 300–800 words. Fiction, especially retold folktales and legends, to 800 words. Poetry, serious and light verse, to 100 lines.

　　Payment: Fiction and nonfiction, $.20–$.25 per printed word. Poetry pays on an individual basis.

　　Comments: "All manuscripts are reviewed by the American Museum of Natural History in New York before being published."

FRESH VOICES, c/o Lynn Minton, Box 5103, Grand Central Station, New York, NY 10163-5103. Appears weekly as a column in Sunday newspaper magazine sections.

　　Needs: Responses from teenagers around the country, especially based on personal experience, to a question posed each week in the column. Previous questions include: "Teens: Are Drugs and Drinking a Problem at Your School Functions?" and "What Do You Want Your Friends to Say About You at Your 10th High School Reunion?"

　　Submission Guidelines: Include daytime phone number.

　　Comments: "Every letter is read, but personal replies regrettably are not possible."

*FROGPOND, P.O. Box 767, Archer, Florida 32618-0767. E-mail: kenneth@afn.org. Editor: Kenneth C. Liebman. Published four times a year. Sample $5.

　　Needs: Original, unpublished haiku and senryu from traditional to contemporary.

　　Submission Guidelines: Submit poetry in groups of 5–20 on one or two sheets of 8½" x 11" paper. Do not send single poems. Do not use titles. Include author's name and address at the top of each page.

　　Payment: One contributor's copy.

　　Comments: *Frogpond* is the official publication of the Haiku Society of America. HSA also sponsors the Nicholas A. Virgilio Memorial Haiku Competition for High School Students. See Contest List for information.

THE FUDGE CAKE, Francora DTP, P.O. Box 197, Citrus Heights, CA 95611-0197. Editor: Jancarl Campi. Published bimonthly. Subscriptions $10, sample or single copy $3.

　　Needs: Fiction and poetry written by students ages 6–17.

　　Submission Guidelines: Short stories to 300 words. Poems to 30 lines. Submit copies (not originals) of 1–5 pieces. Type or hand print manuscript, and include author's name, age, phone number, and address on the top right-hand corner of each piece. Include SASE for notification, but manuscripts will not be returned.

　　Payment: One contributor's copy.

Comments: *The Fudge Cake* often critiques rejected manuscripts. The magazine also contains a pen-pal network listing in each issue through which writers can correspond and comment on their work. Writers should indicate with their submissions if they want to be listed in the pen-pal network.

*GIRLS' LIFE, 4517 Harford Road, Baltimore, MD 21214. 410-254-9200. Fax: 410-254-0991. Editors: Kelly A. White, Michelle Silver. Published bimonthly. Sample copy $5.

Needs: Articles on topics of interest to adolescent girls.

Submission Guidelines: Query first with descriptive story idea. All stories are assigned by editors. Articles 700–2,000 words.

Payment: $150–$800.

*GLIMMER TRAIN STORIES, 710 SW Washington Street, Suite 504, Portland, OR 97205. 503-221-0836. Fax: 503-221-0837. Web: www.glimmertrain.com. Editors: Susan Burmeister-Brown and Linda Davies. Published quarterly. Subscription $29.

Needs: Literary fiction. No children's stories.

Submission Guidelines: Stories 1,200–7,500 words. Include cover letter, with list of publications, with manuscript. Submit manuscripts in January, April, July, and October.

Payment: $500 and 10 contributor's copies for first publication rights.

Comments: *Glimmer Train Stories* is a highly competitive market and one that only very exceptional young writers should submit to. The publication also sponsors a contest open only to new writers. See Contest List for information.

*THE GOLDFINCH, State Historical Society of Iowa, 402 Iowa Avenue, Iowa City, IA 52240. Editor: Amy Ruth. Published quarterly. Sample $3 plus $1.50 shipping.

Needs: Essays based on themes connected to aspects of Iowa history. Special section of writing by children and teenagers.

Submission Guidelines: Send SASE for list of upcoming themes and special guidelines for student submissions.

*HANGING LOOSE, c/o High School Editor, 231 Wyckoff Street, Brooklyn, NY 11217. Published three times a year. Subscription $17.50, sample $7.50 plus $1.50 postage and handling.

Needs: Fiction and poetry by writers of high school age.

Submission Guidelines: Submit 1–3 short stories, 3–6 poems, or an equivalent combination in order for the editor to get a good sense of the contributor's work. Type all manuscripts. Include a brief biographical sketch.

Payment: $10–$15 plus 3 contributor's copies.

Comments: *Hanging Loose* devotes a section of the magazine to the work of high school writers. Hanging Loose Press also publishes individual collections of fiction and poetry. Among their publications are two anthologies—*Bullseye* and *Smart Like Me*—work by high school writers selected from the pages of *Hanging Loose* magazine.

*THE HIGH SCHOOL SENIOR, INC., P.O. Box 11098, Pittsburgh, PA 15237-9737. E-mail: hssm@nauticom.net. Published monthly. Subscription $71.40.

Needs: Fiction, nonfiction, especially opinion pieces, and poetry by high school age writers.

Submission Guidelines: Include with each submission name, address, phone number, age, grade, the name and address of high school, and any relevant biographical information.

Comments: Submissions to the magazine are eligible to win the Short Story Contest and the Poetry Contest.

THE HIGH SCHOOL WRITER, Senior High Edition/Junior High Edition, P.O. Box 718, Grand Rapids, MN 55744-0718. 218-326-8025. Editor: Roxanne Kain. Published monthly September–May. Subscription (25 copies) $59.95.

Needs: Fiction, nonfiction, and poetry written by high school students and junior high and middle school students *of subscribing schools.*

Submission Guidelines: Manuscripts should be under 2,000 words. Type and double-space and include, in this order, at the top of the first page, author's name, school name and address, author's grade. Also include a statement of originality and author's signature.

Payment: "Each month one student whose work appears in this edition of the *High School Writer* will be chosen to receive a trophy."

Comments: Only students of subscribing schools are eligible to submit their work. Writers should indicate junior or senior high edition on envelope.

*HOBSON'S CHOICE, P.O. Box 98, Ripley, OH 45167. 513-392-4549. Published bimonthly. Editor: Susannah West. Subscription $12, sample $2.50.

Needs: Fiction and nonfiction with a focus on science fiction, fantasy, and technology. Interested in positive and plausible science fiction and fantasy stories, especially those with strong female characters. Wants articles of scientific and technological interest, including profiles, interviews, reviews, and how-to pieces.

Submission Guidelines: Short stories from 2,000 to 10,000 words. No specified length for nonfiction. Include name, address, title, and word count on first page. Include title and author's last name on following pages.

Payment: $.01–$.04 per word.

Comments: *Hobson's Choice* is a magazine for both older teenagers and adults. The editor provides a detailed packet of information containing submission guidelines and tips for writers of science fiction, fantasy, and technology. Send $1.50 and SASE for this material. Guidelines only for SASE.

*HOPSCOTCH: THE MAGAZINE FOR GIRLS, The Editor, P.O. Box 164, Bluffton, OH 45817-0164. 419-358-4610. Fax: 419-358-5027. Editor: Marilyn Edwards. Published bimonthly. Subscription $15, sample $3.

Needs: Fiction, nonfiction, and poems for girls ages 5–12. Nonfiction is used 3 to 1 over fiction and is most often used when accompanied by black and white photographs.

Submission Guidelines: Fiction to 1,000 words. Nonfiction to 750 words on such topics as pets, sports, hobbies, crafts, careers, etc. Include cover letter and SASE with complete manuscript.

Payment: Minimum $.05 per word for fiction and nonfiction. $10 for accompanying photo. Minimum $10 per poem.

Comments: Send SASE for guidelines and list of upcoming themes.

HOW ON EARTH!, P.O. Box 339, Oxford, PA 19363-0339. 717-529-8638. Fax: 717-529-3000. E-mail: HowOnEarth@aol.com. Published quarterly by the Vegetarian Education Network. Subscription $18, sample $6.

 Needs: Feature articles, essays, poetry, and food reviews by and for youth ages 13–24 "who support compassionate, ecologically sound living." (See Comments below.)

 Submission Guidelines: Feature articles from 1,000–2,000 words. Essays, interviews, and creative writing from 400–800 words. Food reviews from 300–700 words. Include name, address, phone number, and age on first page of submission and name on every page following. Include a title for each submission or state that it should remain untitled. Attach a *HOE! Questionnaire* to each submission (unless it is already on file). Questionnaires are available at above address. If possible, include with submission a 3.5" disk copy with name of the word processing program used.

 Payment: Several contributor's copies.

 Comments: "*How On Earth!* covers a variety of environmental, animal, and social justice issues while encouraging activism and empowerment among youth who are concerned about the Earth and all beings. *HOE!* recognizes that a vegetarian diet is an essential component of compassionate, sustainable living, so vegetarian recipes, nutrition advice, and lifestyle information are important features of this magazine." All submissions must be consistent with the magazine mission statement. Adult submissions are very limited. Send SASE for submission guidelines and information about special departments and upcoming themes.

INK BLOT, 7180 McCliggot, Saginaw, MI 48609. Editor: Margaret Larkin. Published monthly. Subscriptions not available at this time, sample $1.

 Needs: Fiction, personal essays, articles, and poetry by young writers.

 Submission Guidelines: Short stories and articles up to 500 words. They must fit on one page. Poetry up to 50 lines. Include name, address, age, grade, and name of school on submission.

 Payment: One contributor's copy if SASE is included with submission.

 Comments: "*Ink Blot,* a monthly, six-page, 8½" x 11" newsletter, designed to provide an outlet for the creative talents of those wishing to contribute. It provides an opportunity for writers wishing to receive a byline upon publication."

*IOWA WOMAN, P.O. Box 680, Iowa City, IA 52244-0680. Editor: Joan Taylor. Published quarterly. Subscription $20, sample $6.95.

 Needs: Fiction, personal essays, articles, book reviews, and poetry by female writers.

 Submission Guidelines: Fiction up to 25 pages, especially with female protagonists. No specified length for nonfiction or poetry. Address poetry—up to five poems—to Debra Marquart, Poetry Editor. Type and double-space submissions and include a cover letter. Young writers should mention their age in the letter.

 Payment: $5 per page plus two contributor's copies.

 Comments: "We publish many writers and artists each year for their first time, and welcome the opportunity to provide a nationally recognized forum for women's literature and the arts." Though this is a competitive market, *Iowa*

Woman is interested in work by young women and also has a special column "Under 21" for young writers. The magazine also sponsors an annual fiction, creative nonfiction, and poetry contest with a December deadline. Send SASE for submission and contest guidelines.

KIDS' BYLINE: A MAGAZINE FOR KIDS BY KIDS, P.O. Box 1838, Frederick, MD 21702. 301-695-5963. Fax: 301-845-7959. Published bimonthly. Subscription $15.

> **Needs:** Fiction, nonfiction, and poetry by students grades 2–12.
>
> **Submission Guidelines:** Include author's name, address, phone number, and age on manuscripts. School name is optional. Seasonal material should be submitted four months in advance.
>
> **Payment:** Three contributor's copies.

KID'S WORLD, 1300 Kicker Road, Tuscaloosa, AL 35404. 205-553-2284. E-mail: dkm.alageol@genie.com. Editor: Morgan Kopaska-Merkel. Published quarterly. Subscription $3, sample $1.50. (Make checks payable to David Kopaska-Merkel.)

> **Needs:** Fiction and poetry by writers under age 18.
>
> **Submission Guidelines:** Fiction from 75–500 words. Include name, address, and age on submission.
>
> **Payment:** One contributor's copy.

*LISTEN MAGAZINE, 55 West Oak Ridge Drive, Hagerstown, MD 21740. 301-791-7000, ext. 2534. Fax: 301-790-9734. Editor: Lincoln Steed. Published monthly. Subscription $24.97, sample $1 and SASE.

> **Needs:** Teen-oriented articles and stories. Five basic types of articles appear in *Listen:* narratives, factuals, positive alternative, personalities and organizations, and self-help and social skills.
>
> **Submission Guidelines:** Submissions should be 1,000–1,200 words. Include author's social security number. Encourages submission on disk.
>
> **Payment:** $.05–$.10 per word.
>
> **Comments:** "*Listen* encourages development of good habits and high ideals of physical, social, and mental health. It bases its editorial philosophy of primary drug prevention on total abstinence from alcohol and drugs."

THE LOUISVILLE REVIEW, Children's Corner, 315 Bingham Humanities, University of Louisville, Louisville, KY 40292. 502-852-6801. Editors: Sena Jeter Naslund, Karen J. Mann. Published biannually. Sample $4.

> **Needs:** Fiction and poetry from students grades K–12 with "unusually fresh imagery, striking metaphors and natural rhythms" for "Children's Corner."
>
> **Submission Guidelines:** Include author's name, address, and parental permission to publish.
>
> **Comments:** "The Children's Corner" is a regular feature of this journal.

MAJESTIC BOOKS, P.O. Box 19097, Johnston, RI 02919. Fiction Editor: Cindy MacDonald. Sample $3.

> **Needs:** Fiction by writers under age 18 to be published in softcover bound anthologies of short stories by children.
>
> **Submission Guidelines:** Short stories up to 2,500 words. Include cover letter with age of author and SASE. "Originality is a must!"
>
> **Payment:** One free copy of the book.

THE McGUFFEY WRITER, 5128 Westgate Drive, Oxford, OH 45056. Published three times a year. Subscription $10, sample $3 and SASE with $.78 postage.

Needs: Fiction, essays, and poetry by students grades K–12.

Submission Guidelines: Typed or handwritten submissions accepted. Include author's name, address, grade, and school on every page. A teacher, parent, or responsible adult must sign the first page for verification.

Comments: Because of space limitations, the editor may take excerpts from any work longer than two double-spaced pages.

MERLYN'S PEN, P.O. Box 910, East Greenwich, RI 02818-0910. 800-247-2027. Fax: 401-885-5222. E-mail: Merlynspen@aol.com. Published annually in a reproducible format. Subscriptions $29.

Needs: Fiction, essays, reviews, and poetry by students grades 6–12.

Submission Guidelines: Authors may send up to three works at a time. Page limit is eighteen typed and double-spaced pages. Submissions must include Merlyn's Official Cover Sheet (available in magazine). $2 postage/handling fee for each submission if school or student subscribes; $5 fee for nonsubscribers. SASEs not required. Teachers may send one envelope of the work of several students, using one Cover Sheet per student and including the $2 fee per student.

Payment: $10 for works of one magazine page or more; $5 for shorter works. Three contributor's copies.

Comments: *Merlyn's Pen* responds to every writer with a constructive critique. *Merlyn's Pen* also offers "The Merlyn's Pen Literary Magazine Contest and Critique" as well as "The Merlyn's Pen Mentors in Writing Program." Contact above address for more information.

THE NAKED PLANET, A Small Literary Journal with a Big Purpose, Suite 577, 9461 Charleville Blvd., Beverly Hills, CA 90212. Editor: Joan Lobenfeld. Published quarterly. Sample $1.

Needs: Fiction, poetry, and "anything creative" by writers ages 13–19.

Submission Guidelines: Short stories to 1,200 words. Poetry to fifteen lines. Include name, address, phone number, and age on manuscripts.

Payment: Contributor's copies.

Comments: *The Naked Planet* also includes articles by teachers on writing and creativity.

*NEGATIVE CAPABILITY, 62 Ridgelawn Drive East, Mobile, AL 36608. 334-343-6163. Fax: 334-344-8478. E-mail: necap@aol.com. Editor: Sue Walker.

Needs: Fiction and poetry.

Submission Guidelines: Send one story or three to five poems at a time. Include name and address and phone/fax/e-mail address on manuscript. Include SASE.

Comments: *Negative Capability* also sponsors poetry and fiction contests. Send SASE for more information. *Capability News* (published monthly, $7 a year) offers articles on writing and information on various national writing contests.

THE NEW GIRL TIMES, 215 West 84th Street, New York, NY 10024. 212-873-2132 or 800-560-7625. E-mail: Nugrltim@aol.com. Editor: Miriam Hipsh. Published monthly. Subscription $12.

Needs: Articles, reviews, and poetry by girls.

Submission Guidelines: Send SASE for list of possible article topics. Suggested topics include animal rights, sexism and racism in schools, being a tomboy, young activists for social change, etc. Editor Miriam Hipsh welcomes calls from girls at the above 800 number to discuss other possibilities. Include name, address, phone, and age on all submissions.

Payment: Free subscription to the magazine.

Comments: Girls whose work is published are considered reporters on the newspaper.

*NEW MOON: THE MAGAZINE FOR GIRLS AND THEIR DREAMS, P.O. Box 3620, Duluth, MN 55803-3620. 218-728-5507. Fax: 218-728-0314. E-mail: newmoon@newmoon.duluth.mn.us. Published six times a year. Subscription $25, sample $6.50.

Needs: Fiction, articles, essays, reviews, and poetry for girls ages 8–14.

Submission Guidelines: There are many departments which young writers can contribute to including "Herstory," "Global Village," "Dream A Dream," and "Check It Out." Send SASE for submission guidelines and upcoming editorial themes. Include name, age, and address on submission.

Comments: An editorial board of girls ages 8–14 makes the final decisions about material appearing in *New Moon.*

*OATMEAL STUDIOS, P.O. Box 138-MA6, Rochester, VT 05767-0138. 800-628-6325. Fax: 802-767-9890. Editor: Dawn Abraham.

Needs: Humorous greeting card and notepad ideas that appeal to a range of interests and ages.

Submission Guidelines: Submit original lines on 3" x 5" index cards, one idea per card. Put both outside and inside message on one side of card. Include name and address on the back of each card. Type or print neatly. Include SASE.

Payment: $75 for each idea.

Comments: Oatmeal Studios will accept a batch of cards from a class of students. Put all the ideas from a class together and submit with a short note introducing the class. Contact above address for specific guidelines and samples.

*OUTDOOR ACTION, 774 S. Placentia Ave., Placentia, CA 92870. 714-572-2255. Fax: 714-572-1864. Editor: Dan Sanchez. Published nine times a year.

Needs: How-to articles on outdoor activities including camping, mountain biking, canoeing, and hiking.

Submission Guidelines: Articles 1,500–3,000 words. Send queries to Marie Loggia.

Payment: $350–$800.

Comments: *Outdoor Action* is a competitive market, but its focus on young outdoor enthusiasts makes it a possible market for excellent writers with real knowledge of and experience in a particular outdoor activity.

*OUT OF THE CRADLE, Box 129, South Paris, ME 04281-0129. 207-743-6738. Happenings Editor: Sandra K. Dennis. Published quarterly. Subscription $16, sample $4.50 plus $1.50 postage and handling.

Needs: For "Happenings" Department, a special section of the journal reserved for student work—stories, essays, and poetry.

Submission Guidelines: Stories and essays up to 500 words. Teachers who send student work from assigned topics should send no more than three of the best pieces.

Comments: *Out of the Cradle* has a special interest in student writers as evidenced by the "Happenings" Department. However, older students may also want to individually submit high quality fiction and poetry to other sections of the journal. Send SASE for those guidelines.

*POETRY USA, Fort Mason Center, Landmark Building D, San Francisco, CA 94123. Published quarterly. Subscription $10.

Needs: Poetry, particularly "shorter, more accessible poems."

Submission Guidelines: Submit no more than three poems. Include name, address, phone number, and e-mail address if available. Include SASE.

Comments: *Poetry USA* is a publication of the National Poetry Association at phone 415-776-6602 or Web site http://204.162.243.25/national_poetry/npahome.html.

RASPBERRY PUBLICATIONS, INC., P.O. Box 925, Westerville, OH 43086-6925. 800-759-7171. Fax: 614-899-6147.

Needs: Book-length manuscripts written and illustrated by children from pre-school through high school. These works can be fiction or nonfiction.

Submission Guidelines: Picture books must contain a minimum of sixteen pages; non-picture books must contain a minimum of forty-eight pages. Because there are very specific guidelines for the preparation of a book-length manuscript, students should send SASE for Writing Guidelines. Authors must also enclose a Manuscript Submission Form.

Payment: Publishing contract and royalties.

Comments: There are no deadlines for manuscript entries. Raspberry Publications also sponsors "Raspberry Crime Files" and "Raspberry Romances," two series designed for longer fiction manuscripts. See Writing Guidelines for more information.

READ, "In Your Own Write," 245 Long Hill Road, P.O. Box 2791, Middletown, CT 06457-9291. 860-638-2400. Eighteen issues per year. Subscription $8.75 (for ten issues or more), $29.95 (for one).

Needs: Poetry and very, very short stories for students ages 11–18 for the "In Your Own Write" column.

Submission Guidelines: Stories should be no longer than one page. Pieces involving humor or suspense are of special interest. Include name, address, age, school name and address, and teacher's name. Do not send SASE as no materials are returned.

Comments: *Read* also sponsors a number of writing contests. See Contest List.

*ROSEBUD, P.O. Box 459, Cambridge, WI 53523. 608-423-9780. Editor: Roderick Clark. Published quarterly. Subscription $18, sample $5.50 plus $1.25 postage.

Needs: Fiction, articles, profiles, and poetry that "fit the tone" of rotating departments. Departments include "Mothers, Daughters, Wives" (relationships), "Anything Goes" (humor), "Voices in Other Rooms" (historic or of other culture), "The Jeweled Prize" (concerning love), "I Hear Music" (music), and many others.

Submission Guidelines: Fiction and nonfiction from 1,200–1,800 words. Type and double-space manuscripts, and include author's name at the top of each page. Include SASE.

Payment: $45–$195 plus two contributor's copies.

Comments: Send SASE for complete list of departments and submission guidelines.

*SEVENTEEN, 850 Third Avenue, New York, NY 10022. 212-407-9700. Fax: 212-935-4237. Features/Fiction Editor: Joe Bargmann. Published monthly.

Needs: Fiction relevant to teenagers and articles on subjects of interest to teenagers. Also for "Voice," the section of *Seventeen* devoted to young writers, true stories, opinion essays, personal essays, book reviews, humorous pieces, and poetry.

Submission Guidelines: Fiction from 1,000 to 4,000 words for readers ages 13–21. Type, double-space and include SASE. Send to "Fiction Editor." Nonfiction from 800 to 2,500 words. Type, double-space, and include SASE. Include phone number. Send to "Articles Editor." "Voice" submissions should be no more than six pages. Send no more than three poems. Include name, address, birth date, and phone number as well as SASE. Send to "Voice." "'Voice' is your section—a chance for you to speak about what matters to you in your own individual style."

Payment: Fiction, $500–$1,500. Articles, payment rate varies.

Comments: *Seventeen* also sponsors an annual fiction contest for young writers. See Contest List.

*SHADOW, P.O. Box 5464, Santa Rosa, CA 95402. 707-542-7114. E-mail: brianwts.@aol.com. Submissions Editor: Lisa M. Boone. Published quarterly. Sample $7.50.

Needs: Fiction focusing on teenagers and teenage issues.

Submission Guidelines: Submit stories under 10,000 words. Include cover letter with name, address, phone number, Social Security number, brief biography, and any previous publications. Include SASE.

Payment: Two to three contributor's copies.

Comments: *Shadow* will frequently comment on work if a SASE is included.

SHARDS, Quabbin Poetry Club, Quabbin Regional High School, P.O. Box 429, 800 South Street, Barre, MA 01005. 978-355-4651. Published annually.

Needs: Poetry by Massachusetts high school students.

Submission Guidelines: Send up to five poems. Include author's name and name of school in upper right-hand corner. Include Submission Form with manuscript. (Call or send SASE for form.) Do not include SASE. Only accepted works will be acknowledged.

Payment: Two contributor's copies. All poems are eligible for five $10 awards for excellence.

Comments: The deadline for submission is usually mid-April with publication in September. Call or write for specific information.

*SHOW AND TELL MAGAZINE, 2593 North 140 West, Sunset, UT 84015. Editor: Donna Clark. Published monthly. Subscription $22 for twelve issues and six special fiction collections.

    Needs: Fiction (no horror) and poetry.

    Submission Guidelines: Fiction preferably no more than 2,000 words. Include word count and genre on manuscripts. Include cover letter with some information about where your story came from, why you wrote it, etc. Include a four-to twelve-line biography as it would read if it were published. Poetry up to thirty lines. Include name and address on each page. Include a four-line biography. No cover letter is necessary. Include SASE.

    Payment: Fiction, $5. Poetry, one contributor's copy.

    Comments: *Show and Tell* writes personal reply letters and critiques every submission. *Show and Tell* also sponsors two annual contests. See Contest List.

*SKIPPING STONES: A MULTICULTURAL CHILDREN'S MAGAZINE, P.O. Box 3939, Eugene, OR 97403. 541-342-4956. Published five times a year. Subscription $20, sample $5.

    Needs: Fiction, essays, and poetry that promote "multicultural awareness, nature and ecology, social issues, peace and non-violence." For readers ages 7–18.

    Submission Guidelines: Fiction and nonfiction to 750 words. Poetry to thirty lines. Submission in languages other than English encouraged. Submissions may be typed or handwritten. Include cover letter, with focus on author's cultural background, dreams for the future, etc. Include SASE.

    Payment: One to three contributor's copies.

    Comments: *Skipping Stones* is particularly interested in work by students in social studies, geography, and language arts classes and in cultural and community centers. Also interested in submissions by foreign exchange students.

SKYLARK, "Young Writers" Department, c/o Purdue University, Calumet, 2200-169th Street, Hammond, IN 46323. Published annually. Single copy $7.

    Needs: Fiction, essays, and poetry by students for "Young Writers" section.

    Submission Guidelines: Stories and essays should be short. Send no more than six poems. Type and double-space submissions. Include author's name, address, age, and name of school in upper left-hand corner of first page. Submissions from those under eighteen years old should include a statement from teacher or parent verifying the originality of the work. Include SASE. No simultaneous submissions. Manuscripts read from November 15–April 30.

    Payment: One contributor's copy.

    Comments: The "Young Writers Section" is a regular feature of *Skylark*.

*THE SOW'S EAR POETRY REVIEW, 19535 Pleasant View Drive, Abingdon, VA 24211-6827. 540-628-2651. Editor: Larry K. Richman. Published quarterly.

    Needs: Poetry by young writers.

    Submission Guidelines: Send one to five poems. On each page, include name, address, name of school, and grade. Include a cover letter with some information about the author—interests, activities, etc. Include SASE.

Comments: "In most regular issues of our magazine . . . we print two or three poems by young poets. We receive many more poems than we can print, by both young and adult poets."

STONEFLOWER LITERARY JOURNAL, 1824 N. New Braunfels, Suite 191, San Antonio, TX 78209. Editor: Brenda Davidson Shaddox.

Needs: Fiction and poetry by young writers to age sixteen for a section of the journal devoted to writing by young people.

Submission Guidelines: Fiction to 1,000 words. Poetry to twenty-five lines. Submissions may be typed or handwritten. Include name, address, age, school, and grade on the top of all manuscripts. Send a separate biographical page with author's name in upper left-hand corner. Include information on hobbies, participation in school activities, prior publications or honors, etc. Include SASE.

Payment: Fiction, $5. Poetry, $2. If submission is part of a class project, a copy of the journal will be provided to the school library.

Comments: "Submissions will be reviewed according to age group (work by a child of ten will only be compared to works by other children in that general age group and not to works by 16-year-olds, for example)." *Stoneflower* will accept submissions from a number of students by a teacher.

STONE SOUP, The Magazine by Young Writers and Artists, P.O. Box 83, Santa Cruz, CA 95063. 800-447-4569 or 408-426-5557. Fax: 408-426-1161. E-mail: gmandel@stonesoup.com. Web: http://www.stonesoup.com/. Editor: Gerry Mandel. Published five times a year. Subscription $24, sample $4.

Needs: Fiction, personal narratives, literary essays, book reviews, and poetry by young writers ages 8–13.

Submission Guidelines: Fiction and nonfiction from 150–2,500 words. Send cover letter, including information on how the author came to write the piece. Include SASE.

Payment: $10 plus two contributor's copies.

*STORY, 1507 Dana Ave., Cincinnati, OH 45207. 513-531-2222. Fax: 513-531-1843. Editor: Lois Rosenthal. Published quarterly. Subscription, $22, sample $6.95, 9" x 12" SASE plus $2.40 postage and handling.

Needs: Fiction of the highest quality.

Submission Guidelines: Stories to 8,000 words. Include SASE. Send SASE for submission guidelines.

Payment: $1,000 for stories, $750 for short shorts, plus five contributor's copies.

Comments: This is a highly competitive market. *Story* also sponsors a variety of fiction contests. See the publication for detailed information.

*THE SUN, A Magazine of Ideas, 107 N. Roberson Street, Chapel Hill, NC 27516-9908. 919-942-5282. Editor: Sy Safransky. Published monthly. Subscription $32, sample $3.50.

Needs: Fiction, essays, opinion pieces, interviews, and poetry.

Submission Guidelines: Fiction and nonfiction to 8,000 words maximum. Submit up to six poems. Use standard format. No simultaneous submissions.

Payment: Fiction, $200. Nonfiction, $100–$500. Poetry, $25. Also two contributor's copies and a complimentary one year subscription.

Comments: Although *The Sun* is a competitive adult market, it may be an appropriate market for especially talented older students.

*'**TEEN MAGAZINE,** 6420 Wilshire Blvd., Los Angeles, CA 90048-5515. 213-782-2950. Fax: 213-782-2660. Editor: Roxanne Camron. Published monthly. Sample $2.50.

Needs: Fiction and nonfiction related to teen interests and problems.

Submission Guidelines: Stories from 2,500–4,000 words typed and double-spaced with female, teenage protagonist. For nonfiction, query in quick summary or outline form with SASE. Send resume and published clips. "Subject matter and vocabulary should be appropriate for an average 16-year-old reader."

Payment: Fiction, $200 and up.

TEEN VOICES, c/o Women Express, Inc., P.O. Box 116, Boston, MA 02115. 617-262-2434. Fax: 617-262-8937. E-mail: womenexp@teenvoices.com. Web: http://www.teenvoices.com. Published quarterly. Subscription $20. Also group rates and "Teens on Tight Budgets" rates available. Contact above address.

Needs: Fiction, essays, articles, letters, and poetry for, by, and about teenage women.

Submission Guidelines: Include name, address, phone number, and age on manuscript. Attach a brief biography and photo. If submission should be published without author's name, indicate that.

Comments: "Young adult women are encouraged to express themselves in creative ways that nurture confidence and self-esteem."

TEXAS YOUNG WRITERS' NEWSLETTER, P.O. Box 942, Adkins, TX 78101-0942. E-mail: tywn1@aol.com. Editor: Susan Currie. Published nine times a year. Subscription $10, sample $1.

Needs: Fiction, essays, and poetry by young writers ages 12–19.

Submission Guidelines: Short stories, personal experience and humorous pieces 3–4 pages long. Essays of a more serious nature 3–4 pages long. Poetry up to 55 lines. Type and double-space. Include brief biography and SASE.

Payment: Five contributor's copies for fiction and nonfiction. Two contributor's copies for poetry.

Comments: *Texas Young Writers' Newsletter* also includes articles written by adults for young writers about writing and publishing.

***THEMA,** Box 74109, Metairie, LA 70033-4109. 504-887-1263. Editor: Virginia Howard. Published three times a year. Subscription $16, sample or single issue $8.

Needs: Fiction and poetry related to the premise specified for the particular issue.

Submission Guidelines: Short stories fewer than 20 double-spaced pages. Submit no more than three poems per theme. For stories and poems, "the premise must be an integral part of the plot, not necessarily the central theme but not merely incidental." Previous themes have included: "A visit from the imp," and "Too proud to ask." State premise on title page. Do not put author's name on any page beyond page 1. Send SASE for upcoming themes and deadlines.

Payment: Short story, $25. Short-short story (up to 900 words), $10. Poetry, $10.

360° MAGAZINE, P.O. Box 25356, Washington, DC 20007. 202-628-1836. Fax: 202-628-1843. E-mail: mag360@aol.com. Published three times a year. Distributed free to over 1500 school and youth organizations. Subscription $10 for students, $15 all others.

Needs: Fiction, essays, articles, opinion pieces, and reviews by teenage writers.

Submission Guidelines: Submit manuscripts to one of four departments: "Degrees"—500–700 word pieces, personal experience and opinions, related to issue's theme; "Endpoints"—500–700 word opinion pieces on controversial issues; "Rhythms"—reviews on CDs, bands, movies, and books; "Tangents"—short stories, creative essays, lyrics, and poetry. Send submissions to above address *Attn: Submissions*. Send SASE for upcoming themes and submission guidelines.

Comments: "*360°* is the nation's only opinion magazine written and edited entirely by teens. Today more than ever young people need a forum to discuss social issues that concern them." Students can also apply for a position as Youth Editor on the magazine's editorial board.

*THUMBPRINTS, 928 Gibbs Street, Caro, MI 48723. Editor: Janet Ihle. Published monthly. Subscription $9, sample $.75.

Needs: Fiction, short articles, and poetry, especially around stated themes. Submissions, however, are not limited to the themes.

Submission Guidelines: Fiction and articles to 500 words. Short fillers from 50–100 words. Poetry to 32 lines. Articles are more likely to be accepted if they pertain to writing or to the monthly theme. Send SASE for theme list and guidelines. Previous themes have included: "The One Who Got Away," "Winter White," and "Thoughts on Writing."

Payment: One contributor's copy.

THE 21ST CENTURY, Box 30, Newton, MA 02161. 617-964-6800. E-mail: The 21stCen@aol.com. Published monthly. Distributed to 1,700 high schools throughout New England and New York.

Needs: Fiction, nonfiction (in various categories, see below), and poetry by high school students.

Submission Guidelines: Label submission according to category: Fiction, Nonfiction, Opinion, Community Service, Review, Science and Technology, College Essay. Include name, address, phone number, age, and name of high school on each submission. Work may be published anonymously if so requested, but name, address, etc. must be on the submission. Submissions should be typed and under 2,500 words. No more than one poem per page with name, address, etc. on each page. Include statement, written and signed, stating "This will certify that the above work is completely original." No manuscripts will be returned. Include SASE for *The 21st Century* sticker and free Pepsi coupon. One per student per month.

Payment: *The 21st Century* Woody Pen and a gift certificate from Strawberries and CVS/pharmacy.

Comments: *The 21st Century* also publishes *The 21st Century Poetry Journal* three times a year in fall, winter, and spring. Poetry submissions may be published in either *The 21st Century* or the *Poetry Journal.* The same submission guidelines and payment apply.

TYKETOON YOUNG AUTHOR PUBLISHING COMPANY, 7417 Douglas Lane, Fort Worth, TX 76180. 817-581-2876.

> **Needs:** Books (fiction, nonfiction, and poetry) written and illustrated by students in grades 1–8.
>
> **Submission Guidelines:** "Students should write for their own age group to be competitive." Students/classes may collaborate on manuscript. Bilingual Spanish manuscripts are especially encouraged. Typed or handwritten manuscripts of any length acceptable, unbound, on any size paper. One-third or more of the pages should have illustrations, on one side of the paper only. Send for SASE for very specific guidelines on manuscript preparation. Include SASE large enough to hold book manuscript for manuscript to be returned.
>
> **Payment:** Cash scholarships paid as a royalty on each book.
>
> **Comments:** Tyketoon Publishing Company will offer a personal publisher's critique on any manuscript not selected, if SASE large enough for manuscript is included.

*WATERWAYS: POETRY IN THE MAINSTREAM, 393 St. Paul's Avenue, Staten Island, NY 10304-2127. 718-442-7429. Fax: 718-442-4978. Editors: Richard Spiegal, Barbara Fisher. Published 11 times a year. Subscription $20, sample $2.60.

> **Needs:** Poetry, by poets of all ages, related to monthly themes.
>
> **Submission Guidelines:** Rarely publishes haiku or rhyming poetry. Send SASE for upcoming themes.
>
> **Payment:** One contributor's copy.

WHOLE NOTES, P.O. Box 1374, Las Cruces, NM 88004. 505-382-7446. Editor: Nancy Peters Hastings. Published biannually. Subscription $6, sample, $3.

> **Needs:** Poetry by young writers.
>
> **Submission Guidelines:** All poetic forms acceptable. Submit 2–5 poems. Include name, address, and grade on submissions. Include SASE. No multiple submissions.

*WORCESTER MAGAZINE, "First Person," 172 Shrewsbury Street, Worcester, MA 01604. Published weekly.

> **Needs:** Fiction, nonfiction, and poetry.
>
> **Submission Guidelines:** Fiction and nonfiction to 1,000 words. No manuscripts returned.
>
> **Payment:** Cash payment.

THE WRITE NEWS, Newsletter of the Young Writers Club, P.O. Box 5504, Coralville, IA 52241. E-mail: kidsclubs@aol.com. Published 6 times a year. Club membership (includes subscription) $14.95 a year.

> **Needs:** Fiction, nonfiction, and poetry by writers ages 7–13 who are members of the Young Writers Club.
>
> **Submission Guidelines:** Typed or handwritten manuscript acceptable. Include photo (prefers school photo) and SASE.

Comments: Membership in the Young Writers Club includes membership card and certificate, club pencil, and subscription to *The Write News*, which contains articles on writing and publishing as well as work by young writers. The newsletter also sponsors free contests with prizes for club members.

*WRITERS' INTERNATIONAL FORUM, P.O. Box 516, Tracyton, WA 98393-0516. Editor: Sandra E. Haven. Published bimonthly. Subscription $14, sample $3.50.

Needs: Fiction and essays.

Submission Guidelines: Fiction to 2000 words (500–1500 preferred). "No vignettes, slices-of-life, or character sketches." Essays from 400 to 1,200 words that "make a point or offer some insight." Humor is encouraged. No simultaneous or multiple submissions. Include name and address in upper left-hand corner and word count in upper right-hand corner of page 1. Number pages. Type "End" at bottom of last page. Include cover letter stating the piece's proposed audience and brief information about the author and his or her writing experience. Include SASE.

Payment: $5 (or more for exceptional material) and two contributor's copies.

Comments: *Writers' International Forum* also publishes periodically a special "Juniors Edition" with stories and essays for, about, and/or by writers ages 8–16. Manuscripts for this edition should be marked "for Juniors Edition" and should indicate intended age group. *Writers' International Forum* provides a written critique of manuscripts submitted by subscribers.

THE WRITERS' SLATE, Department of English, East Carolina University, Greenville, NC 27858-4353. Co-editors: Dr. F. Todd Goodson, Lori Atkins Goodson. Published three times a year. Subscription $10.95.

Needs: Fiction, essays, articles, book reviews, and poetry by students grades K–12.

Submission Guidelines: Include name, address, grade, school name and address, and teacher's name on submission.

Comments: *The Writers' Slate* also includes "Conversations," interviews with authors of children's and young adult literature, and "In the Classroom," suggestions for using published writing to encourage student writing.

WRITES OF PASSAGE, Editorial Dept., 817 Broadway, 6th Floor, New York, NY 10003. 212-473-7564. E-mail: WPUSA@aol.com. Web: http://www.writes.org. Published biannually. Subscription $12, sample issue $6.

Needs: Fiction and poetry by writers ages 12–19.

Submission Guidelines: Send up to five poems and/or two short stories. Stories up to five typed, double-spaced pages. Include name, address, phone number, school name and address, and a brief biography (age, interests, etc.) and SASE. Writers may include a photo.

Payment: Two contributor's copies.

Comments: Submissions are considered for both the printed magazine and the Web site. Teachers may submit multiple student submissions in one package. A Teacher's Guide is available with a class subscription.

WRITING!, Student Writing, 900 Skokie Boulevard, Suite 200, Northbrook, IL 60062-4028. 847-205-3000. Fax: 847-564-8197. E-mail: Writing!@weekly reader.com. Web: http://www.weeklyreader.com. Published seven times a year, September-May. Subscription (minimum 15) $8.65 per student.

Needs: Fiction, essays, book reviews, and poetry for Student Writing department by students grades 6–12.

Submission Guidelines: Fiction and essays up to 1,000 words. Include name, address, grade, school name and address, and teacher's name. Include SASE for response.

Comments: *Writing!* includes articles on the craft of writing as well as writing challenges and prompts. The magazine also sponsors contests. See September issue for information or contact above address.

*XTREME: THE MAGAZINE OF EXTREMELY SHORT FICTION, P.O. Box 678383, Orlando, FL 32867-8383. E-mail: rhowiley@aol.com. Editor: Rho Wiley. Published biannually. Sample copy (and fiction guidelines) for 9" x 12" SASE and two first-class stamps.

Needs: Stories of exactly 250 words.

Submission Guidelines: Stories must be exactly 250 words. Include cover letter and SASE. No simultaneous submissions.

Payment: Three contributor's copies.

*YM, 685 3rd Ave., New York, NY, 10017. 212-878-8644. Fax: 212-286-0935. Senior editor: Stephanie Dolgoff. Published monthly. Sample: $2.50.

Needs: First-person articles for female readers ages 14–21. Focus on overcoming obstacles or solving problems.

Submission Guidelines: Articles up to 2,000 words. Guidelines for SASE.

Payment: $.50–$.75 per word for unsolicited articles 1,200–2,000 words.

YOUNG VOICES, P.O. Box 2321, Olympia, WA 98507. 360-357-4683. Editors: Gwen Anderson, Mark Shetterly. Published six times a year. Subscription $20, sample $4.

Needs: Writing by students in elementary through high school. Fiction and essays from 600–3,000 words. Also book reviews and poetry.

Submission Guidelines: Query first, describing story idea. No unsolicited manuscripts. Include name, address, phone number, grade, and school name in letter. Include SASE.

Payment: $5 and contributor's copies.

The Contest List

The Contest List is an alphabetical listing of writing contests. Some are sponsored by magazines, journals, and newspapers; others by various public and private organizations and companies. Each listing begins with the name, address, phone and fax number (when available) of the contest and/or group sponsoring it, followed by a brief description of the contest. The section called "Guidelines" gives information about the contest, including eligibility requirements, entry fees, and deadlines. "Prizes" describes the awards for winning entries. The final section, "Comments," includes any other additional information that may be helpful to teachers and young writers.

A few words of advice and caution to students interested in entering writing contests:

1) Always send a SASE for up-to-date contest information and entry forms. Although care has been taken to ensure that the following information is accurate at this time, contests, even more so than publications, are very much subject to change, and writers should always get the most recent contest information before submitting manuscripts. Deadlines especially change from year to year.

2) Always follow the rules of the contest *exactly*. Any variation may cause an entry to be disqualified. Be particularly aware of the deadline.

3) Consider the cost of the contest, if there is one. If an entry fee seems too expensive, look for another contest/market.

4) Unless otherwise specified, writers should assume that only original, unpublished manuscripts may be submitted. The only exception would be for works that have been published in small, in-school publications.

THE ACORN, 1530 7th Street, Rock Island, IL 61201. Series of seven student contests throughout the year. Send SASE for themes and deadlines.
    Guidelines: Prose submissions of no more than 300 words. Include name, address, and age or grade on entry. Entry fee: Three $.32 stamps per contest.
    Prizes: One year subscription to *The Acorn* in each of the following grade groups: K–2, 3–6, 7–8, and 9–12. One winner will be chosen for each group.
    Comments: Entry into contests serves as permission to publish winning entries.

*AIM: AMERICA'S INTERCULTURAL MAGAZINE, P.O. Box 20554, Chicago, IL 60620. 312-874-6184. Short fiction contest for unpublished story that "embodies our goals of furthering the brotherhood of man through the written word."
    Guidelines: Maximum length 4,000 words. Type entry. Deadline: August 15.
    Prizes: $100 and publication in fall issue.
    Comments: *Aim* especially encourages entries by new writers.

AMERICAN HISTORY COMPETITION, Dongan Patent Lodge #1134, Box 441, Medford, NY 11763. 516-588-6244. Historical short fiction, biographies, and research papers, especially on the Masonic teachings of freedom, tolerance, and brotherhood.

   Guidelines: Open to high school and college students. Entries up to 5,000 words. Type and double-space manuscripts. Deadline: April 19. "Submissions will be evaluated on creativity, effort, thought and originality."

   Prizes: $100 for first prize. Smaller cash awards for runners-up. All submissions will be considered for publication in the lodge's journal.

AMHAY LITERARY CONTEST, The American Morgan Horse Association, P.O. Box 960, Shelburne, VT 05482-0960. 802-985-4944. Fax: 802-985-8897. Literary contest, essay or poetry, connected to Morgan horses, for writers under the age of 22 by October 1. Send SASE for specific theme and deadline and entry form.

   Guidelines: Essays to 1,000 words, or poetry. Include entry form. Deadline: October 1. Entries judged on style, originality, grammar, spelling, and punctuation. No manuscripts returned.

   Prizes: $25 to the winner in both categories. Ribbons awarded to first through fifth place winners in each category.

THE ARMCHAIR SAILOR ANNUAL WRITING COMPETITION, 543 Thames Street, Newport, RI 02840. E-mail: armchair@seabooks.com. Essay contest with special category for writers under the age of 16 (as of July 1).

   Guidelines: Essays of 2,000–6,000 words on "the sea and man's relationship to it." Type in 10pt, double-spaced with 1" margins. Number pages at bottom center. Do not staple pages. Include cover page marked "Armchair Sailor Annual SeaStory Competition" with title, author's name, address, phone, and short biography underneath. Include verification of age. No manuscripts returned. Entry fee: $15. Deadline: July 1.

   Prizes: $500 for first prize in junior division.

THE AYN RAND INSTITUTE ESSAY CONTEST, *Anthem* Essay Contest, P.O. Box 6099, Inglewood, CA 90312. Essay contest for 9th and 10th graders based on one of three topics related to Ayn Rand's *Anthem.* Send SASE for topics.

   Guidelines: Essays from 600–1,200 words. Include stapled cover sheet with name, address, name and address of high school, topic selected (#1, 2, or 3), year of graduation from high school, and (optional) name of teacher most helpful in writer's development of skills. No manuscripts returned. Deadline: April 1. Winners notified by May 31. Submissions judged on style, content, and an understanding of the philosophical meaning of the novelette.

   Prizes: First prize $1,000. Ten second prizes of $200. Twenty third prizes of $100.

   Comments: A Teacher's Guide to *Anthem* and contest flyers are available at no cost from The Ayn Rand Institute, P.O. Box 6004, Inglewood, CA 90312.

THE AYN RAND INSTITUTE ESSAY CONTEST, *Fountainhead* Essay Contest, P.O. Box 6004, Inglewood, CA 90312. Essay contest for 11th and 12th graders based on one of three topics related to Ayn Rand's *The Fountainhead.* Send SASE for topics.

Guidelines: Essays from 800–1,600 words. Include stapled cover sheet with name, address, name and address of high school, topic selected (#1, 2, or 3), year of graduation from high school, and (optional) name of teacher most helpful in writer's development of skills. No manuscripts returned. Deadline: April 15. Winners notified by May 31. Submissions judged on style, content, and an understanding of the philosophical meaning of the novel.

Prizes: First prize $5,000. Five second prizes of $1,000. Ten third prizes of $500.

Comments: A Teacher's Guide to *The Fountainhead* and contest flyers are available at no cost from The Ayn Rand Institute, P.O. Box 6004, Inglewood, CA 90312.

BAKER'S PLAYS HIGH SCHOOL PLAYWRITING CONTEST, 100 Chauncy Street, Boston, MA 02111. 617-482-1280. Fax: 617-482-7613. Playwriting contest for high school students. Plays "should be about the 'high school experience,' but may also be about any subject and of any length, so long as the play can be reasonably produced on the high school stage."

Guidelines: Include with the manuscript the signature of a sponsoring high school drama or English teacher. Manuscripts must be typed, firmly bound, and include SASE. Multiple submissions and co-authored plays are accepted. Deadline: January 31. Winners notified in May. "Awards are based on merit and if no submission warrants an award, no prizes will be given."

Prizes: First prize $500 and publication by Baker's Plays. Second prize $250 and Honorable Mention. Third prize $100 and Honorable Mention.

Comments: It is suggested that entries receive a production or public reading before they are submitted.

*BARBARA MANDIGO KELLY PEACE POETRY AWARDS. Send to: Nuclear Age Peace Foundation Peace Poetry Awards, 1187 Coast Village Road, Suite 123, Santa Barbara, CA 93108. 805-965-3443. Web: http://www.napf.org. Poetry contest that seeks "to encourage poets to explore some aspect of peace and the human spirit." Three divisions: Adult, Youth 13–18, and Youth 12 and under.

Guidelines: Send two typed copies of up to three poems of under 40 lines. For youth categories, include name, address, phone, and age in upper right-hand corner of one copy; the other copy should be anonymous. No manuscripts returned. Deadline: June 30.

Prizes: First prize in each youth category is $250.

*BULWER-LYTTON FICTION CONTEST, Department of English, San Jose State University, San Jose, CA 95192-0090. Annual contest that asks entrants to create the worst possible opening sentence to a novel in a variety of genres.

Guidelines: Submit sentence of any length (suggested length under 60 words) on an index card with the sentence on one side and the entrant's name, address, and phone number on the other. Entries are judged by genre—western, science fiction, mystery, romance, etc. Deadline: April 15.

Prizes: Computer equipment and possible publication.

BYLINE STUDENT CONTESTS. Send to: Student Page Contests, *Byline*, P.O. Box 130596, Edmond, OK 73013-0001. Monthly contests October-May with specific theme and genre for students grades 1–12. Send SASE or see magazine for listing. Subscription $20, sample copy $4.

Guidelines: All manuscripts must be typed. Include name, address, age, and grade in top right-hand corner of first page. Include teacher's signature at bottom of first page verifying originality of work. Entry fee: $1. No manuscripts returned.

Prizes: Cash payment and number of awards varies depending on contest. Usually three awards of $5–$25 plus publication.

CARING INSTITUTE ART OF CARING ESSAY CONTEST, Caring Institute, 513 C Street NE, Washington, DC 20002-5809. Essay contest for students grades 7–12.

Guidelines: Submit an essay or short story up to 1,000 words or a poem on a topic related to caring. The piece should express the writer's interpretation of caring. Include completed entry form. Deadline: November 22.

Prizes: Finalists will be named in each grade level and receive an award certificate. Three winners will be chosen from the finalists. First place receives a $100 savings bond; second place a $75 savings bond; third place a $50 savings bond.

Comments: The Caring Institute provides detailed information on its work and also information on photography and poster contests. Request materials at above address.

CYBERKIDS/CYBERTEENS CONTEST, 298 Fourth Avenue, #401, San Francisco, CA 94118. Fiction contest open to students ages 7–16 in two divisions (7–11 and 12–16).

Guidelines: Short stories up to 15 typed, double-spaced pages. Include entry form. One entry per person. Send SASE for entry form (may be photocopied). Deadline: December 31. Finalists will be published and voted on at cyberkids.com and cyberteens.com from mid-January to March.

Prizes: First prize receives a WebTV subscription and Sony or Philips set-top box, three software prizes, and $100. Second prize receives two software prizes and $50. Third prize receives one software prize and $25.

DISCOVER GOLD ESSAY CONTEST, The Gold Institute, 1112 16th Street N W, Suite 240, Washington, DC 20036. Essay contest for students grades 10–12 on the uses of gold.

Guidelines: Essays of 5–10 pages (exclusive of bibliography) should discuss the uses of gold in our daily life. Each essay should include at least five references from research sources. Type and double-space manuscripts with 1" margins. Include name, grade, address, phone, school name and location, teacher's name, and how entrant learned about the contest in the upper right-hand corner. No manuscripts returned. Deadline: April 15. Winners notified in May.

Prizes: First-place winner receives $750 and a U.S. Mint-issued one-ounce American Eagle gold bullion coin. Second-place winner receives $500 and the gold bullion coin. Third-place winner receives $250 and the gold bullion coin.

First- and second-place winners also receive a two-day trip to Washington, D.C. Each winner's school receives a $1,000 donation for the science department.

EF EDUCATIONAL TOURS. Send to: EF Ambassador Scholarship Program, EF Educational Tours, EF Center Boston, One Education Street, Cambridge, MA 02141-1883. 800-637-8222. E-mail: scholarships@ef.com. Web: http://www.eftours.com. Writing contest for students in North America in grades 9–12. Writers should submit an essay that "highlights their plan for global or local change."

Guidelines: Essays on a particular theme. Send SASE for specific guidelines and application. Deadline: January 31.

Prizes: Up to one student from each state selected to travel on a ten-day expenses-paid educational tour of Europe.

EMERSON COLLEGE JOURNALISM AWARDS, Emerson College, Office of Admission, Journalism Award, 100 Beacon Street, Boston, MA 02116-1596. 617-578-8600. Fax: 617-824-8609. E-mail: admission@emerson.edu. Web: http://www.emerson.edu/admiss. International writing competition for high school student journalists.

Guidelines: Students may submit one entry in each of the following categories: Newswriting, Feature Writing, and Editorial. Send photocopy or original. Include cover sheet with name, address, birth date, native language, school name and address, grade, name of newspaper faculty advisor, category/categories entered, URL of school's newspaper (if applicable). Deadline: April 1.

Prizes: First prize $250. Second prize $100. Third prize $50. Ten Runners-up and twenty-five Honorable Mentions will also be awarded.

EMERSON COLLEGE SECONDARY SCHOOL WRITING AWARDS, Emerson College, Office of Admission, Writing Award, 100 Beacon Street, Boston, MA 02116-1596. 617-578-8600. Fax: 617-824-8609. E-mail: admission@emerson.edu. Web: http://www.emerson.edu/admiss. International creative writing competition for high school students.

Guidelines: Submit fiction, essays, plays, and poetry, one entry per student. Fiction and essays to twenty pages. Poetry to three poems. Plays either the first act or entire one-act plays. Type and double-space entry. Include cover sheet with name, address, phone number and/or fax number, birth date, grade, school name and address, and name of current English teacher. No manuscripts returned. Deadline: March 31.

Prizes: First prize $250. Second prize $100. Third prize $50. Ten Runners-up will receive one-year subscription to *Ploughshares.* Twenty-five Honorable Mentions will receive one issue of *Ploughshares.*

*F/J WRITERS SERVICE CONTESTS, c/o F/J Writers Service, P.O. Box 22557, Kansas City, MO 64113-0557. Various writing contests open to all age groups. Includes Fall Fiction Contest. Also special Junior Writers Contest.

Guidelines: Send SASE for contest list, rules, and required Entry Form. No entry fees.

Prizes: Cash awards from $5–$100.

FULBRIGHT YOUNG ESSAYISTS AWARDS, Send to: Alliance for Young Artists & Writers, Inc., 555 Broadway, New York, NY 10012-3999. 212-343-6493.

Web: http://www.usia.gov/education/fulbright50/contest.htm. Essay contest open to students in grades 7–12.

Guidelines: Students select from three questions stated on the entry form which "explore international issues and cross-cultural experiences." Send or call for application, guidelines, and essay information. Deadline: January 19.

Prizes: Twelve scholarship awards, $500–$2,500 bonds redeemable upon graduation. Winners honored at a Washington, D.C., ceremony.

*GLIMMER TRAIN SHORT-STORY AWARD FOR NEW WRITERS, Glimmer Train Press, 710 SW Madison Street, Suite #504, Portland, OR 97205. 503-221-0836. Fax: 503-221-0837. Fiction contest "open to any writer whose fiction hasn't appeared in a nationally distributed publication with a circulation over 5,000."

Guidelines: Short stories from 1,200 to 7,500 words. Type and double-space manuscripts. Staple pages together. Include name, address, and phone number on first page. Write "Short-Story Award" on outside of envelope. No manuscripts returned. Entry fee: $11 for up to two stories mailed in same envelope. All entrants receive a copy of the issue in which the winning entry is published. Two contests: February/March and August/September. Contact for specific deadlines.

Prizes: First prize $1,200 and publication in *Glimmer Train Stories*, and 20 copies of that issue. Second prize $500. Third prize $300.

GUIDEPOSTS YOUNG WRITERS CONTEST, 16 East 34th Street, New York, NY 10016. 212-251-8100. Essay contest open to high school juniors and seniors.

Guidelines: Submit a *true*, first-person story to 1,200 words about a memorable or moving experience the author has had. Type and double-space manuscripts. Include name, address, phone number, and school name, address and phone number. Write "Young Writers Contest" on manuscript. No manuscripts returned. Deadline is usually the Monday after Thanksgiving. Send SASE for guidelines or see October issue of *Guideposts*.

Prizes: First prize: $6,000 college scholarship and portable electronic typewriter. Second prize: $5,000 college scholarship and portable electronic typewriter. Third prize: $4,000 and portable electronic typewriter. Fourth through Eighth prizes: $1,000 college scholarship and portable electronic typewriter. Ninth through Twenty-fifth prizes: Portable electronic typewriters.

*HIGHLIGHTS FOR CHILDREN, Fiction Contest, 803 Church Street, Honesdale, PA 18431. 717-253-1080. Editor: Kent L. Brown Jr. Annual fiction contest open to children and adults. Themes vary each year. Contact: Beth Troop.

Guidelines: Stories to 500 words for children to age 8, and stories to 900 words for children ages 9–12. Include SASE. Send SASE for guidelines and specific theme. Submit manuscripts between January 1 and February 28.

Prizes: Three $1,000 cash prizes and publication in *Highlights*.

THE HOWARD NEMEROV CREATIVE WRITING AWARDS, Washington University, Campus Box 1122, One Brookings Drive, St. Louis, MO 63130-4899. Fiction and poetry contest for high school juniors and seniors.

Guidelines: Each student may send a single entry. Type manuscript. Include name, address, social security number, school name and address, and genre (fiction or poetry) in upper right corner of each page. No manuscripts returned. Deadline: February 28. Awards announced in May.

Prizes: Three awards of $250 each in fiction. Three awards of $250 each in poetry.

*INTERNATIONAL IMITATION HEMINGWAY CONTEST, PEN Center West, 672 S. LaFayette Park Place, Suite 41, Los Angeles, CA 90057. 213-365-8500. Contest parodying the writing of Ernest Hemingway open to all writers.

Guidelines: Submit a one-page (500 word) parody of Hemingway. Piece must be funny and include a mention of Harry's Bar. Deadline: March 1.

Prizes: Winner receives round-trip airfare for two to Florence, Italy, for dinner at Harry's Bar & American Grill.

KAPLAN/NEWSWEEK "MY TURN" ESSAY CONTEST, 810 7th Avenue, New York, NY 10019-0767. Essay contest for students grades 9–12.

Guidelines: Send SASE for specific topic and entry form. Essays from 500–1,000 words. Type and double-space manuscripts. Staple entry form to essay. Put entrant's social security number in upper right-hand corner of each page. Do not include name on the essay. Deadline: March 7.

Prizes: Ten $1,000 college scholarships. First-prize winner also receives a free Kaplan PSAT/SAT/ACT course, book, or software product. Ten winners and twenty honorable mentions will be published in a Newsweek Education Program book.

KOREAN INFORMATION CENTER. Send to: Essay Contest, Korean Information Center, 2370 Massachusetts Ave., N. W., Washington, DC 20008. 800-841-3692. 202-797-6343. E-mail: korinfo@koreaemb.org. Essay contest open to high school students (grades 9–12) on topics that "encourage Americans to better understand the emergence of Korea in the modern world and America's relationship with Korea."

Guidelines: Send SASE for specific topics and application form. Essays to 750 words. Type and double-space manuscripts. No manuscripts returned. Essays "judged on the basis of topic interpretation, style, grammar and originality." Deadline: May 31. Winners notified in the summer.

Prizes: Grand prize $3,000 scholarship and one-week trip for two to Korea. First prize (2) $2,000 scholarship and electronic product. Second prize (5) $1,000 scholarship and electronic product. Third prize (10) $500 scholarship and electronic product.

Comments: This contest includes a separate category for teacher entries. Send SASE for topics and application form.

THE LONGMEADOW JOURNAL, c/o Robert and Rita Morton, 6750 Longmeadow Avenue, Lincolnwood, IL 60646. 312-726-9789. Short-story contest for writers between the ages of 10 and 19.

Guidelines: Short stories to 3,000 words. Type and double-space manuscripts. Include name, address, age, and school name. Include SASE. Deadline: December 31. Winners announced in May.

Prizes: First prize $175 and publication. Second prize $100 and publication. Five third prizes $50 and publication. Twenty stories will be published.

Comments: If the writer of a winning story includes the name and address of a teacher, librarian, dean, or advisor instrumental to him or her in entering the contest, that person will receive a special award of $50.

LOUISE LOUIS/EMILY F. BOURNE STUDENT POETRY AWARD, Poetry Society of America, 15 Gramercy Park, New York, NY 10003. 212-254-9628. Fax: 212-673-2352. Web: http://www.poetrysociety.com. Poetry contest for students grades 9–12.

    Guidelines: Submit poetry of any length. Include cover page with name, address, phone number, school name and address, name of award, and title, first line and number of lines of poem. Type award name in upper right corner of every poem submitted. Entry fee: $1 for single entry (payable to Poetry Society of America); $10 per high school for an unlimited number of student poems. No manuscripts returned. Submissions accepted October 1–December 21.

    Prizes: Awards will be given.

MARYKNOLL MAGAZINE STUDENT ESSAY CONTEST, Student Essay Contest, P.O. Box 308, Maryknoll, NY 10545-0308. Essay contest for students in grades 7–9 (Division I) and grades 10–12 (Division II).

    Guidelines: Write an essay of 500–750 words describing a peacemaker—yourself, someone you know, or someone you have read about. Describe why that person is a peacemaker and what he/she has done to promote peace. Type and double-space or handwrite manuscript and staple pages. Include name, grade, teacher's name, and school name, address, and phone. Include student's name on each page. Specify appropriate division. Deadline: December 1.

    Prizes: In each division, first prize is $1,000, second prize is $300, third prize is $150.

MAY FAMILY NATIONAL ART & WRITING CONTEST, United States Holocaust Memorial Museum, Attn: Art & Writing Contest, 100 Raoul Wallenberg Place SW, Washington, DC 20024-2150. Writing contest for students grades 7–12 designed to "help students consider aspects of Holocaust history that have contemporary resonance."

    Guidelines: Send SASE for specific theme and entry form. Submit writing (research paper, story, poem, essay, play, or newspaper article) of up to 2,000 words. Type and double-space manuscripts. Two age divisions: grades 7–9 and grades 10–12. Deadline: May 2.

    Prizes: First place is an expense-paid trip to the Holocaust Museum, a selection of books, a gift certificate to the Museum Shop, and a certificate of achievement. Second prize is a selection of books, a music CD, a gift certificate to the Museum Shop, and a certificate of achievement. Third prize is a selection of books, a gift certificate to the Museum Shop, and a certificate of achievement. Each of the winning schools will receive a gift certificate.

MISSISSIPPI VALLEY POETRY CONTEST, P.O. Box 3188, Rock Island, IL 61204. Poetry contest open to poets of all ages with special student division.

    Guidelines: Students may submit one to five poems, maximum 50 lines per poem, on any subject. Entry fee: $3. Include name, address, grade and school as of September of the year in which entering in top left-hand corner of each page. In top right-hand corner state "Student Division." No manuscripts returned. Entry period from January 1 to April 1.

Prizes: High school award $75. Junior high award $75. Elementary school award $50. Winners are invited to attend an Awards Night.

NANCY THORP MEMORIAL POETRY PRIZES, Hollins College, P.O. Box 9677, Roanoke, VA 24020-1677. 540-362-6317. Poetry contest for female high school or preparatory school juniors or seniors.

Guidelines: Submit no more than two poems, each on a separate sheet. Entries must be submitted by a member of the faculty or administration of author's school. Type manuscript, and include name, year of graduation from high school, faculty sponsor's name, school, and name and address of parents or guardians. No manuscripts returned. Deadline: December 13. Winners notified in February.

Prizes: First prize $50 and an all-expenses-paid trip to the Hollins campus to meet resident and visiting writers. Two second prizes of $25 each. Winning poems will be published in the spring issue of *Cargoes*, the literary magazine of Hollins College.

NATIONAL CHILDREN'S CREATIVE WRITING CAMPAIGN, Children's Creative Writing Awards, P.O. Box 999, Cooper Station, New York, NY 10276. 212-228-3041. Fax: 212-228-6574. Writing contest for students ages 4–14.

Guidelines: No specific guidelines for submissions, but stories are judged on originality, imagination, and plot. Request entry form at above address. Deadline: February 9.

Prizes: All entrants receive a Certificate of Creative Writing Excellence. Finalists and semi-finalists receive special personalized certificates and media recognition. Finalists receive a $100 U.S. Savings Bond and their schools receive contributions to the library.

NATIONAL COUNCIL OF TEACHERS OF ENGLISH (NCTE) ACHIEVEMENT AWARDS IN WRITING. Send to: Achievement Awards in Writing Program, NCTE, 1111 W. Kenyon Road, Urbana, IL 61801-1096. 800-369-6283 or 217-328-3870. Ext. 221. Annual writing competition for juniors in high school sponsored by the National Council of Teachers of English.

Guidelines: Teachers should request information and a nomination form at the above address by October 16. The form for requests can also be found in the September *English Journal.* Students participate by writing impromptu and edited essays on topics selected by NCTE. Deadline for entering: January 23.

Prizes: Certificates of achievement and possible publication. Award winners' names and those of their high school are sent to college directors of admissions, state supervisors of English, and NCTE leaders.

NATIONAL COUNCIL OF TEACHERS OF ENGLISH (NCTE) PROMISING YOUNG WRITERS PROGRAM. Send to: Promising Young Writers Program, NCTE, 1111 W. Kenyon Road, Urbana, IL 61801-1096. 800-369-6283 or 217-328-3870. Ext. 221. Annual writing competition for eighth-grade students sponsored by the National Council of Teachers of English.

Guidelines: Teachers should request a brochure and entry information at the above address before December 1. The form for requests can be found in *English Journal.* Eighth-grade students submit samples of their best writing and one impromptu theme on a topic selected by NCTE. Entry fee: $5 per nominated student. Deadline: January 10.

Prizes: Winners receive certificates of achievement. All entrants receive certificates of participation.

NATIONAL ENDOWMENT FOR THE HUMANITIES, NATIONAL ESSAY CONTEST, 1100 Pennsylvania Avenue NW, Washington, DC 20506. 800-NEH-1121. Essay contest for American citizens or legal residents enrolled in grades 10–12 on topics related to American identity and ideals. Sponsored by the National Endowment for the Humanities and the Voice of America.

Guidelines: Send SASE for specific essay question and contest brochure. Essays from 350 to 500 words. Type and double-space manuscript, and submit three copies. Include separate information page stapled to essay with name, address, phone number, grade, and school name. Also type, sign, and date statement of originality as described in guidelines. No manuscripts returned. Deadline: November 20.

Prizes: Ten prizes for finalists, including trips to Washington, D.C., for an awards ceremony. Winning essays will be broadcast on Voice of America. One grand-prize winner will receive a $5,000 college scholarship and an Apple computer.

Comments: This contest encourages students to look at the essay question from a variety of perspectives. The contest brochure offers examples. The competition also encourages students whose first language is not English to submit essays in their native language with their own English translation.

NATIONAL FOUNDATION FOR ADVANCEMENT IN THE ARTS. Send to: NFAA/ARTS, 800 Brickell Avenue, Suite 500, Miami, FL 33131. 800-970-ARTS or 305-377-1148. E-mail: nfaa@nfaa.org. ARTS is a national program which recognizes the work of high school seniors and/or those who are either 17 or 18 years old on December 1 in a variety of arts including Writing.

Guidelines: Writers may submit work in the following categories: Poetry, Short Story, Selection from Novel, Expository, Play or Script for Film or Video. A portfolio of work is required. Send SASE for registration form. Then submit registration form and fee (entry fee: $35 for regular entries to October 1; $25 for early entries to June 1) to receive ARTS Application Packet for appropriate discipline.

Prizes: Up to 20 award candidates in each of the eight disciplines. Prizes include cash grants, all-expenses-paid trips to Miami to work with renowned artists, access to scholarship opportunities, and nomination to the White House Commission on Presidential Scholars.

Comments: Teachers should request ARTS materials early in the school year since there is lengthy process involved in preparing entries. Registration forms, printed in NFAA/ARTS information booklets, may be duplicated.

THE NATIONAL WRITTEN AND ILLUSTRATED BY . . . AWARDS CONTEST FOR STUDENTS, Landmark Editions, Inc., P.O. Box 4469, 1402 Kansas Avenue, Kansas City, MO 64127. Annual contest for students ages 6–19 requiring entrants to both write and illustrate a book.

Guidelines: Students may enter in one of three age groups: 6–9 years old, 10–13 years old, or 14–19 years old. Each entry, 16–24 pages in length, 11" x 8" in size, must be written and illustrated by the entrant. Entries must include official Entry Form and be submitted by a teacher or librarian. Include return book mailer with sufficient postage for return of manuscript. Entry fee: $1. Deadline: May 1. Send SASE for complete rules and guidelines for preparation of manuscript.

Prizes: Three winners, one from each age category, will receive publishing contracts with royalties and an all-expenses-paid trip to Kansas City to assist in production of their books.

Comments: Landmark Editions, Inc., also publishes *Written & Illustrated by . . .* by David Melton, a teacher's manual with step-by-step instructions to help students write, illustrate, and produce children's books. Request brochure of publications from address above. For guidelines, send SASE with $.64 postage to NWIB Awards Contest, c/o Landmark Editions Inc., P.O. Box 270169, Kansas City, MO 64127.

THE NICHOLAS A. VIRGILIO MEMORIAL HAIKU COMPETITION FOR HIGH SCHOOL STUDENTS. Send to: Tony Virgilio, Nick Virgilio Haiku Association, 1092 Niagara Road, Camden, NJ 08104. Haiku contest for students ages 13–19 enrolled in high school in September.

Guidelines: Submit up to three haiku. Each haiku must be typed in triplicate on front of 3" x 5" index cards. Type name, address, age, grade level, and school name and address on the back of one of the cards for each haiku. No manuscripts returned. Deadline: November 30.

Prizes: Cash awards. Publication in *Frogpond*. The high school of each student winner will receive a one-year subscription to *Frogpond*.

NORTHFIELD MOUNT HERMON SUMMER SCHOOL SHORT STORY SCHOLARSHIP CONTEST. Send to: Short Story Contest, Northfield Mount Hermon, Summer School, Drawer 5100, Northfield, MA 01360. 413-498-3290. Short story contest for students in grades 9–12.

Guidelines: Submit one or more short stories from 3 to 15 double-spaced pages with margins of 1" or more. Include cover sheet with name, grade, home address, phone number with area code, and school name, address, and phone number. Include SASE. No entry fee. Deadline: December 15. Entries returned with decision letter by March 15.

Prizes: Winning entrant will receive a full scholarship (includes tuition, books, room and board) for the six-week summer session Creative Writing course at Northfield Mount Hermon School. All entrants receive a catalog describing Summer School opportunities.

OUTSIDE MAGAZINE, "The Adventure Grants," 400 Market Street, Santa Fe, NM 87501. 505-989-7100. Fax: 505-989-4700. Web: http://outside.starwave.com. Essay contest for teams of students ages 12–17 describing an expedition/adventure they would like to take in North America.

Guidelines: Send a letter of no more than 2 pages typed describing "the adventure of your dreams." Questions to answer include: Where does your team want to go, and why? Why do you and your team think you can do this? How will your trip help the environment? Send SASE for complete guidelines. Deadline: April 21.

Prizes: Winning team will receive training, equipment, and logistical support to complete the expedition.

Comments: "A panel of judges made up of the world's best explorers (adults and kids) will award the grant to the expedition that best combines exploration, conservation, and adventure." *Outside Magazine* provides Teacher Guides. Request at the address above.

OXFAM AMERICA'S NATIONAL STUDENT ESSAY CONTEST, Oxfam America, Attn: Fast Contests, 26 West Street, Boston, MA 02111. 800-597-FAST. E-mail: oxfamfast@igc.apc.org. Essay contest for students in grades 6–8 and grades 9–12.

Guidelines: Write an essay (or sometimes a letter) of 500 words or less on a stated topic related to hunger and poverty. Contact above address for specific topic. Include name, age, grade, teacher's name, and school name, address, and phone. Deadline varies yearly.

Prizes: Winners and parent/guardian will be brought to Oxfam America awards ceremony.

Comments: Oxfam America also offers free of charge supplementary activities and material to teachers.

THE PIRATE'S ALLEY FAULKNER PRIZES FOR CREATIVE WRITING, "High School Short Story," 632 Pirate's Alley, New Orleans, LA 70116-3254. 504-524-2940. Fax: 504-522-9725. Short story contest for Louisiana high school students.

Guidelines: Submit short story less than 10,000 words. Type and double-space manuscripts. Include entry fee of $10 and a completed entry blank. Send SASE or call for entry forms and competition rules. Entries may be submitted from January 1–April 1.

Prizes: Winner and three runners-up will be selected. $750 prize and a sterling medal for winner, and $250 award to sponsoring teacher.

PRINCETON UNIVERSITY SECONDARY SCHOOL POETRY CONTEST. Send to: Princeton Poetry Prize, Creative Writing Program, 185 Nassau Street, Princeton University, Princeton, NJ 08544. Poetry contest for high school juniors.

Guidelines: Eleventh-grade students may submit up to three poems. Include name, address, and phone number on each poem. No manuscripts returned. Deadline: March 1.

Prizes: First prize $500. Second prize $250. Third prize $100.

PRINCETON UNIVERSITY TEN-MINUTE PLAY CONTEST. Send to: Princeton Ten-Minute Play Contest, Theatre and Dance Program, 185 Nassau Street, Princeton University, Princeton, NJ 08544. Playwriting contest for high school juniors.

Guidelines: Eleventh-grade students may submit one ten-minute play. Include name, address, and phone number on manuscript. No manuscripts returned. Deadline: March 1.

Prizes: First prize $500. Second prize $250. Third prize $100.

PROFILE IN COURAGE AWARD ESSAY CONTEST, The John F. Kennedy Library Foundation, Profile in Courage Award Essay Contest, Columbia Point, Boston, MA 02125. 617-436-9986. Essay contest open to students in New England, New York, New Jersey, and Pennsylvania.

Guidelines: Submit an essay of no more than 1,000 words on some aspect of political courage. Type and double-space manuscripts, and include a list of sources. Send two copies. Include a title page with name, address, phone number, name and address of school, and names and phone numbers of school principal and two teachers. Deadline: March 3.

Prizes: Each winner will receive a $2,000 scholarship and be invited to the Kennedy Library to participate in the John F. Kennedy Profile in Courage Award ceremony. Winning essays will be published in the John F. Kennedy Library Newsletter.

PROJECT: LEARN MS, MSAA Scholarship Essay Competition, P.O. Box 187, Oaklyn, NJ 01807. 800-LEARN-MS. Annual "nationwide scholarship essay program for high school students to promote awareness and education of Multiple Sclerosis as well as raise crucial funds needed to provide services to those afflicted with the disease."

Guidelines: Call above number for contest question and registration/sponsor form. One essay per student in grades 10–12. Essays of 500–1,000 words must be typed and double-spaced and include a title page. Entries must include completed registration/sponsor form and at least $7.50 in prepaid sponsorship. Deadline: May 27.

Prizes: One Golden Scholarship of $7,000 to the college of choice. Nine Silver scholarships of $1,000 to the college of choice. All winners also receive award plaques. (Students may also earn prizes—televisions, sweatshirts and T-shirts—by raising money for MS.)

Comments: Project: Learn MS also provides information on MS with the registration packet.

READ. Send to: Bowler Poetry Contest, Weekly Reader Corporation, 200 First Stamford Place, P.O. Box 120023, Stamford, CT 06912-0023. 203-705-3406. Ann Arlys Bowler Poetry prize for students grades 6–12.

Guidelines: Students in grades 6–12 may submit up to three poems no longer than one page each in any poetic genre. Type all submissions. Include Entry Coupon stapled to back of entry. Send SASE for complete guidelines and Entry Coupon. No manuscripts returned. Deadline: December 12.

Prizes: Six national winners receive $100 each, a medal of honor, and publication in *Read*. Six semi-finalists receive $50, a certificate, and the possibility of publication.

READ. Send to: Letters About Literature, *Read Magazine,* Weekly Reader Corporation, 200 First Stamford Place, P.O. Box 120023, Stamford, CT 06912-0023. 203-705-3449. Essay contest about literature for students in grades 6–12.

Guidelines: "Select a book you read recently about which you have strong feelings. Write a letter of 1,000 words or fewer to the author, explaining what the book taught you about yourself." Avoid plot summaries. Send signed letter with Entry Coupon. Send SASE for complete guidelines and Entry Coupon. Deadline: December 6.

Prizes: Grand-prize winner and parent/guardian receive an all-expenses-paid trip to Washington, D.C., and publication in *Read.* Nine national finalists receive cash awards.

READ. Send to: *Read* Writing and Art Awards, Weekly Reader Corporation, 200 First Stamford Place, P.O. Box 120023, Stamford, CT 06912-0023. 203-705-3449. Fiction and Essay contest for students grades 6–12.

    Guidelines: Submit short stories up to five typed, double-spaced pages for middle and high school readers. Submit essays in first-person point of view up to five typed, double-spaced pages. Attach Entry Coupon to back of entry. Write category on the envelope. Send SASE for complete guidelines and Entry Coupon. Deadline: December 5.

    Prizes: First-place winners in each category receive $225. Second-place winners in each category receive $75. Third-place winners in each category receive $50. Winners and honorable-mention recipients receive a certificate of excellence, and their work will be eligible for publication in *Read.*

RESPECTEEN SPEAK FOR YOURSELF, Letter Writing Contest, Lutheran Brotherhood, 625 Fourth Avenue South, Minneapolis, MN 55415. 800-984-9427. Web: http://www.luthbro.com. Letter writing contest for students in grades 7–8 to "encourage students' examination of issues and their participation in the democratic process."

    Guidelines: Students in grades 7 and 8 must write a letter to the U.S. representative in their district which discusses an issue affecting young people on a national level and which proposes a solution. The letter should be 150–300 words and follow standard letter format. Original letter must be sent to the entrant's U.S. representative. Contest entry must include Contest Entry Form. Send or call for specific guidelines and Contest Entry Form. Deadline: January 31.

    Prizes: Awards given at congressional district level and state level. Various awards include certificates, savings bonds, trips to Washington, D.C., and participation in the RespecTeen National Youth Forum.

    Comments: RespecTeen sends teachers a complete curriculum packet with contest information as well as detailed materials about the American political process. Call above number for materials.

RIVER OF WORDS, P.O. Box 4000-C, Berkeley, CA 94704. 510-433-7020. Fax: 510-848-1008. E-mail: row@irn.org. Web: http://www.irn.org/irn/. National environmental poetry contest for students grades K–12 sponsored by the International Rivers Network.

    Guidelines: Poetry to 32 lines on the theme of the contest. (1996 theme was Watersheds.) Include name, address, grade, and teacher's name on manuscript. Attach completed Contest Entry Form. Write or call for complete guidelines and Contest Entry Form. Deadline: March 4. Winners announced April 1.

    Prizes: Winners receive round-trip airfare to Washington, D.C., accommodations, and some meals for self and one parent/guardian in April. Winners will read poems at an Earth Day celebration.

    Comments: Teachers may request a Teacher's Guide with contest guidelines and entry forms.

SCHOLAR GYPSY PRESS, P.O. Box 350, North Falmouth, MA 02556. Poetry contest open to Massachusetts high school students.

Guidelines: Submit original poetry of up to 20 lines. Type entries and include name, address, school, and grade. Include SASE. $1/poem entry fee for response. No simultaneous submissions or previously published poems. Deadline: June 1.

Prizes: First prize $250. Second prize $150. Third prize $50. Possible publication for best submissions.

SCHOLASTIC WRITING AWARDS, The Scholastic Art and Writing Awards, c/o Alliance for Young Artists and Writers, Inc., 555 Broadway, New York, NY 10012. 212-343-6493. Writing awards in a variety of categories for students in grades 7–12 in two divisions (grades 7–9 and 10–12).

Guidelines: Send SASE in early fall for complete guidelines and entry form and deadlines. Entries are accepted in seven categories: Short Story, Short Short Story, Essay/Nonfiction/Opinion Writing, Dramatic Script, Poetry, Humor, Science Fiction/Fantasy, and Writing Portfolio. Processing fee: $3. No manuscripts returned.

Prizes: Scholarships and cash awards from $100–$5,000, grants, certificates, and publishing opportunities.

Comments: Because requirements are so specific and varied, teachers should request guidelines and information as early in the school year as possible.

SEVENTEEN MAGAZINE ANNUAL FICTION CONTEST. Send to: Fiction Contest, *Seventeen*, 850 Third Avenue, New York, NY 10022. 212-407-9700. Fiction contest for writers ages 13–21.

Guidelines: Short stories up to 4,000 words that would interest readers of *Seventeen*. Writers may submit as many original stories as they want. Type and double-space manuscripts. Include name, address, phone number, birth date, and signature on the top right-hand corner of the first page of each story. Deadline: April 30.

Prizes: First prize $1,000 and possible publication. Second Prize $500. Third prize $250. Five honorable mentions $50.

*SHOW AND TELL. Send to: Thomas Conger, Editor, P.O. Box 11087, Salt Lake City, Utah 84147. Two annual contests open to all writers.

Guidelines: For "Holiday Fiction Contest": short stories on the theme of Thanksgiving and Christmas. Entries to 2,500 words. Entry fee: $5 per story. Stories may be sent between January 1 and September 30 each year. Specify contest name on envelope. For "Don't Forget To Write Contest": fiction and poetry about healthy male/female relationships. Fiction to 3,000 words. Poetry to 50 lines. Entry fee $5 per story; $5 per 1–5 poems. Entries may be sent between February 14 and December 31 each year. Specify contest name on envelope.

Prizes: Fiction Grand prizes $50. Poetry Grand prizes $25. Fiction honorable mentions $25. Poetry honorable mentions $15.

SKIRBALL ESSAY CONTEST, 635 S. Harvard Blvd., Suite 214, Los Angeles, CA 90005-2511. 213-381-1719. Annual essay contest for high school students grades

10–12 sponsored by the Skirball Institute on American Values, a division of the American Jewish Committee.

Guidelines: Students in grades 10–12 must respond to a question focusing on their roles as citizens of the United States. Send SASE for specific question, application, and guidelines. (1996 question: "What Does U.S. History Teach Us About the Role of Immigration in the Creation of American Society?") Essays between three and four pages must be typed and double-spaced and include footnotes and bibliography when appropriate. Include name and essay title on each page. Submit essay and application in duplicate. Deadline March 15. Winners announced in May.

Prizes: Grand prize $5,000 and trip to Washington, D.C., for winner and sponsoring teacher. First prize $1,000. Second prize $500. Fifty third prizes $100.

Comments: "The first 100 teachers to submit their students' essays in a group as a class project will receive the recently published *American Heritage College Dictionary, Second College Edition* as a gift from Houghton Mifflin Company."

SWACKHAMER PEACE ESSAY CONTEST. Send to: Nuclear Age Peace Foundation, 1187 Coast Village Road, Suite 123, Santa Barbara, CA 93108-2794. 805-965-3443. Fax: 805-568-0466. Web: http://www.napf.org. Essay contest "seeking suggestions for constructive approaches to the problems of war and peace" open to high school students.

Guidelines: Essays 500–1,000 words based on a specific topic related to problems of war and peace. Send SASE for specific topic and guidelines. Type and double-space manuscripts. Include name, address, phone number, school, grade, and age on cover page. Do not put name on any other page. Include bibliography. Submit original and one copy. Deadline: June 6. Prizes awarded in September.

Prizes: First prize $1,500. Second prize $1,000. Third prize $500. The prize-winning essay will be published by the Nuclear Age Peace Foundation and sent to the President of the United States, the Secretary-General of the United Nations, and other world and national leaders. It may also be published in newspapers, magazines, and broadcast networks.

TAMPA WRITING SCHOLARS COMPETITION, Writing Scholarships, Department of English, The University of Tampa, 401 W. Kennedy Blvd., Tampa, FL 33606-1490. 813-253-3333. Ext. 6229. Competition open to high school seniors with an overall GPA of 3.0 or higher *and* SAT I score of 1180 or higher or an ACT score of 26 or higher who have special talents in English or writing.

Guidelines: Submit a portfolio of poems (5–10), a short story, a play, an essay (1,500–3,000 words), or a combination (up to 15 pages). Include an autobiography (300–500 words) and a high school transcript. Entry period is from January 1 to February 15.

Prizes: Five to fifteen winners will be published in a national anthology *Writers for a New Millennium*. Winners will receive a copy of the book, a certificate of national distinction, and scholarships of up to $28,000 over four years to study English or writing at the University of Tampa.

VEGETARIAN RESOURCE GROUP'S ANNUAL ESSAY CONTEST, The Vegetarian Resource Group, P.O. Box 1463, Baltimore, MD 21203. 410-366-8343.

E-mail: The VRG@aol.com. Essay contest for students ages 6–18. Three divisions: ages 14–18; ages 9–13; ages 8 and under.

Guidelines: Submit a two- to three-page essay on any aspect of vegetarianism. Base the essay on interviewing, research, and/or personal opinion. Include name, address, phone number, grade, school, and teacher's name. Deadline: May 1.

Prizes: One $50 savings bond in each age division.

Comments: The Vegetarian Resource Group provides material on vegetarianism to teachers. Request material at the above address.

VERY SPECIAL ARTS, PLAYWRIGHT DISCOVERY PROGRAM. Send to: Playwright Discovery Program, Very Special Arts, Education Office, The John F. Kennedy Center for the Performing Arts, Washington, DC 20566. 800-933-8721. Fax: 202-737-0725. E-mail: rachelg@vsarts.org. Web: http://www.vsarts.org. Playwriting contest for writers under the age of 25 who have a disability. The script must "examine the way disabilities shape the human experience."

Guidelines: There are two categories: Category I—18 years of age and under; Category II—19–25 years of age. Submit two typed copies of a script that explores the theme of disability. Include completed application form and SASE. Deadline April 14.

Prizes: Winning plays will be professionally produced. Winner will have an one-on-one session with a professional playwright and will receive cash awards (Category I—$500, Category II—$2,500). Winners and chaperone/guest receive a trip to Washington, D.C., to be honored at the premiere.

Comments: Very Special Arts Playwright Discovery Program provides detailed information both on disabilities and on writing plays. Request with guidelines. Also available to purchase are copies of prize-winning scripts by young playwrights from 1984–present.

"WHO'S YOUR HERO?" NATIONAL ESSAY CONTEST, c/o Conari Press, 2550 Ninth Street, Suite 101, Berkeley, CA 94710. 510-649-7175. Fax: 610-649-7190. Annual contest focusing on heroes of American youth. Open to young people ages 6–18 who are participants in an agency affiliated with the National Collaboration for Youth (i.e., Boy Scouts of America, Girl Scouts of the USA, YMCA, YWCA, American Red Cross, etc.). Send SASE for contest topic and list of affiliated agencies.

Guidelines: Guidelines vary depending on particular topic. Include Participant Information Form and Release of Information Form. Deadline: March 30.

Prizes: Complimentary copy of anthology of winning essays plus a disposable camera.

WILLIAM J. GAGE ANNUAL STUDENT ZINC ESSAY CONTEST, American Zinc Association, 1112 16th Street NW, Suite 240, Washington, DC 20036. Essay contest for students grades 7–12 "to increase awareness of zinc in our lives, and to highlight the importance of minerals in our society."

Guidelines: There are two age groups: category one—grades 7–9; category two—grades 10–12. Essays of 5–10 pages (exclusive of bibliography) should discuss the importance of zinc in our society and our daily lives. Each essay should include at least five references from research sources. Type and double-space manuscripts with 1" margins. Include name, grade level, address, phone number, school name and address, teacher's name, and how entrant learned about contest in upper right-hand corner of page one. Submit two copies. No manuscripts returned. Deadline: March 31. Winners notified in May.

Prizes: One winner chosen in each category. Each winner receives $200 Savings Bond and airfare and accommodations for self and parent/guardian/teacher for two-day visit to Washington, D.C., in June or July. Science department of each winner's school receives $100.

"WORLD" CONTEST, "Changing My World," P.O. Box 696, Asheville, NC 28802. 704-254-8111. Essay contest for students ages 8–18 sponsored by the Writers' Workshop.

Guidelines: There are two age groups: ages 8–12 and ages 13–18. Submit an essay of 10–20 double-spaced pages describing a problem the writer would like to change and possible solutions. Essay should include research and opinion supported by fact. Include name, address, birth date, and phone number. Include SASE. Entry fee: $5. Deadline: February 25.

Prizes: First prize $100. Second prize $75. Third prize $50. Five Honorable Mentions. Winners published in newsletter.

*WORLD'S BEST SHORT SHORT STORY CONTEST, English Department, Florida State University, Tallahassee, FL 32306-1036. 904-644-4230. Short short story contest open to all writers.

Guidelines: Submit short short stories of no more than 250 words, one typed, double-spaced page. Entry fee: $1 (payable to *Sun Dog*). Include SASE for copy of prize-winning story. Deadline: February 15. Winner announced May 15.

Prizes: $100 and box of Florida oranges. Winner and finalists will be published in *Sun Dog: The Southeast Review.*

WRITE LYRICS CONTEST, Scholastic Inc., 555 Broadway, New York, NY 10012-3999. Song lyric contest for students in grades 6–12. The contest is usually offered in the following Scholastic publications: *Junior Scholastic, Scope, Literary Cavalcade, Action,* and *Choices.*

Guidelines: Submit a single, completed song lyric. No music is required. Include a completed entry form signed by student and teacher. (See magazine or write to above address.) "Entries will be judged on their creativity, clarity, and quality of thinking and language, *not* on music, length, or presentation." Deadline: April 4. Winners notified in April.

Prizes: Grand-prize winner receives a concert at his or her school by a major recording artist. (Previous artists include 10,000 Maniacs, Jackson Browne, Tracy Chapman, and Indigo Girls.) Grand prize and first runners-up receive computer equipment. All winners, including twenty-five second runners-up, receive autographed CDs.

Comments: This contest is held periodically. See magazine or contact above address for next "Write Lyrics Contest." Scholastic, Inc. also provides a Teacher's Guide with classroom activities and a cassette to develop students' songwriting skills.

*WRITER'S DIGEST WRITING COMPETITION, 1507 Dana Avenue, Cincinnati, OH 45207-9966. 513-531-2690. Fax: 513-531-1843. Writing contest sponsored by *Writer's Digest* open to all writers.

   Guidelines: Categories for submissions include: Personal Essay, Feature Article, Literary Short Story, Mainstream/Genre Short Story, Rhyming Poem, Non-Rhyming Poem, Stage Play, and Television/Movie Script. Fiction and nonfiction to 2000 words. Poetry to 32 lines. Scripts, send first 15 pages plus synopsis. Entry fee: $8 per manuscript. Send manuscript with official Entry Form (see magazine or request with SASE) and fee. Type and double-space. Include name, address, phone number, competition category, and intended market or audience in upper left-hand corner of first page. Type exact word count on first page of fiction and nonfiction. Deadline: May 31.

   Prizes: Grand-prize winner receives an expenses-paid trip to New York City to meet editors and agents, and computer equipment. Other awards in each category include cash prizes, Writer's Digest Books, *Writer's Digest* subscriptions, and certificates.

THE WRITERS FOUNDATION'S AMERICA'S BEST SCHOLASTIC WRITING COMPETITION. Send to: America's Best Scholastic Competition, c/o The Writers Foundation, 3936 S. Semoran Blvd. #368, Orlando, FL 32822. Fax: 407-894-5547. Web: http://www.solutions.ibm.com/write. Writing contest open to students grades 1–12. Three divisions: high school (grades 9–12); middle school (grades 6–8); elementary school (grades 1–5).

   Guidelines: Categories for high school submissions include: Scriptwriting (Screenplay and Television), Short Fiction (any genre), Poetry, Songwriting, Original Sitcom, and Novel. Students may enter as many times as they want but should send all submissions in one envelope. Entry fee: $3. Categories for grades 6–8 submissions include: Create a Television Show, and Creative Fiction or Nonfiction (up to 1,250 words). No entry fee. One submission per student. Send SASE for application and specific guidelines in each category. Include signed application and entry fee with each submission. Write grade level on outside of envelope. Deadline: June 7.

   Prizes: For high school competition, each category will have 50 finalists. Winners in each category will receive an IBM Thinkpad. For middle school competition, winners in each category will receive a $500 U.S. Savings Bond and America's Best certificate. Five runners-up will receive a $50 U.S. Savings Bond and America's Best certificate. Winners and runners-up receive Sara Lee coupons.

YOUNG PLAYWRIGHTS FESTIVAL NATIONAL PLAYWRITING COMPETITION, Young Playwrights Festival, Dept. L, 321 West 44th Street, Suite 906, New York, NY 10036. 212-307-1140. Fax: 212-307-1454. Playwriting contest for young writers eighteen-years-old or younger as of October 15.

   Guidelines: Submit script of any style, subject, and length. Type and number pages and staple together. Include title page with name, birth date, address, and phone number. Entrant may submit more than one script. Collaborations up to three writers are accepted if all writers are under 18. No manuscripts returned. Send SASE for complete guidelines. Deadline: October 15.

Prizes: Selected playwrights will participate in the professional production of their plays in New York City and will receive transportation, accommodations, and a royalty.

Comments: All entrants receive a written evaluation of their plays.

Appendix B
Electronic Submissions

A whole new world of publishing opportunities is opening up to writers, thanks to the World Wide Web. Not all writers welcome this, bemoaning what may be the decline of printed books and the permanency of words on a page. But for young writers, the opportunities offered on the Internet are new, fast-paced, and exciting, befitting the energy of their generation. A colorful screen filled with the words of her peers from around the country and around the world can motivate even the most disinterested writer to tap out her own words, send them out to the world, and see, almost instantaneously, their potential impact on readers.

What follows is a very abbreviated list of some of the Web sites offering publishing opportunities and/or resources presently available to young writers. These entries have been chosen to suggest the variety of opportunities out there, and in no way attempt to provide a complete listing. Frequently any one such address can serve as a jumping-off point as it will offer connections to other publications, particularly the newest "zines." Many magazines and journals are also starting to appear both in print and on the Internet and allow writers to submit their work either by regular mail or e-mail.

One caution to teachers and writers: as quickly as printed publications may change—appearing and disappearing or altering their format, seemingly overnight—electronic publications change even faster, literally in the blink of an eye. It takes time, effort, and the willingness to wander down the information highway to find new publishing opportunities. But most students love the journey and find their interest in both writing and reading piqued by their travels.

http://www.inkspot.com
Inkspot is one of the best Web sites for writers of all ages, offering information both on the craft of writing and on publishing as well. Resources for Young Writers is a part of Inkspot, providing information of special interest to young writers, including listings of workshops and associations, E-zine and online writing opportunities, and other Web sites of interest to young writers.

http://www.kidnews.com
ISN KidNews is an international student newswire interested in receiving stories, articles, reviews, profiles, and creative work from students. Located at the University of Massachusetts–Dartmouth, the service seeks to give young writers, especially young journalists, the chance to showcase their own writing as well as to learn from the work of other student writers. Writers can submit their work directly on the screen or send it using e-mail, being sure to include name, address, grade, age, and school name and address. E-mail: powens@cape.com.

http://www.quill.net
The Quill Society is an online writing club for writers between the ages of 12 and 24. Young writers can read the work of their peers, share their own work, and receive constructive criticism and editing suggestions. This site also offers an e-mail magazine to both help and entertain young writers.

http://www.lehigh.net/zuzu/direct.html
Zuzu's Petals Literary Resource offers a wide variety of material of interest to writers of all ages. Of particular interest are detailed listings of little and literary journals.

http://www.woodwind.com:80/cyberteens/index.html
Cyberteens Connection includes an online zine *Zeen* which accepts submissions from teenage writers around the world. Submissions may include stories, articles, opinion pieces, poems, reviews, and music compositions. Include age and address. Cyberteens Connection also sponsors an International Writing and Art contest for students ages 7–16.

http://www.kidpub.org/kidpub/
KidPub WWW Publishing accepts writing by students ages 8–14.

http://www.yam.regulus.com/
The Young Author's Magazine Internet Classroom offers a variety of educational opportunities. There is also a Poetry Submission Center and a Short Story/Essay Submission Center for writing by students in grades K–12.

http://ipl.org/
Internet Public Library sponsors an annual writing contest. See both Youth and Teen Division Writing Contest Pages.

http://www.nypl.org/branch/teen/vox.html
Wordsmiths: Teen Voice @ Teen Link, sponsored by the New York Public Library, is open to all teenagers ages 12 to 18. Submit up to three poems or two short stories (no more than five typed pages). Include name

and age. Send e-mail submissions to teenlink@nypl.org. For notification of when your work is printed, include mail address and/or e-mail address. Selected entries are posted on the Web page for at least two weeks.

http://www.writes.org
Writes of Passage—The Online Service for Teenagers is an online source for students and teachers. This site expands on the *Writes of Passage* literary journal and gives young writers the chance to write and share stories, poems, and essays. Interviews with writers, writing tips, interactive writing activities, and the WP Teachers' Guide are also offered.

http://www.realkids.com/club.html
Young Writer's clubhouse provides useful information for young writers on the craft of writing. There is also a "Teachers' Lounge" as a resource for classroom teachers.

Appendix C
Resources for Young Writers

There are many publications—books, magazines, journals, and newsletters—of interest to young writers. Though generally not geared specifically to students, these publications provide market listings and offer technical advice that is very appropriate for young writers. My students enjoy browsing through these books and magazines, not only because they provide valuable information, but also because they make the readers feel that they are truly part of the writing world.

Although no teacher could be expected to purchase and/or subscribe to all of these publications, many are available through libraries and through the Internet. The periodicals are particularly valuable in offering up-to-date information about the publishing world and are often the best sources for learning about new writing contests and awards. The following list features a sampling of such publications. The listing includes the name, address, phone/fax numbers, subscription information, and a brief description of each. Publications that focus primarily on writing and publishing are marked with an asterisk(*).

*AWP CHRONICLE, The Associated Writing Programs, George Mason University, Tallwood House, Mail Stop 1E3, Fairfax, VA 22030. 703-993-4301. Fax: 703-993-4302. http://web.gmu.edu/departments/awp. Published six times a year. Subscription $20, single copy, $3.95. *AWP Chronicle* offers news, essays, articles, and interviews on writing for teachers and writers. Each issue includes lists of awards, grants, and publishing opportunities.

*BYLINE, P. O. Box 130596, Edmond, OK 73013. 405-348-5591. Published 11 times a year. Subscription $20. *Byline* takes a special interest in new writers and offers valuable information for those just starting to publish. The magazine includes fiction and poetry, articles on writing, conference lists, and new markets.

THE COUNCIL CHRONICLE, National Council of Teachers of English, 1111 W. Kenyon Road, Urbana, IL 61801-1096. 800-369-6283. 217-328-3870. Published five times a year. Subscription available as part of NCTE membership. Individual membership $30. *The Council Chronicle*, NCTE's official newspaper, provides up-to-date information on newsworthy issues, trends, and events of interest to English language arts teachers. Contest and publishing opportunities for student writers are frequently noted.

ENGLISH JOURNAL, National Council of Teachers of English, 1111 W. Kenyon Road, Urbana, IL 61801-1096. 800-369-6283. 217-328-3870. Published eight times a year. Subscription $20; you must join NCTE to subscribe to *English Journal*. Individual membership $30. *English Journal* is the journal of the Secondary Section of NCTE. It offers articles, opinion pieces, and reviews focusing on reading, writing, and oral language for middle school and junior and senior high English teachers. Contests and publishing opportunities for student writers are frequently noted.

*HOW TO WRITE IRRESISTIBLE QUERY LETTERS, by Lisa Collier Cool. Writer's Digest Books, 1507 Dana Avenue, Cincinnati, OH 45207. 513-531-2222.

*INTERNATIONAL DIRECTORY OF LITTLE MAGAZINES AND SMALL PRESSES, Dustbooks, P. O. Box 100, Paradise, CA. 95967. 800-477-6110. This directory, updated annually, lists over 6,000 magazine and book publishers of work in all genres. Dustbooks is an excellent source for small press information. Other Dustbooks publications include the *Directory of Poetry Publishers* and *Small Press Review*, a monthly periodical.

*POETS & WRITERS, 72 Spring Street, New York, NY 10012. 212-226-3586. Fax: 212-226-3963. E-mail: pwsubs@pw.org. Web: http://www.pw.org. Published six times a year. Subscription $19.95; single copy, $3.95. *Poets & Writers* focuses primarily on fiction and poetry and includes essays, articles, and interviews by poets and short story writers. The magazine also provides extensive lists of grants, awards, and publication opportunities.

TEACHER MAGAZINE, Suite 250, 4301 Connecticut Avenue NW, Washington, DC 20008. 202-364-4114. Published eight times a year. Subscription $17.94. *Teacher Magazine* focuses on people and trends in education in all disciplines. The magazine offers a monthly listing "For Your Students" which provides information on various contests, scholarships, and internships for students.

*TEACHERS & WRITERS MAGAZINE, Teachers and Writers Collaborative, 5 Union Square West, New York, NY 10003-3306. 212-691-6590. Published five times a year. Subscription $16 (free subscription with Teachers & Writers $35 basic membership). *Teachers & Writers Magazine* offers practical ideas and innovative strategies for the teaching of writing.

*THE WRITER, 120 Boylston Street, Boston, MA 02116-4615. 617-423-3157. Editor: Sylvia K. Burack. Published monthly. Subscription $28. *The Writer* offers articles on writing techniques, interviews with authors, market news, and special monthly market lists.

*WRITER'S DIGEST, 1507 Dana Avenue, Cincinnati, OH 45207. 513-531-2222. Editor: Thomas Clark. Published monthly. Subscription $27, single copy $2.99. *Writer's Digest* offers feature articles on writing techniques along with monthly columns on writing in the various genres. The magazine also provides up-to-date market information.

*WRITER'S DIGEST BOOKS—MARKET BOOKS, 1507 Dana Avenue, Cincinnati, OH 45207. 513-531-2222. Published annually. Writer's Digest Books publishes a number of books listing publishing opportunities for various markets (some include a CD-ROM Electronic Edition). The books also offer articles on the basics of writing for publication. These books include *Writer's Market,* which lists markets for fiction, articles, poetry, plays, scripts, and novels; *Novel & Short Story Writer's Market; Poet's Market*; and *Children's Writer's & Illustrator's Market.*

Appendix D
Sample Formats for
Cover Letters and
Manuscripts

Sample cover letter for a publication with a particular interest in the work of young writers:

```
000 Street
City, State  Zip Code
(Area code) Telephone number
Date


Sandra K. Dennis
Out of the Cradle
Box 129
South Paris, ME 04281-0129


Dear Ms. Dennis:

Enclosed please find my essay "Lady's Choice" which I would
like to submit to the "Happenings Department" of Out of
the Cradle.

I am a fifteen-year-old sophomore at Wachusett Regional
High School in Holden, MA.  I enjoy writing and photogra-
phy, and I work on my school newspaper.

Thank you for your consideration.  I look forward to hear-
ing from you.

Sincerely,

(signature)

Jane Smith
```

Sample cover letter for a general publication (includes information on publishing credits):

```
000 Street
City, State  Zip code
(Area code) Telephone number
Date


Dr. Stanley Schmidt
Analog Science Fiction & Fact
1540 Broadway
New York, NY 10036
```

Dear Dr. Schmidt:

Enclosed is my short story "Spin Blank" for your consideration. I am an avid reader of *Analog* and feel that this story focusing on a futuristic medical technology might be of interest to you.

My publication credits include local publications as well as a short story in *Hobson's Choice* this past spring.

I look forward to your reply. Thank you for the attention you give my manuscript.

Sincerely,

(signature)

Jane Smith

Poetry manuscript sample format:

```
Maria Megnin                                              18 lines
000 Street
City, State  Zip code
(Area code) Telephone number
SS #000-00-0000



BODY CAST

by

Ria Megnin

Were you to touch me I would turn away
and no contact made
would burn deeper than our separate skins.
It's hard to explain why I feel this way
but I don't trade
my defenses for your gummy grins.

It has everything to do with how
I always felt
the lives that dance and swirl and be
in this full and empty house
could melt
and disappear without a thought for me.

So please don't move for my embrace.
We've shared
quite keenly too much unspoken pain
alone together in this place.
Love bared
would only complicate the name.
```

Prose manuscript sample page—Page 1:

Wylie Culhane   612 words
000 Street
City, State Zip code
(Area code) Telephone number
SS #000-00-0000

BLOOD & SWEAT

by

Wylie Culhane

I can still feel her soft voice in my ear, "Everything is fine, darling. I'd never let them hurt you." She'd whisper this over and over again until I wasn't quite sure if it was me she was trying to reassure or herself. After all she didn't know these horrible people; they only liked me. They came to me almost every night, torturing me with their bloody hands. But I'd always awake before the blood tainted my pale white flesh. My mother was always there to comfort me; she'd sit beside me and gently wipe the pearls of sweat from my forehead. I loved the way she curled up next to me as I rested on my side, with her chest against my back and her knees tucked so they fit perfectly with the backs of mine. Like two pieces of a puzzle, mother and daughter. Often times I'd awake in the morning with face raw from the past night's tears and hair encrusted with salty sweat. My mother was never there. The only trace of her was the faint scent of her lilac soap left behind on my pillowcase. And still, mixed with the aroma of my stale sweat, it never really smelled like her . . .

Prose manuscript sample page—last page:

Culhane - 3

. . . All I want to do is run. When I start I never want to stop—it's a race and I'm determined to win. The brisk air feels good against my sweaty face and the muffled thud of my feet against the solid earth reminds me that I am here and I am real. I have finally learned to run from the bad people in my world. I have learned to let the sweat drip into my eyes though it stings and to accept the blood that stains the soles of my sneakers.

THE END

Author

© 1997 Photography by Winthrop Inc.

Susanne Rubenstein lives and teaches in central Massachusetts. A graduate of Tufts University, she has taught high school English for twenty-two years, and she also conducts workshops for young writers. She has been involved with both the Boston Writing Project and the Western Massachusetts Writing Project, and she serves on the Editorial Board of the Massachusetts Field Center for Teaching and Learning. She strongly believes that teachers of writing should be writers themselves. Her work has appeared in *The Worcester Review, Teacher Magazine*, and other periodicals. She is currently at work on a collection of short stories.

This book was typeset in Avant Garde and Baskerville by
Electronic Imaging.
The typeface used on the cover was Comic Sans.
The book was printed on 50-lb. Williamsburg Offset by Versa Press.